The Dennis Nilsen Tapes

In Jail with Britain's Most Infamous Serial Killer

By MICHAEL MORLEY

CORONET

First published in Great Britain in 2021 by Coronet
An Imprint of Hodder & Stoughton
An Hachette UK company

This paperback edition published in 2021

1

Copyright © Michael Morley 2021

The right of Michael Morley to be identified as the
Author of the Work has been asserted by him in accordance
with the Copyright, Designs and Patents Act 1988.

A CIP catalogue record for this title is available from the British Library

Paperback ISBN 9781529370713
eBook ISBN 9781529371710

Typeset in Electra LH by Palimpsest Book Production Ltd,
Falkirk, Stirlingshire

Printed and bound in Great Britain by Clays Ltd, Elcograf S.p.A.

Hodder & Stoughton policy is to use papers that are natural, renewable
and recyclable products and made from wood grown in sustainable forests.
The logging and manufacturing processes are expected to conform to
the environmental regulations of the country of origin.

Hodder & Stoughton Ltd
Carmelite House
50 Victoria Embankment
London EC4Y 0DZ

www.hodder.co.uk

'I kept their bodies beneath the floorboards and brought them out for my rituals, for my fantasies. I'd wash them, cover them in talcum powder, dress and undress them, take them to bed and be with them.'

Dennis Andrew Nilsen

In memory of Don Dovaston, Robert Ressler and Roy Hazelwood. True gentlemen and wonderful criminal investigators who made the world a better and safer place.

'I began to exchange letters with Mike Morley, the producer, all of which passed through the official censor, so the prison authorities could have been in no doubt as to what was being proposed and required. Then a date was fixed for a preliminary meeting to be followed by a filming session a week later.'

Dennis Nilsen, *History of a Drowning Boy* (2021)

'Be aware that when you interview Nilsen, he will be arrogant and demanding and will seek to control the agenda from the get-go. You'll have to take great care not to let him get into your head. And if he does get in, then you will have to take even greater care to get him out again.'

Former FBI profiler Robert Ressler

'I would say that Nilsen is mad in the soul, that's the best way I can think of putting it. He's certainly not mad in the head. Intellectually, he's perfectly able to plan, to devise things and see things through to fruition.'

Author and Nilsen confidant, Brian Masters

CONTENTS

BEFORE WE CONTINUE . . .

There are things you need to know.

The interview I recorded in Albany Prison with Dennis Nilsen breached long-standing Home Office policies that banned such offenders from ever appearing on TV.

It so enraged the British government of the day, that they spent a fortune in taxpayer's money hauling me through both the High Court and the Court of Appeal, in failed eleventh-hour efforts to obtain injunctions that would have prevented the public ever seeing a frame of it.

But this book is more than the story of that interview and the landmark legal victory.

It is a unique investigation into the mind and crimes of Dennis Andrew Nilsen. The first of its kind to take in three decades of expert analysis, including the serial killer's own correspondence with me, my full notes from our recorded interview, the 2021 publication of his autobiographical accounts in *History of a Drowning Boy* (begun and written partly on a typewriter I provided), Brian Masters' classic biography of him, Russ Coffey's insightful book into his life, the views of leading psychological profilers from the FBI, an insight from one of Britain's most respected chief forensic pathologists, plus collated information from countless medical and legal records on the serial killer.

I am not a Nilsen biographer, not a clinician who assessed

him as mad or bad, not a psychiatrist who treated him, not a former detective who arrested him, nor a previous friend, cellmate or lover of Dennis Nilsen.

The observational lens I have studied him through is wider than the one used by all those individuals. A more encompassing and more familiar one. I am an author and award-winning investigative television journalist*, trained in sifting lies from the truth, in finding dark secrets and crimes that people hoped they had hidden and would never be exposed.

I've spent my entire career researching difficult subjects, many scientific, medical and criminal, with a view to interpreting them for easy understanding.

To reach conclusions on Nilsen, I've followed the same rigorous research processes that in the past have led me to presenting evidence that resulted in both people being prosecuted and convicted for serious crimes in English and international courts, and innocent people being freed from jail in the UK and the US.

My method of investigation has always been the same. Personally examine the main sources. Verify everything said and everything found. Check as many times as possible before even thinking of calling anything a fact. Run all the facts past the leading experts in the field. Then, and only then, is there

---

* I edited/executive produced network current affairs such as ITV's *The Cook Report*, *The Tuesday Special* and *Big Story*. I was head of current affairs for Carlton Television and chief creative officer for Sony Pictures Television International Productions. Awards include: Royal Television Society Documentary Awards: *The Hunt for Baby Abbie*, *Caution Our Hands Are Tied*, *Barry's Blues*, *Central Weekend*, *It's Your Shout*, *Savaged*; Bafta Nomination: *Murder in Mind*; Science Writers' Fellowship Award: *A Shred of Evidence*; British Medical Association Documentary Awards: *Dying to Eat*, *Let Me Die*; Charleston Film Festival 'Gold' Award: *Justice for Lynn*.

solid ground to take a stand on, a viewpoint to form and a reliable perspective to share.

I believe I've managed that in this case, and as an internationally published crime fiction novelist* I hope I've done it in a way that provides a fascinatingly gripping story, as well as a new insight into some of the most terrible of crimes of modern times.

From 1993 to the autumn of 2020, I hadn't written or spoken publicly about Dennis Nilsen. Had I not been approached by highly respected programme makers producing a documentary for global release, I would have remained silent.

My Nilsen experience – preparing for that interview, filming it, and the aftermath – had not been pleasant. And as I told both the director and producer of the intended film, I really had no desire to reopen that chapter of my life. Ghosts had been laid to rest. I'd moved on.

My silence would have continued had Donna, my wife and partner of almost twenty-seven years, not pointed out that we had a twenty-one-year-old son who, just graduating from university, had his sights set on entering the world of media. 'Maybe you should help them,' she said. 'If Billy was chasing interviewees, you'd hope someone would give him "a little of their time". So maybe you should.'

Partners the world over fully understand how loaded the word *maybe* is when spoken by the love of your life. So, the next time the dutifully persistent producer of the documentary called and asked for my cooperation, I consented.

What no one realised, was that I was giving up far more than time. I was giving up 'closure'.

In preparing for the Nilsen interview, which had been part

---

* Books written as Michael Morley: *Spree, Viper* and *Spider*. Under the pseudonym Sam Christer: *House of Smoke, The Stonehenge Legacy, The Rome Prophecy, The Turin Shroud Secret, The Camelot Code, The Venice Conspiracy.*

of a much bigger documentary about recent developments of offender profiling in the UK and how they contrasted to the FBI's long-established Behavioral Science Unit, I had completely immersed myself in the life and crimes of one of the world's most notorious murderers.

I had consulted police officers, psychiatrists, psychologists, psychological profilers and pathologists. I had wanted to know not only why this man had killed so many people and had sex with their dead bodies, but what emotions he'd experienced, what remorse, what regrets, and what circumstances in his life had led him to fantasise about murder and necrophilia.

I had wanted to *understand*.

I remember all too well some solid advice given to me by pioneering FBI profiler, Robert Ressler, the man credited with coining the term 'serial killer'.

'To understand a serial murderer, to make sense of why they do what they do, you have to think like them. I don't mean that you have to read about it and *imagine* what it was like. I mean, you must put yourself in the killer's position and envision yourself committing the crime, strangling, shooting, or stabbing the victim. What are you thinking when you kill? What will you do next? How much time do you have before someone comes? How much cleaning up, covering up do you have to carry out? Are you going to leave the body where it is, or move it? How are you going to exit the crime scene without someone seeing you? How will you make sure you haven't left any evidence behind?' Without drawing breath, he added, 'You must think about how you might have felt when you were planning the murder – how you felt while you were doing it – were you excited, disappointed, frightened? Did it live up to your expectations? If you *really* want to know about a murderer then you must get so close to the unsub's behaviour that you can answer all those questions. So close that when you arrest them, you already think how they think. You know if they're lying or holding back. You know if there are more victims, or even accomplices to the crimes.'

In Nilsen's case, I tried my utmost to follow Bob Ressler's advice. I did my level best to add some of the techniques of profilers to my skills as an investigative crime journalist, so I could better understand Nilsen and what motivations lay behind his crimes.

Such an effort to understand is not without problems.

Like certain police officers involved in the case, after all these years, I am still occasionally awakened by Nilsen-related dreams and I will never be able to forget some of the things he said, wrote, or did during my investigation.

Such was my desperation to be free of all thoughts of Dennis Nilsen, that on the 26 January 1993, I was already on a stool in a hotel bar, getting seriously drunk at 10.40 p.m. that wet, winter night, when as scheduled, ITV screened my documentary *Murder in Mind*, including selected sections of the interview I had recorded with the killer.

In the documentary, watched by a record number of viewers, Nilsen described in chillingly emotionless detail how he lured young, male victims to his London homes, killed them and kept their bodies for sex and for companionship, often talking to the corpses and watching television with them propped up alongside him.

The edited extract of interview was a bare and relatively benign four minutes, out of what had been almost four hours of truly soul-destroying and awfully precise recollections of murder, sexual fantasies, necrophilia, sodomy, dismemberment, boiling and burning of human flesh and callous disposal of human remains.

Those few minutes had been chosen, not because they had been the most sensational or shocking (far from it), but because they had been the most appropriate in beginning to demonstrate that Nilsen was more than the monster the media had crudely painted. More than just the dangerous criminal the police and courts had rightly apprehended and sentenced.

He was all those things.

But he was also intelligent. Immensely articulate. Argumentative. Creative. Well-informed. Hugely manipulative. Generous. Needy. And even humorous.

Dennis Nilsen didn't only 'appear' to be normal. At times, he *was* normal. That's how he got away with committing murder after murder.

Single male. Intelligent. Humorous. Creative. Good cook. Generous. Into music, films and photography. Likes a laugh and a drink.

Sounds almost like the perfect dating profile.

Add in the facts that he had his own place, always worked hard and paid his bills on time, then those seeking such a partner could be forgiven for seeing him 'as a keeper'.

And that was the whole point of my documentary.

Serial killers are not outwardly identifiable.

Their behaviour does not overtly betray their murderous activities. Nilsen, for goodness' sake, had been a policeman. None of his badge-wearing colleagues raised a red flag about any of his activities. Nor did anyone he worked with in the army or the civil service.

Offender profiling is about recognising that many fine qualities can genuinely exist in a person, but that person may also harbour fantasies about drowning you, strangling you, and keeping your body for months on end, to bathe and dress, to place in chairs around their house and to make the centre of depraved sexual rituals.

Single male. Necrophile*. Into strangling and drowning. Keeps bodies under floorboards. Stacks dismembered limbs in bags and boxes. Boils heads on stoves and flushes flesh down drains.

Now, that's not likely to go down well on any dating platform.

I've made the ludicrous comparison because those two extremities co-existed in Nilsen and I know he was not unique. In the following pages, you'll meet many more men like him.

And there are plenty of other Nilsens in our modern-day societies. Serial killers still to be detected. Balancing similar extremities of personality. Appearing to be normal.

Hopefully, we can identify signs that give away who they are and what they might do.

Such signs were certainly there in the life of Dennis Andrew Nilsen. He described many of them in his letters to me and detailed them in my interview with him. I uncovered more during my research and analytical discussions with psychologists, profilers and people who knew him well.

Because of the Court of Appeal ruling that the hours of Nilsen tapes that hadn't been included in the documentary would remain forever unseen by the public, I never made the follow-up programme I had planned. It was one that would have concentrated solely on Nilsen.

The programme would have used the expertise of two of the finest FBI profilers in the world – Robert Ressler and Roy Hazelwood, the man who literally wrote the FBI handbook on catching serial sexual offenders and sadists – to help us

---

* The term "necrophile" was probably coined in 1850 by Belgian psychiatrist Joseph Guislain when lecturing about the case of Françoise Betrand, the Vampire of Montparnasse.

know who Nilsen really was and why he committed such depraved crimes.

I'd given the intended documentary the working title 'The Dennis Nilsen Tapes – Profiling Britain's Most Disturbing Serial Killer', and though I never got to make it, I did do all the research, and those two profilers did provide valuable and exclusive analysis. Analysis that will now be made public for the first time.

Before we begin this investigation, please keep in mind the victims and survivors of Nilsen's crimes, and their loved ones. Nilsen's actions ended lives, ruined dreams, caused lifelong trauma and tragedy. Few of the murdered were subject to any police investigations at the time they went missing. Many of them would have survived had Nilsen been caught earlier.

The day before his execution, Ted Bundy, one of the world's most infamous serial killers, warned Bill Hagmaier, the FBI special agent sent to interview him for more information about his crimes, 'If you want to catch the big fish you must be willing to go under and into the deep water to catch them.' When Hagmaier replied he wanted to proceed with the interview, Bundy warned him, 'Then I'm gonna take you under with me.'

Take a deep breath.

You are about to go under.

1

THE INTERVIEW – PART I

I'd never been to the Isle of Wight.

As a child born in the northwest of England, the most exotic resorts I'd visited during the annual summer holidays were the coastal towns of Blackpool and Southport.

Occasionally, if my adoptive parents had felt a little flush with cash, then there'd be a coach trip to North Wales and the magic of visiting a castle in either Conway or Caernarfon.

But no one I knew had ever holidayed on the Isle of Wight.

Northern, working-class families did not go to haunts like Cowes, home to probably the oldest and largest sailing regatta in the world. The nearest most of us got to sailing boats, were the miniature motorised ones you hired for next to nothing and remotely steered across a lake in a Manchester park.

Many years later, in the autumn of 1992, it came as something of a shock to me to learn that this apparently idyllic southern isle, with its breathtaking coastal scenery, verdant landscape of fields and multicoloured chines, this highly praised UNESCO Biosphere Reserve, was also home to three of Britain's most infamous prisons – Parkhurst,* Albany and Camphill.

Now, these were places that I *did* know about.

---

* Dennis Nilsen was sent to Parkhurst in 1991, moving to Albany a short time later.

Albany and Parkhurst were two of the few jails in the UK that held Category A prisoners – dangerous offenders such as kidnappers, murderers and terrorists. Parkhurst was one of the toughest jails known to tabloid journalists and their readers. This was where gangland killers, Reggie and Ronnie Kray and serial murderers such as the Yorkshire Ripper, Peter Sutcliffe, had been sent.

Camphill was more a Borstal, a bootcamp for juveniles, where it was hoped a short, sharp judicial shock might stop a young offender turning into a career criminal.

And then there was Albany.

The place where paedophiles like former glam-rock star Gary Glitter were sent. A place that in 1992 housed a Vulnerable Prisoner Unit, containing, among many other murderers, Dennis Andrew Nilsen.

Nilsen had killed at least a dozen young men. He'd lured them to his flat in London, plied them with drink and then strangled or drowned them. Afterward, he'd kept their corpses and carried out a variety of sexual rituals on them until decay demanded he desisted.

I had spent many months making arrangements to interview him for a TV documentary I was producing on the psychological profiling of serial killers, finally securing permission on the basis that it would also be used in teaching police detectives about how to better understand – and apprehend – such murderers.

En route, I'd thought a lot about the man I was about to meet. Not just about his crimes and his victims, but about what he might look and sound like on camera. How he might behave once the recording was underway. How he might even decide to pull out at the last moment, just for the hell of it. Just to show he could still exert some power and control over invaders from the world outside, the world that had come to despise and incarcerate him.

And I had seen many photographs of his unimposing face and long, lanky frame. They'd been plastered over the front pages of the national press from the moment he'd been arrested after blocking the drains of his London flat with the crushed bones and boiled flesh of his final victims.

The dutiful hacks of Fleet Street, researchers for TV shows and subsequently crime authors had found virtually everyone he'd ever had contact with, and begged and bribed them out of an entire library of Nilsen material. Without ever reading a word about Nilsen, you could, through the endless gallery of published photographs, know exactly what kind of life he'd lived.

I recalled an endearing head-and-shoulders shot of a smiling, chubby-faced six-year-old Nilsen, complete with primary school collar and tie, his short back and sides haircut side-parted and neatly combed so he'd looked his best.

Then, there had been a spindly, standing-to-attention, teenage Soldier Nilsen, trying to look like a man-of-action. His thin legs had been spread defiantly apart, booted feet planted at ten and two o'clock, his hands tucked behind the back of his tightly buttoned-up uniform, his chin held high, head of thick hair topped by a peaked cap, scrawny shoulders pinned back, pigeon-chest puffed out.

The first sign of Adult Nilsen appeared in a picture of him looking awkwardly toward the photographer. He was dressed in chef's whites, his hair, presumably for hygiene reasons, hidden in a chequerboarded hat bearing the insignia of the Army Catering Corps.

The most surprising shot was that of PC Nilsen. It was in black and white, taken some time back in the seventies. He was dressed in full Metropolitan Police uniform, complete with a pointy, shiny-badged black helmet and thick chinstrap. The huge helmet cast an ominous shadow over his eyes, and his lips were clamped almost humorously together.

But the images that I remembered most were captured after his arrest.

There's the full-length Prisoner Nilsen shot, taken in a police station, showing him in an open-necked shirt and dark unbelted trousers. He's not so much staring straight into the lens, but through it – as though contemplating the people who might in future give it their attention. And even more strikingly, there is a snapped shot of him, taken through the barred window of a police van during his trial at the Old Bailey. He is smartly dressed in a light-coloured jacket, plain shirt and Windsor-knotted tie, wearing large, owlishly round, metal-rimmed spectacles. What's fascinating here is the pleasure twitching his lips and the fascinated glaze in his eyes as he stares out at the crowd of snappers desperate for him to simply look their way so they can get their shots of him.

I've seen this look a thousand times – and so have you.

It's on the face of every wannabe, snapped for the first time by paparazzi.

Shock, followed by relief.

It's the 'I can't believe all those people have come to see me' look.

It's an expression common to most modern-day wannabes who've been catapulted from obscurity by a TV reality show into the spotlight of the public eye and the front covers of tabloid magazines.

It's the 'Thank God people are at last taking some notice of me' look.

This is Celebrity Nilsen.

I'd studied all these photographs and his phases of life before my first meeting with Nilsen at Albany Prison on the Isle of Wight. The face-to-face had been arranged, not only to try to put him at ease, but also to get the measure of him and work out just how he might perform on camera. That might sound an unnecessary exercise, but I'd had an awful experience a few years earlier in America that had resulted in me vowing never again to begin an on-screen interview without having a personal meeting beforehand.

I'd been making a documentary called *A Shred of Evidence* and had secured exclusive cooperation from the scientist who had invented genetic fingerprinting, Professor Alec Jeffreys* from Leicester University.

During filming, I'd come across the case of Gary Dotson, a man jailed in Illinois for a rape that he'd always claimed he hadn't committed. Dotson had been in jail for about half a decade when his supposed victim Cathy Crowell Webb confessed that as a teenager she'd had consensual sex with her boyfriend and, frightened she might be pregnant, told her ultra-strict parents she'd been raped. The police took her through a book of mug shots and under, pressure she'd picked Dotson, who had some minor criminal convictions. Despite her recantation and public calls for his release, the local judiciary chose not to believe Cathy's story and kept him in jail.

I asked Professor Jeffreys if he would DNA-test clothing that the prosecution had presented as being stained with Dotson's semen, to forensically prove whether he was guilty or not. He agreed to do so, and I fixed the transfer of evidence with the prisoner's attorney, Thomas Breen, on the condition

---

* Professor Alec Jeffreys was knighted in 1994 for services to genetics.

13

that I got to meet Dotson on camera in prison and tell him the results of the test. Professor Jeffreys carried out the genetic examination and was able to say beyond a shadow of a doubt that the semen wasn't Dotson's.*

He was innocent.

Post-haste, I flew to America with the good news and a camera crew. Accompanied by Tom Breen, we were admitted to the prison and walked through to a visiting area, deep inside the jail.

As guards unlocked and swung open a ceiling-to-floor iron door, I instructed the cameraman and sound recordist to begin filming. I made my way toward Gary, a slight, shy man, with the test news envelope in my hand.

'This –' I told him, holding it out – 'is DNA evidence that proves, categorically, that you're innocent and should be freed from jail.'

I waited for his emotional reply.

Waited.

And waited.

Finally, Gary looked up and struggled to speak. Not because he was overcome, but because he had a terrible stammer that no one had mentioned. One worsened by moments of extreme stress. Had I known of his nervousness, I would never have pressured him like that. I'd have filmed the historic moment with his lawyer instead.

The Dotson experience had been an invaluable lesson in not taking things for granted.

In 1992, as I boarded the ferry taking passengers from main-

---

* Sir Alec Jeffreys' DNA evidence led to Gary Dotson being freed from prison in 1989. Three years later, he was officially pardoned by the Governor of Illinois. This was the first legal case in the world where DNA resulted in a convicted man's innocence being proved and him being freed from jail.

land Britain across the Solent to the island, I hoped Dennis 'Des' Nilsen did not have a stammer.

I also wondered what had been going through the murderer's mind when he'd made the same boat journey, knowing that behind him was his life as a free man, and ahead lay years of incarceration that would only end when he drew his final breath.

Children were laughing on the decks around me, pointing excitedly at the fast-approaching cliffs, occasionally glancing backwards at the long, white wake churned by the ferry engines, their young minds fizzing with fun and adventure.

Were they literally walking in Nilsen's footsteps as they excitedly ran the deck and gazed in wonder at the water?

I hoped not.

Indeed, I persuaded myself that the police and prison service must have used different and more secure vessels, some hulk of a Dickensian prison ship, or more likely a modern speed-boat, to cross from the mainland.*

Crossing the Solent took less than an hour. Within another twenty minutes I'd reached the outskirts of Newport and the bland block of former military barrack buildings that consti-tuted Albany Prison.

Behind a high concrete wall lay a perimeter road, locked gates, and an inner security ring of wire fencing, topped with misshapen, tumbling coils of razor wire. Beyond it were five ugly four-storey cell blocks that housed around a hundred prisoners.

Other inmates, more trusted ones, seemed to be held in makeshift units around the grounds and near several flat-roofed single-storey buildings that served as administration offices.

---

* In 2021 I learned that Nilsen had taken the same ferry across the Solent.

Beyond the car park, I met up with Home Office psychologist, Paul Britton. From reception, we were led through electronically operated inner gates along labyrinthine corridors. After at least nine barred doors had been unlocked, the visual austerity of the building was overwhelmed by the uniquely sour stench of masculine confinement.

Male jails are architectural skunks.

You cannot mistake or escape their pervasive stink. They are smoulderingly revolting. All your primal senses tell you that you are not in a healthy place. Your inner voice screams – *No good can come from being here – you should get out as quickly as you can!* Jail odours hang in your hair like nesting spiders, they settle in the weaves and creases of your skin and stay long after showering or bathing.

When we reached the point where the segregation block and E wing joined, we were led through a door into what I expected to be an interview room or visiting area.

It was neither.

We entered a dusty, small storage room, virtually devoid of daylight, filled with filing cabinets, sacks of waste marked 'confidential', stacks of suicide prevention manuals for officer training purposes, and, fortuitously, a table and chairs. It was hard to think that any effort had been made on our behalf and I took the lack of preparation to be an expression of official contempt for Nilsen and perhaps the media world in general.

After what seemed an eternity, the door opened, and Dennis Nilsen was escorted in by a sullen guard who said nothing then quietly exited.

The man left behind was a flesh-and-blood compendium of all the photographs I'd seen and studied of him, as a child, soldier, policeman and civil servant in a job centre. Albeit a somewhat frayed and faded version.

His sun-starved skin was corpse-white, and he was taller than I had expected. Edging on thin and bony rather than athletic. A great flop of thick hair crested the left lens of a pair of large round glasses acutely reminiscent of the ones pictured in the police van. He was dressed in a blue pin-stripe shirt with thick, rolled up cuffs and beneath it a plain white T-shirt. His blue jeans were old and tatty, as were his black trainers. In a different place, outside in the real world, he could have passed for a scruffy academic.

He tilted his head and examined us in a way that reminded me of that memorable shot of him as an army cook. In the photograph, his right hand had held a long, razor-sharp knife while prepping food on a chopping board.

An innocent moment caught on camera.

Since then, that same hand had murdered at least twelve innocent people.

It had strangled. Drowned. Dismembered.

'I'm Des,' he said, his right hand still hovering. 'Who am I talking to? Who's who? Who does what?' This was Civil Servant Nilsen, taking charge, asserting himself.

'Mike. Mike Morley.' His handshake was soft and limp. His bony, nicotined fingers wrapped gently around mine and I found myself gripping tightly, thinking quite irrationally that it might somehow negate the uncomfortable feelings I was experiencing. 'This is Paul, Paul Britton.'

'Good morning,' said the softly spoken forensic psychologist. 'Please have a seat.' He gestured to a chair we'd positioned opposite our own, across a metal table that I had cleared of files and rubbish.

'I didn't know a damned thing about this today,' Des complained as he settled down. '*They* told me nothing.' He

17

planted his thin, pale forearms on the table and looked from one of us to the other, his eyes demanding an explanation.

We didn't have one. I presumed from the barely civil way we'd been treated that he was held in even more contempt by prison authorities than we were.

'The purpose of our visit today is just to chat,' Paul announced. 'We'll do the interview tomorrow.'

For a moment, Nilsen looked angry. He tilted his head again and weighed us up, much in the way that I imagined he listened to comments job-seekers made when he'd interviewed them. Finally, he sighed away the tension that had stiffened his shoulders, and said, 'Tomorrow? Oh, well, alright, whatever. I'm yours. I've nothing else to do. Have you got any smokes?'

Oh shit!

How could I have forgotten? I'd learned everything there was to know about this man and could recall every landmark in his life but had forgotten his requested cigarettes.

'I'm sorry, Des,' I said, using first name terms as a means of building bridges. 'It's *my* mistake.' I literally held my hands up. 'It was on my to-do list. I know you specifically mentioned wanting them in your very first letter, but I just forgot. I'll get some when we take a break.'

'Marlboro Lights.'

'I know.'

This is not going well, I admitted to myself.

We're stuck in a crap room where no one feels at ease.

Nilsen was pissed-off before he even came in here because of poor communication and now I've riled him further.

Paul began explaining how the day and the interview would progress.

Nilsen interrupted. 'With no disrespect,' he said, in the way that people always do when they're about to be downright rude, 'I much prefer Dr Anthony Clare.* I'm sure you know your job but I'm a fan of his. I listen to him on Radio 4, on – *what* is it called – *The Psychiatrist's Chair* – that's it. He's got a good way about him.'

Oh my, talk about throwing the cat among the pigeons. That little riposte came out of nowhere. Acid-tongued Des clearly has no filter. Who does he think he is, some celebratory guest?

'Yes, Dr Clare is very good,' Paul replied with disarming honesty and a genuine smile. 'I also greatly enjoy his radio programmes.'

I can't describe how much I'd wished I'd had a camera rolling at that moment. This little exchange would have been TV gold. All my fears about Nilsen being as poor an interviewee as Gary Dotson had evaporated.

As the two of them continued sizing each other up, I remembered that Nilsen was himself both a seasoned interviewer as well as interviewee. Long before the weeks, maybe months, of police interrogation that followed his arrest, he had conducted years of interviews with job centre visitors, many of whom no doubt tried to deceive and manipulate him. He knew the Q&A game every bit as well as Paul.

Pearls of truth took patient fishing.

People had to be put at ease and their trust won before they opened up.

Ask the tough questions too soon and they clam-up quicker than a mussel in a bowl of icy water.

But not in Des Nilsen's case. Oh no. He had no intention of conforming to normal interview rules, as we were about to find out.

---

* For almost twenty years, the Irish psychiatrist presented the show on the BBC, probing celebrities about their professional and personal lives, gently deconstructing their personalities and exploring their motivations and values.

'People in here have said to me, "Des, with most of your victims, you carried out the perfect murder, you'd got away with it." But I'd never got away with any of them. Right after the first one, I knew I'd done it and I could never get away from that, I could never get away from me knowing. Right after that, I relinquished my union post. I had lost conviction. How could I get up and tell people what they should be doing, after I'd done that? I had such a dark secret to keep, how could I look people in the eye and make statements about what's right and what's wrong? I just couldn't do it.'

Again, I wished we'd been filming. That one reply raised so many questions – was he telling us the truth? Did he really feel like that, or was he just wanting us to think he had a conscience, a set of morals?

I could see from Paul's face that he was concerned Nilsen was opening up too soon and that might damage tomorrow's plan to take him through his life in a much more structured and clinical fashion.

Our dilemma was put on hold when a prison officer opened the door and brought in two mugs of tea plus sugar and milk. As he started to leave, I caught up with him in the doorway, and presuming I had just witnessed another bad mannered and petty act of trying to make Nilsen feel worthless, I quietly asked why *he* hadn't been brought a cup of tea. I was told it was prohibited by regulations, and was a precaution taken for our safety because the prisoner could throw the hot liquid at us or attack us with the mug.

I came away shaking my head. If Nilsen wanted to attack us – which I very seriously doubted – then he could easily grab one of the mugs just put down in front of him. *What made his own cup of tea more dangerous than ours?* What I'd witnessed just didn't make sense.

I returned to the table and explained, 'Apparently, prison regulations mean you can't be given a hot drink when you're with us.' I turned my mug around. 'You can have mine if you like.'

'No thanks. I'll have a smoke instead. There are no prison regulations against that.' Nilsen fished several dog ends out of his pocket, along with a slim, makeshift lighter (for obvious reasons gas lighters were banned in Albany). It seemed to comprise of a roller wheel from an old lighter and a piece of metal that worked as a flint, plus a thin strand of floor mop that served as a wick. Deftly, he produced a spark and seconds later was sucking nicotine with the relief of an allergy sufferer jabbed with an EpiPen.

'I'm addicted to these.' He blew out smoke. 'They'll be the death of me.' He held the stub and gave it his considered admiration. 'I'll probably die of these things before anything else.'

A fervent non-smoker, Paul discreetly moved from the table, dodging the vast grey nicotine fog Nilsen miraculously produced from the small cigarette in the airless room. I'd spent years elbow-to-elbow with chain-smoking newsroom hacks, so was not quite as affected.

Nilsen waited for his moment, then when Paul was out of what he considered to be hearing distance, he leaned forward and quietly asked, 'Is he any good? Is he really the best for this job of yours?'

'He is,' I said, unhesitatingly, fully aware that it would please Nilsen to disrupt whatever plans we had for tomorrow.

Once the dog end had been discarded, Paul sat back at the table and politely explained how tomorrow he would want Des to tell his life story in his own words in his own time, running from early childhood to present day, including the offences he had committed and how he had felt about them.

21

I could see that none of this fazed Nilsen. To the contrary, he was impatient to get on with it. He immediately began telling us about how homophobic he'd found the police service and how lonely he'd felt after leaving the army. Paul shut him down, stressing once more that these were things he'd really like to hear about – but *tomorrow*, not today.

Nilsen took no notice.

He went off again, this time disclosing how painful it had been to keep his homosexuality a secret and his lifelong difficulties in forming meaningful relationships.

'It's been the same in prison,' he said. 'You could always go in someone else's cell if all you wanted was a quick fuck, a one-night stand, but love has not been on the cards. I've only really been in love three times. You never get over it . . .'

Paul again used his psychological skills to end the monologue.

By now, I was struck by the difference in how Nilsen expressed himself in person, to how he had done in writing – a process that he said he found 'cathartic and meditative'. He spoke very directly and clearly, with a Scottish accent softened by many years in London. Face-to-face, he was still the confident, complaining and controversial person I'd discerned from his letters. But he got to the point much quicker.

At first, I thought this brevity was because when asked a question in person, he simply had less time to respond. Less time to dress up an answer in the clothes of his own self-justifying philosophy. But then I realised I was wrong. I had underestimated him. He was talking in soundbites. He understood that television didn't have the time for long answers – and if he gave one, then it would either be edited down to fit the programme, or it would be cut out.

One thing for sure, Nilsen would make an incredible TV interviewee.

Lunch, apparently, comes very early in jail. Prisoners rise early, eat early, and are locked down early. It's a regime that I suspect suits those working there more than those locked up.

Regulations at Albany meant Category A prisoners, of which Nilsen was one, had to be fed between 11.30 a.m. and 1.30 p.m., so at exactly 11.30 a.m. the garrulous Scot was stopped mid-sentence and marched back to his wing in the Vulnerable Prisoners Unit.

Unlike most other men in the building around us, Paul and I were free to come and go as we pleased. We both jumped at the chance to get out of jail – for a short time at least.

Fresh air never felt so good.

I'd visited and filmed in all manner of prisons before Albany, including the notorious 'Wendy House' inside Lincoln Prison – essentially a jail within a jail – a segregation of the country's most violent men, moved there because they'd caused so much trouble in other prisons they couldn't be safely contained. I'd spent time recording a documentary called *Lifers* at the jail, something of a misnomer because although the men were all murderers, they would eventually be released on license, unlike Nilsen, who was on a special Home Office list decreeing he'd never be freed.

Without exception, I'd always stepped outside prison walls and instantly felt more alive than ever before. You suddenly don't mind the cold, the rain, the wind, the noise of traffic or the overcast skies. You don't mind, because you suddenly realise that you have taken the wonder and joy of these amazing things for granted, and how much of a punishment it would be to have them denied you – for months – for years – or in Nilsen's case, for life.

During our 'escape' from Albany, I asked Paul what his first impressions were.

'He's working on an image,' he said. 'We're seeing the person he is, and the person he'd like to be. From our point of view, that is very important to recognise.'

I certainly recognised it. Nilsen wanted to appear to be open and truthful by revealing graphic details about himself, but every comment would be calculated to either hide something or present a better version of himself.

By 1.30 p.m. we'd gone through security checks and were back in our seats, awaiting Nilsen's return.

Fifteen minutes later, we were still waiting.

Had he decided to pull out of the project?

Had he reflected on my forgetfulness about the cigarettes and decided to teach me a lesson by not turning up?

Had his dislike for Paul Britton run deeper than I'd detected, and he was no longer going to cooperate with us?

Or, worse than any of those things, had he been attacked by other prisoners and was now being treated for his injuries?

An attack was a real possibility. Soon after being jailed for his crimes, an inmate at Wormwood Scrubs stabbed Nilsen in the face, creating a deep wound that ran from his left ear to his mouth. Several times that morning I'd seen him finger the shiny scar as he formulated a reply.

By 1.55 p.m. I had grown sure that something serious had happened and restlessly paced the dusty room, while Paul sat quietly reading notes.

'They said one thirty. We're here and he isn't. What do you think is going on?' I asked in a way that I'm sure betrayed my deepest fears.

'Don't read too much into it,' Paul cautioned, without looking up. 'No one has told us Nilsen isn't coming, so be patient.'

I wasn't certain whether I'd been reassured or admonished.

One thing *was* certain: I had no control and no power in here. And that made me even more nervous. The success of documentaries largely depends upon directors and producers ensuring everything happens in a certain way, at a certain time and in a certain place, with certain people all playing very certain parts. Shooting schedules are not possible without these basics being in order. Camera crews, production managers, interviewers, researchers, and a hidden cast of dozens of other people rely on this exacting process.

Mine was being shredded.

I didn't know where my interviewee was. I had no way of communicating with him. If he started to change his mind and wanted to pull out, I had no chance of sitting with him and talking him out of it.

2 p.m. came.

My nerves jangled.

The door opened.

A guard nonchalantly led Nilsen into the room.

'We've been waiting since half past one,' I blurted.

The prison officer gave me a couldn't-care-less look and left.

'I was ready at half past,' Nilsen chipped in, eager not to miss out on an opportunity to complain. 'They just chose not to bring me down until now.'

There was no point debating the delay. We handed over the pack of twenty Marlboro Lights that I'd bought.

'Thanks,' Nilsen said, positioning them on the table close to his homemade lighter. He side-eyed me. 'Can you bring two packs tomorrow?'

'Of course,' I replied, guessing nothing would ever be quite right for him. He'd always want more. Or less. Or different.

The afternoon session followed the same pattern as the morning. Paul and I tried to check facts, dates, sequences of events and get a reading on his personality, his truthfulness, and areas that he might find too uncomfortable to discuss.

There were none. Silence was the only thing he seemed to find uncomfortable. He was hugely cooperative and never stuck for words.

'I like being the centre of attention,' he told us – as though that was something we never could have guessed. 'I like being number one. I like being special, but I hate competition. I'll avoid competition like the plague.' He addressed me directly, 'I hope this programme is going to be of value to you.' And then he turned to Paul. 'I hope *you* come out of it with some theory, some knowledge and understanding because it would be good to know that I'd done something good.'

We were both mentally processing this remark when Nilsen continued, 'Look at Hitler. Hitler wouldn't have been happy with Europe. He wouldn't have been happy with the world. He would have to have destroyed it eventually.'

My eyebrows were still rising in surprise and I was expecting him to expound some messiah theory, when he added, 'There are similarities between the two of us, both of us have personality orders.' He looked to Paul again. 'And it all goes back to childhood, doesn't it?'

Now we were on dangerous ground. He'd gone from spouting profundities about himself, to asking vital questions about what had made him the man he was. Questions we absolutely wanted him to address, but not now. Not today.

Paul decided to call time on our get-together. It was earlier than we'd planned but it was clearly necessary. He waited until Nilsen ended a sentence about his heightened sense of self-awareness, and announced, 'Well, thank you for speaking to us today.' He stood and stretched out his hand to hasten the goodbye. 'I'd like to call it quits for today.'

Nilsen recognised the cue. He quickly got to his feet, smiled politely, and shook the psychologist's hand.

Then he sat down again.

Leaving Paul standing.

Nilsen blanked him. Cut him off as expertly as a guilty politician passing a crowd of journalists shouting questions. Eyes fixed firmly on mine, he asked, 'So when is this programme going out then? When will everyone get to see it?'

I could hardly ignore him, so I answered as briefly as possible. 'It's still to be scheduled – but given all the editing and post-production that needs to be done, I guess it'll air early next year.'

He looked disappointed, then added, 'I love television. Well, more films really. I've watched *Man for All Seasons* over and over. I used to do lots of filming, you know, home movie stuff, but good – *really good.* I burned reels and reels of film. The only stuff that was saved was the duff bits, the bits I never thought anything of. I never had any training or anything like that, but give me a camera and I could look through the frame and know what the camera wanted.'

As he paused, I got to my feet, so he was now the only one sitting. 'I really think we have to leave all this until tomorrow.'

Thankfully, Nilsen followed suit. But he hadn't finished. 'I hope you're not going to use any of that weird lighting. I don't want to look like a bloody monster. I want to look interesting. However you shoot it, make me look interesting.'

2

LETTERS FROM HELL

In 1992, I received the first of what I would come to regard as Letters from Hell.

It was correspondence destined to dramatically change my life by enabling me to create a piece of TV history, an event that hasn't happened since, and is unlikely to ever happen again.

But that initial letter would also be a catalyst for outbreaks of depression and unimaginable nightmares. The type of REM-wreckers that wake you in the black hours of the morning with a pounding heart and a cold sweat. The type so graphic, you don't even want to tell your family you endured.

The missive was lodged in the middle of a mundane stack of morning mail delivered to the small, glass-fronted first-floor office I occupied as head of current affairs in the Nottinghamshire HQ of Central Television, one of the biggest independent broadcasters in Europe.

I had absent-mindedly ripped open the envelope, paying more attention to my usual at-desk breakfast of lukewarm canteen tea and blackened toast, leaving buttery fingerprints on the edge of what I had imagined were the inconsequential pages I laid out in front of me.

The sender turned out to be Britain's most prolific serial killer of the time. A man who'd been jailed more than a decade earlier, and despite proclaiming himself to be 'the murderer of the century', had largely been forgotten about by the public and the mainstream media. Neither he nor I realised it, but this letter was going to put us both in the spotlight and turn him into the most talked-about English murderer since Jack the Ripper.

My interest piqued as I read the sender's name, along with his obligatory prison number in the top right corner of cheap paper that smelled strongly of cigarettes. I had recently contacted Dennis Nilsen but had not expected a response, yet alone so swift a reply to the vital question I had asked him.

My eyes scanned line after line of what amounted to a long, disjointed, intellectual ramble that changed every few sentences and touched on everything from his distrust of the police, '. . . *most of whom ran roughshod through rules, regulations and common decency*', to psychiatrists and psychologists, '. . . *their minds twisted by over-thinking the unthinkable and failing to think of anything original*', to his dislike for other prisoners, '. . . *the community in here is daily proof that there is not always wisdom in crowds but there is always danger and thuggery*', and for prison itself, '. . . *for a free spirit like me, the denial of liberty is a living hell*'.

Finally, amid all the vitriol, I saw what I was hoping for. Confirmation that Dennis Nilsen was '. . . *enthusiastically disposed toward participation in the proposed Central Television project*'. He said he would make himself available to us whenever his presence was required '. . . *subject to the constraints, trials and tribulations imposed daily and unpredictably upon me by my incarcerators*'.

Oh my God, I thought. *He's said yes.*

He's agreed to do it.

In my introductory letter, I'd been very clear that as well as a part of the interview being screened on network television in the UK, the *entirety* of it would be used by police forces up and down the land, to learn how to better understand and more quickly capture offenders such as himself.

Given Nilsen's known contempt for the police (which he said had started while serving as a PC and became entrenched during his treatment after being arrested), I'd convinced myself that their involvement may well be a reason why he would decline.

But he hadn't.

Quite the contrary.

'*I have no time for tawdry tabloid voyeurism,*' he wrote, '*but I welcome the prospect of a professional and proper exploration of my life for many reasons, primary of which is my belief that what may be discovered will transpire to be of intellectual merit synchronous with my own commitment to ongoing self-reflection regardless of how painful such an endeavour is, or how inadequate I may prove to be in performing it. Much academic fog has been created around me by various authors, and I have long been of the opinion that it would be good if something useful came out of this sorry mess, so I am trusting that everyone involved will work towards that end.*'

Sorry mess.

Those two words hit me like punches that I hadn't seen coming.

Sorry mess.

What an astonishingly understated way of describing how he murdered at least a dozen young men.

Sorry mess.

The words hadn't been carelessly chosen. The entire letter had been assiduously composed. They simply gave away how he felt toward his victims and their loved ones. Nothing. He felt nothing for them. He completely lacked empathy.

And the line, *'I am trusting that everyone involved will work towards that end.'* It smacked of the kind of proclamation a pompous, out-of-touch boss might write in a company-wide end-of-year letter to a workforce.

Nilsen added, *'I have long been amazed at the public interest in me, my life and all matters of the macabre. I question though whether the so-called ordinary public really care to see that I am less than the monster the newspapers would have me be.'*

It was hard not to agree with him. We all are indeed interested in the macabre. It is human nature to try to understand matters of death that frighten and revolt us. It is how we face mortality and overcome our fears. The darker the crime, the brighter the light needed to examine it.

'I know nothing about the man you say you have assigned to the role of interviewer,' he had continued, *'and I can only trust, in the unlikely event that the authorities allow your project to proceed, that he comes properly prepared. I would counsel you to take measures to secure such preparation because as you will discover, I am a unique individual and require unique attention if any interrogation of my behaviour is to bear fruits of genuine worth.'*

Despite the pomposity and verbosity of his comment, I knew Mr Dennis Nilsen of Albany Prison was absolutely right. There was a lot of Home Office red tape that prevented me directly asking him questions – and the reasons for this will shortly become apparent – so, I had told Nilsen that the interview would be carried out by a very senior clinical and forensic psychologist, Paul Britton. The only problem was, Paul was also an exceptionally busy psychologist, which meant he might not have the time to do all the preparation he would like or need.

For my own peace of mind, I would have to make sure that I could not only brief him properly, but I would also have close to hand everything there was to know about Nilsen and his self-acclaimed uniqueness, in case we needed to refer to it.

But there were other problems.

Much bigger ones.

In America, TV interviews with infamous serial killers had long been commonplace. It was relatively simple to set up. A phone call to the prisoner's lawyer, a letter of explanation to the prisoner asking for consent, a filming request form to the governor and away you go.

But not in the UK.

In Britain, such interviews had never taken place.

Prison governors did not have the autonomy to grant such access, and the Home Office strangled such ideas at birth, saying it was against their policies.

But Nilsen has said yes.

He was willing to be interviewed.

I consoled myself with this fact. It was a good start.

I re-read the letter. Now that I wasn't simply speed-reading for a yes/no answer to my request to interview him, certain passages started to grab my attention.

'*Contextually, my offences will, under proper examination, and in clinical perspective, be clearly shown to be more than the sole result of my own physical actions. They will be identified as having been fashioned, as much as by everything and everyone around me, as by myself, for I too have been fashioned by forces other than solely my own. Those of higher intellects will understand the justification of me saying that society should have stood alongside me in the dock when I was held to account, for society formed me far more dangerously than I had formed myself. Thus, it is, that my sicknesses are no more or less than the secondary infections of society's own sicknesses. Imprisonment is not a way to end endemic societal sickness. The disease that afflicted me and a pantheon of others has resisted such impotent measures for centuries, continues to do so, and will prosper in perpetuity unless met with a manner of thinking more modern than today's "lock 'em up and throw away the key" approach.'*

This, I would eventually learn from other letters, extracts from books and plays he told me he was 'working on', plus graphic drawings he doodled of himself and his victims, was typical of Nilsen's provocative and philosophically chaotic thinking. There was a valid point in there, fighting to escape a maze of self-serving verbosity.

Whenever he wrote about his crimes, he always mitigated his actions by claiming there was a reason why events, people or circumstances had '. . . *caused me to act so lethally out of character and so hideously inhumanely'*.

'*I am fully culpable for my actions,*' he wrote, '*for those I hurt and those I killed, and I do not seek to evade such responsibility. Murder had become a ritual driven by my own emotions and though I was aware of it, like all who consciously exercise a lack of willpower and become immersed in harmful habits, I found myself entranced, swept along by a sexual and emotional momentum that rendered me unable to stop.*'

When I later showed this section of the letter to a behavioural scientist, he said simply, 'One of his final words is *unable*. If you swap that for *unwilling*, then you get the true picture.'

Nilsen also wrote, '*There were times when I was attracted to the ritual and times when the thought of it sickened me. It often turned out to be like a person you had lusted after and*

33

spent the night with, only to find in the morning you were sickened by the sight of them and by the recollection of what you'd done.'

He added, *'There were even times when I had not given thought to the ritual only to find it had already begun and was progressing. I am under no illusion though that it was my ritual and I do not deny such ownership.'*

The day I received the first letter, I took his use of the word 'ritual' to be a synonym for 'murder'.

My mistake.

It was both different and more complex than that. I was to later discover that to Nilsen, murder was not the end of his crime, but the beginning. To him, it was simply a means of keeping someone permanently captive, so he could indulge in a whole sequence (ritual) of sexually and emotionally charged acts (undressing, bathing, redressing, abusing, etc.) without his victim resisting.

Reading and trying to understand Nilsen's letters became the psychological equivalent of standing in an old photographic darkroom endlessly watching pictures appear in dishes of developing fluid. His choice of words, the old-fashioned layout and the spidery handwriting all gave me a fuzzy but nonetheless highly informative snapshot of the author's personality.

His penmanship was strong and quick, unhesitatingly confident like a doctor's and as difficult to read. All his words slanted a little forward and individual letters were joined together by loops and upward diagonals. The pen pressure was mainly consistent but increased when he wrote about the police. The writing showed maturity – and his spelling, grammar and vocabulary were of a high educational standard.

His turns of phrase were often colourful, complex and verbose.

'People who say I am incapable of emotion know nothing of the emotions of death, of mortido,* of my unique feelings.

'Like half-witted vandals with cans of aerosol colours, the tabloid press has painted me as an icon of evil.'

'My imprisonment has no societal value; it is human storage. I am moved around with disdain and neglect, like a toxic package that everyone knows will never be delivered anywhere other than the graveyard.'

'From my experiences, there is nothing of rehabilitative value in the current prison system. I have received no therapy or counselling that has shed, for me or for others, any useful light on my thoughts, my actions or my state of mind, let alone any identification of personality problems and possible solutions to my inadequacies.'

'It saddens me that I am shown and seen solely for what I have been imprisoned for, not for who I am, and not for the good things I did, the kind things I did, the brave, courageous and generous things I did. I am so much more than the error of my ways.'

'It is an indictment on the Police and their prejudiced practices that they failed so many young men for so many years. Had they done their jobs as proficiently as they professed, then the engine of my actions would have been halted much earlier and lives would have been saved.'

---

* 'Mortido' is a psychoanalytical term referring to unconscious self-destruction and aggression, the desire to destroy life, both in oneself and others. Psychoanalysts claim there are two drivers of human personality – libido (creative) and mortido (destructive). Ego-mortido is experienced as pain and a fear of the unknown.

His letters often seemed to have been devised as a deliberate attempt to display his intelligence.

Perhaps he was firing a warning that he wanted to be taken seriously?

Treated with some degree of respect?

Not talked down to or underestimated?

In one letter to me, he politely asked if it was possible to provide him with a typewriter and ribbons, as he wished to send me other documentation, insisting: *'The amount of correspondence I am compelled to instigate or reply to has become more than pen and hand can adequately manage.'*

I apologise now to all those people across the world who received unwanted letters from him. I did send a typewriter. And he very probably wrote to you on it. It was a very fine one that we had kept as a spare in our newsroom. For good measure, I included a plentiful supply of ribbons and hefty slab of A4 paper.

In giving his consent to participate in the documentary I was making, Nilsen added some final instructions to send stamps and paper if I wished to continue corresponding with him – oh, and cigarettes if, as I intended, I secured permission from the prison and Home Office to film him, which he seriously doubted would be given.

He is controlling, I noted.

Agenda-setting. Manipulative. Hungry for attention.

No doubt difficult to deal with.

I wouldn't rule him out of withdrawing at the last minute. Scuppering everything I might put in place, just to show he has the power to do so.

One of the most striking features about his first letter had been his politeness. Not something you immediately associate with a serial killer. For example, he'd begun his reply – *'Dear*

Mr Morley' – addressing me in the way only tax authorities and bill servers tended to.

Intriguingly, he'd signed-off, *'Yours sincerely, Des.'*

Des.

Was he inviting me to reply on first name terms?

Did *I* want to do that?

Such a little thing.

Wasn't it?

Or was being 'routinely familiar' with a man who'd killed at least a dozen people a step too far? Morally wrong? Unacceptable? Unthinkable?

For the first, but by no means the last time, I found my internal voices, one liberal and one conservative, debating the ethics of an unfolding situation.

Surely, whatever anyone calls him, he is still a human being? A man in jail, paying the ultimate price for his crimes. Maybe even trying to come to terms with what he did? Wasn't it entirely acceptable, decent, and just polite to call him Des?

No. It absolutely wasn't. Try monster – that would be more fitting. Murderer. Necrophile. Those are names most of the public still call him. The Muswell Hill Murderer. Why not write back to him using one of those pejorative names and see if he still agrees to be interviewed?

That would be stupid. It would end any chance of getting to see him.

He called himself Des and wants to be known as Des. He really couldn't have made it any clearer.

What about Nilsen's victims? Too much familiarity would be disrespectful to them.

Then Mr Nilsen is the compromise to use. Reply, 'Dear Mr Nilsen, thank you for your letter, etc.' but sign it as Mike. Mirror his style. Nothing will go wrong if you do that.

My voices and I settled on that – *'Dear Mr Nilsen . . .'*

Then I rang my boss and told him the good news.

'Still a long way to go,' he reminded me.

'I know. We'll get there,' I promised, wondering if we ever would.

I put the phone down and guessed that the project would probably be cancelled as soon as I contacted the police, Prison Service or Home Office.

But maybe not.

And maybe was always worth a shot.

If you don't ask – you don't get.

3

THE FILM THAT LED TO THE BOOK THAT LED TO THE PROGRAMME THAT LED TO THE PRISON INTERVIEW WITH DENNIS NILSEN THAT LED TO A WHOLE WORLD OF TROUBLE

Please forgive the lengthy chapter heading. Brevity isn't something I'm blessed with. It does, however, flag up the fact that the road to HMP Albany and the recorded interview with Dennis Nilsen was a circuitous one that needs perspective and explanation.

So here we go.

In early 1991, like millions of other people around the world, I left a darkened cinema, speechlessly impressed by what was destined to be only the third movie in history to win Academy Awards in the top five categories.*

The film was *The Silence of the Lambs*, directed by Jonathan Demme, starring Anthony Hopkins and Jodie Foster. In it, a young FBI cadet (Clarice Starling) is sent to a maximum-security psychiatric hospital to gain the cooperation of a murderous inmate (Hannibal Lecter). She is hunting a serial

---

* Best Director, Best Actor in a Leading Role, Best Actress in a Leading Role, Best Screenplay and Best Sound.

killer called Buffalo Bill, who abducted, killed, and then skinned his victims to make clothing from them.

Aside from the sheer shock, what helped make it a global box-office hit grossing more than a quarter of a billion dollars, was the fact that Hannibal was a brilliant former psychologist who among his highly refined tastes had a penchant for human flesh and organs – 'I ate his liver with fava beans and a nice Chianti.'

Here, for the first time (in my memory at least), was the depiction of a cultured, very intelligent killer who had outwitted the best of US homicide cops. A special department of the FBI called the Behavioral Science Unit (BSU) had to be called in to catch him. Someone with a gift for brevity would put it like this – Lecter was so smart and so evil that the good guys had to turn to him to learn how to catch other bad guys like Buffalo Bill.

It was a great story.

But that was all it was. Right?

Wrong.

I quickly discovered that this fiction had been fashioned from far more shocking fact. There actually was a Behavioral Science Unit* that hunted guys as bad as Lecter and Bill. It was based in Quantico in Virginia, where cinema's Clarice trained as a cadet. People in this unit were, as shown in the film, both FBI agents and psychological profilers. And they actually did visit killers in prison to interview them and learn how to catch others like them.

I remember sitting back at my desk in the TV studios in Nottingham and being amazed at my staggering naivety. Until then, you couldn't have persuaded me that there were people

---

* In 2018 the BSU was renamed as the Behavioral Research and Instruction Unit.

in the world more unspeakably horrible than Ian Brady and Myra Hindley, the Moors Murderers.* I'd never considered that in modern times there were crimes as comparably awful as abducting, sexually abusing and then murdering young children.

Skinning people and making clothes out of their skin?
Cooking and eating human flesh and organs?
Surely not.

I researched the real-life case of Edward Theodore Gein – a graverobber and murderer from Wisconsin who became known as the Butcher of Plainfield. When he was arrested, sheriff deputies searched his farmhouse and found, hung upside down, the decapitated body of one of the several women he'd been suspected of killing.

That discovery, undoubtedly mind-blowing, was nothing compared to the grizzly evidence lying in the rest of the house. The deputies found leggings – cut from human thigh and calf skin, a corset sewn from a skinned female torso, masks made from female faces, a lampshade created from skin and bone, a belt of human nipples and a variety of skulls, organs and genitalia.

The fictional Buffalo Bill that I had found so horrible, turned out to be a toned-down version of Gein.

Journalistically, I was hooked.

I had to know more about these people. More about this world of profiling.

I *needed* to get inside it.

I devoured every article I could find on the BSU and serial offenders. The more information I read, the more I craved.

---

* Brady and Hindley murdered at least five young children, sexually assaulting most of them, then buried their bodies on moorland near Manchester in England between 1963 and 1965.

The unit, I found, was not a new development and had existed long before Thomas Harris had shone his literary spotlight on it.

The division had been formed in 1972 as a political/law-and-order response to a country-wide rise in the rate of murders and sexual assaults. It wasn't until '76 that its pioneering work really began, with senior agents travelling to prisons to interview serial killers and learn from them.

For a solid week, I hammered the work phone, making calls to every police officer, lawyer, social worker, psychiatrist and prison officer in my contact book.

The UK had no national/federal body like the FBI, let alone the BSU. Only a handful of police forces had ever used psychologists when investigating serious crimes, and they were either reluctant to talk about the cases or were dismissive of the results. A senior academic at Surrey University had helped in a rape-murder investigation and off the back of it founded the university's Offender Profiling Research Unit. I marked this down as worth a closer look.

I rang the FBI in Washington.

After days of being bounced through multiple departments, I ended up talking to a weary publicity liaison officer working for the Academy and the BSU. After introducing myself and my company, I cut to the chase. 'I'd like to come to Virginia and film everything you do. I want to contrast the work being done in America to what is being done in the UK.'

I was met with a few seconds of spontaneous laughter, then she gave me a not entirely unexpected response. 'Sir, since *The Silence of the Lambs* came out, we've been snowed under with media access requests. At the moment, I'd say it'd be impossible to accommodate your wishes, but write me exactly what you want, and I'll run it by the folks in the bunker.'

'The bunker' was the term used for the BSU, because it had been started in a cleared-out part of the basement at FBI HQ in Quantico.

I put the phone down, in no doubt that overseas hacks like me were at the back of the queue when it came to granting requests to film. Not a pleasant place to be. And not a position I planned to stay in for very long. I needed leverage. Some way of muscling my way to the front.

A year earlier, I had been granted unprecedented fly-on-the-wall access to Derbyshire Police's CID department and had become the first documentary maker in the UK to film a murder investigation, from the moment a body had been found, to the conviction and imprisonment of the offenders. To do so, I'd had to secure the cooperation of the Crown Prosecution Service, both at local and national level. Fortuitously, the local senior crown prosecutor had turned out to be Paul Bland, a prosecuting lawyer I'd spent endless hours with when I'd been a court reporter in north Manchester. His boss, CCP David Seddon, was open-minded enough to support the project and eventually we'd been given the green light by the head of the CPS, Allan Green.[*]

Aside from the tangle of red tape, it turned out to be a gruelling project, ending in the kind of professional and public controversy that was going to become a regular companion throughout my broadcast career.

General filming parameters had been agreed with the Force's assistant chief constable (Operations), Don Dovaston. A hard-nosed, no-nonsense crook catcher, he'd earned his

---

[*] As a QC in 1983, Allan Green had been the prosecution counsel in Dennis Nilsen's trial at the Old Bailey. He would later become Sir Allan and would then resign after receiving a police caution for kerb-crawling in a red-light district of London.

fearsome reputation on the streets of Liverpool, where he rose to the highly respected position of head of CID with Merseyside Police. I was a street savvy, working-class lad from Manchester who spoke the same kind of language. We'd first met years ago during the Toxteth Riots in Liverpool*, and had formed a friendship outside of work that we kept private and very separate from our professional dealings.

On a murky March morning, I found myself being bleeped on my pager with a number that required me to call Derbyshire Police CID, which I immediately did. A DC informed me that a body of a middle-aged man had been found on the outskirts of Derby city centre, a team was being dispatched as we spoke, and he was about to call a Home Office pathologist to attend the scene.

I left everything and headed to my car with a video camera, in case the coordinator at the TV studios couldn't get a crew to the scene before the body was taken away for a post-mortem examination. These were the days of strong trade unions and 'closed shops', when only cameramen could operate cameras, certainly not journalists, but I would worry about that, and overcome it, later.

It transpired that fifty-year-old Mohammed Rafia had been stabbed forty-seven times inside a car. He was then dumped and left to die in a back street, near an industrial estate not far from Derby city centre.

I filmed everything, from the appearance of the pathologist and his in-situ examination of the body, to the start of forensic evidence gathering and the crime scene search by police. My

---

* The riots in July 1981 sparked by racial tensions and high unemployment, lasted nine days, saw around five hundred arrests and four hundred and fifty police officers injured. Around seventy buildings, mainly targets of arson, had to be demolished afterwards.

professional focus had been so intense, that it wasn't until I'd finished recording and stopped being a television automaton that I connected with the victim on a human level. Here was a man, a human being, who one moment had walked around thinking about his family, friends and what he might have for dinner that night, then the next moment he had ceased to exist.

Mortality.

Someone had reduced his half-century of actions, his life, his laughter and his love for others, to a mass of gaping wounds, untold pain and a bundle of blood-soaked clothes.

Why?

How could someone do such a thing?

Even to my untrained eyes, I could see a number of potentially fatal wounds to the back of his head and front of his legs and body. Either someone had gone crazy, beaten him up, stabbed him, turned him over and stabbed him again, or two people had attacked him. One from the back and one from the front.

The police moved the body from the scene. Transported it quietly, under covers, in silence, with the greatest of respect. As they did so, I saw again the cruel cuts in the corpse, the emptiness in his milky eyes, the hardened blood on his clothes.

Life was so fragile. We took it for granted. Could never imagine it being taken from us in a manner like this.

Dogged detective work would reveal that the stabbing had been ordered as part of what I was horrified to learn was termed an 'honour killing'. Rafia had openly sided with his nephew's wife during a marital dispute and had given her a place to stay when their rows had got too much. The nephew, along with other male relatives, had taken this to be an unforgiveable act of disrespect and had paid a local lowlife to help them murder Rafia and dispose of the body.

The killing had been a bodged affair, and the poor man's assailants ended up soaked in blood and panic. It hadn't taken any incisive policing to track down the murderers, just judicious door-knocking and discreet conversations in the local community.

My crew and I filmed the arrests of all five conspirators and recorded them being taken in handcuffs into the city's police station where they were to be interviewed. Here our access ended, and we waited in the corridors of the police cell block. Word came back that despite the discovery of considerable forensic evidence, all of the men were pleading innocence.

Instinctively, I'd kept a camera in the cell block after the prisoners had been taken to the interview rooms, and it was still filming when they were brought back and locked up for the night. The busy custody sergeant didn't give me a second glance as he walked out of shot back to his desk where paperwork was piling up.

As he disappeared, the face of one of the arrested men appeared through a cell door hatch that had been left open.

The prisoner mouthed something to me.

I stepped forward, expecting him to swear or spit as several of the defendants had done when we'd videoed their arrests.

He didn't.

Instead, he told me, in surprising detail, about his part in the crime and said that all it amounted to was 'jabbing' the dead man several times with a knife.

'Jabbing him in his leg.'

I felt a surge of adrenaline. From the preliminary in-situ post-mortem examination that I'd witnessed, I was aware that this jab to the femoral artery in the thigh had been one of several fatal wounds. What the knifeman thought was a protestation of his innocence was actually a confession to murder. A confession the police didn't have.

I finished filming and headed back to the TV studios.

Even before the on-camera confession, I'd known the material we'd shot that day had been historic. The confession elevated its importance.

As soon as I reached the studios, I had a technician make copies of the video tapes in case they were seized by the police and I rang my boss and then the company's in-house lawyers.

As I was recounting the day's events, I got a message from a secretary, saying there was an officer from Derbyshire Police downstairs *demanding* to see me.

Still on the line, our lawyers confirmed what I already suspected. 'Arrests have been made and charges either brought or are imminent, so the murder case you've been filming is sub judice*, meaning you won't be able to transmit any of the material you just recorded until after the men have stood trial. Expect calls from solicitors. Lots of solicitors. The police, the prosecution and the defence are going to be all over this and there may be accusations that we've interfered in the course of justice.'

I made notes and put the phone down. My euphoria was turning into anxiety. Ignoring the police officer downstairs waiting to see me, which I guessed was not going to be a pleasant experience, I made another call, directly to Don Dovaston.

'Get yourself over here. Now!' the assistant chief constable told me, 'And make sure you bring those bloody tapes with you.'

---

* 'Sub judice' is Latin for 'under judgment', UK law prohibits the pre-trial broadcast of material such as the video confession I'd recorded, as it might influence a jury. Not obeying sub judice is taken as contempt of court and can be punished by an unlimited fine or up to two years imprisonment.

I did. But with copies of the taped confession, not the originals.

For about ten minutes, I sat in Don's office and bit my tongue while he turned the air blue. He left me in no doubt that he was incandescent with rage over what had happened.

Finally, he softened. 'I don't blame you for doing what you did. I know it's your job to get the best footage you can. But legally you've created a real problem for us, and you will probably end up being a witness in the trial.'

'I'm sorry,' I said, knowing the apology was insufficient.

'I just wish my people had done their jobs as well as you'd done yours and this hadn't happened.'

A truce was called.

In the end, the man who'd confessed to me reiterated his story to the police, meaning there'd be no compulsion for me to be a witness at the Crown Court trial, where subsequently all five were found guilty of murder.

In 1991 I was once again in Don Dovaston's office, testing our relationship by asking for his trust and cooperation.

'I know you're involved in a profiling project called CATCHEM,' I told him. 'And I'd like to include it in a documentary I'm going to make about psychological profiling.'

Don pulled a sour face.

I continued. 'I know it's an acronym for Centralised Analytical Team Collating Homicide Expertise and Management. My guess is that it was your idea and you set it up here in Derbyshire because it would be away from the interference of others. And maybe the powers that be were either too slow or too stupid to put the right amount of money and manpower into it.'

I had found out from other sources that the Home Office

and the police were fighting over funds for a whole variety of projects and many initiatives had been put on hold.

'Don, you know that with or without your cooperation I'll find someone to talk about CATCHEM. Maybe they'll champion it, maybe they won't. Can you at least steer me towards the right people, so you get a positive spin on this – that's presuming you still think the project is worth it?'

The ACC let out a long sigh, then said, 'I'm going to ask you a question. One I recently asked a number of heads of CID. Here it is: The body of a young female child is found. She's been sexually assaulted, strangled and her body hidden at the bottom of the large garden of her middle-class family. Who's more than 90 per cent likely to be the killer?'

'Father, stepfather or brother,' I answered immediately.

His eyes brightened and I knew I had been sucker-punched. 'That's what most people say. When people see a child murder on the news they think, "I bet it's the father or stepfather", like you just did.'

I waited for the pay off.

'It isn't.' After a dramatic pause, he continued, 'CATCHEM is a database we are assembling of all child murders going back twenty years. It's a long way from finished, but it already produces statistical profiles of murder situations, and what it tells us is, that if a child's body is found at the family home, then the killer is almost – *almost* – certain *not* to be a member of the immediate family.'

I looked surprised.

'It makes sense when you think about it. If you killed *your* child – your Damian – then you wouldn't leave his body in your own garden. It ties you to the murder scene. You'd move it as far away as you could. At least to another postcode. But if a stranger attacked and killed Damian, then he wouldn't want to be caught with the boy's corpse in his car, so he'd leave it there and make his escape.'

'But fathers and stepfathers *do* kill their children and *do* leave them in the grounds of family homes, don't they?'

'Yes, they do, but it is very, very rare, which is why we remember it, and why I said *almost* and not *always*. My point is, operationally we've traditionally concentrated initial resources into looking at the family first. Now we know that's the wrong thing to do. Going forward, we will still have to look at the family, but in those vital first few days we should be focusing on suspects from further afield.'

'Such as?'

'Visitors to the house. Handymen. Window cleaners. Neighbours. Delivery drivers who regularly drop things off or pass the house on their rounds. People who might frequently see the child coming home alone from school and fantasise about assaulting them.'

I sat in silence, feeling a mixture of confusion and repulsion. In the last few minutes, I'd been asked to contemplate how I might kill my nine-year-old son and dispose of his body. Now my mind was wondering how many perverted milkmen, postmen and couriers might be thinking about sexually assaulting and murdering him.

My speechlessness was also because this was the first time I'd ever been forced to think about murder from the murderer's perspective. It made me exceptionally uncomfortable. As did any contemplation of child murder. I'd covered many such cases, including the Susan Maxwell murder in the Borders and the nationwide hunt and arrest of serial child-killer Robert Black. As a father, I'd always felt gut-punching sympathy for the parents I'd interviewed. But there was no doubt that sympathising with the families of victims was a far more natural mental exercise than thinking as a murderer, something detectives have to put themselves through on a regular basis.

Amid my reflections, I could see the ACC was waiting for me to react to his explanation. 'I'd like to film CATCHEM, see it at work and have you talk about its value,' I said, repeating myself.

'I'm sure you would,' he answered drily.

I knew Don was a leading member of the Association of Chief Police Officers. 'Is ACPO backing it? Is this something that every force is soon going to be using?'

'They are.'

'And *psychological* profiling, are you involved in that?'

He hesitated.

'Do you believe in it?' I asked.

'To an extent. But there are a lot of charlatans putting themselves forward. I need convincing that behavioural opinions bring us more than forensics or statistics.'

'Would you say that on camera?'

He weighed up his response. 'Probably.'

'So CATCHEM then, can I film that, and you and your people talking about it?'

'You *can* – providing we don't have a repeat of what happened in the cell blocks with the Rafia case.' He gave me a withering look. 'I'm going to trust you on this.'

'Thank you.'

'Do you know why I'm going to trust you? It's not because I don't think you'll ever let me down again, it's because I believe the public should know what we're doing to try to protect them. I don't believe in policing in secret.'

'Neither do I.'

Don had long been my litmus test on what was possible and what wasn't when it came to police access, so I shared what was at the back of my mind. 'I'm probably going to go to America to interview a serial killer there, it's fairly easy to get access, and I'm hoping to get the FBI on board. How do you rate my chances of interviewing someone here – like Hindley, Brady, Sutcliffe or Nilsen?'

He smiled and gave me a quick reply. 'Not a chance. Not a hope. They'll never let you near any of those evil bastards.'

I took the 'they' to mean the Prison Service and Home Office.

Don's great detective brain clicked in and he added, 'You should check to see if any prison psychiatrists have interviewed any of them. You might have some luck there, though personally, I hope you don't. I'm in favour of these people being locked away and forgotten.'

The chief constable's staff officer knocked on the door and entered with a reminder that a top-level meeting was about to start.

I gathered my things and said goodbye. As I headed to the door, Don added, 'I have to clear your access to CATCHEM with John Stevens, the chairman of the ACPO Crime Sub-Committee on Offender Profiling. If he gives the okay, then we can discuss dates. I'll let you know.'

I left feeling I'd made a small step forward. And I was hopeful that I'd find some already recorded material on a UK serial murderer.

The following week, I received confirmation that ACPO had green-lit the filming, and Don suggested that if I directly contacted John Stevens then he might be forthcoming about other initiatives.

I did.

It resulted in me travelling north for my first meeting with a man who would eventually move on from his post as chief constable in Northumbria, serve as commissioner of one of the world's most famous police forces, the Met, be knighted for his work, and become Lord Stevens of Kirkwhelpington.

Tall, broad, clean-shaven, with brown eyes, dark hair and a great smile, John Stevens was one of those people I knew the TV camera would just love. He spoke without any hesitation or hint of regional accent. His sentences were soundbite smart, and he was full of enthusiasm. It was clear, even then, that his communication skills alone would propel him to much higher office.

Our meeting went well, and I came away with the knowledge that ACPO had hired an independent consultant psychologist called Paul Britton to review the use of clinicians (profilers) in aiding the investigation of serious crimes. I was also provided with a list of psychologists and psychiatrists who had been used on major investigations (some I already knew about) and been assured that ACPO would cooperate with the documentary I planned to make.

This was more than the breakthrough it seemed.

It was leverage.

I now went back to the FBI in Washington and told them I had secured the cooperation of the Association of Chief Police Officers in the UK and was about to film major breakthroughs they had made in profiling offenders. I added the names of Don Dovaston and John Stevens as references, plus a list of other experts I had filmed with in the UK and US, such as Alec Jeffreys and Tom Breen.

Several weeks passed.

Finally, I received a letter from Quantico saying they'd reviewed my request to film with the BSU team and were willing to cooperate, but they would not grant me access to any live cases. They would, however, arrange for me to meet current and past profilers who'd be cleared to talk about previous cases.

It was more than I'd expected.

4

WE'RE ALL ALMOST NILSEN

There isn't a crime buff on the planet who isn't aware of the fact that serial killers appear to be perfectly normal. For most of the time, they're just like the rest of us. Much more like us than, say, the bonobo, a primate that shares almost 99 per cent of our DNA.

So how alike was I to Dennis Nilsen?

This was the uncomfortable question I faced as I researched the serial killer for the planned documentary.

In 1992, I was thirty-five years old, just two years younger than he'd been when policemen turned up at his home in London with a search warrant and brought his days as a murderer to a close.

Unlike him, I was heterosexual, had been married for more than a decade and had a young son. I was the head of current affairs for the biggest independent television station in the country and strongly believed that I was about as happy as it was possible to get. And I was confident that my wife and family were at least as equally content.

So, nothing like Nilsen.

But hang on. Things are seldom what they seem.

My family was not that happy.

And neither was I.

We just hadn't realised it. Or we were refusing to admit it. Invisible cracks in my marriage would soon permanently open so wide that they'd never close and it would all end in tears and divorce.

For years, I'd ignored signs of growing incompatibility at home by burying myself in work. The harder I worked, the more professional praise and rewards my stupid ego got, and consequentially the longer I remained blind to the damage being caused by my selfish and largely absentee lifestyle.

With hindsight, my inability to see beyond my own emotional needs had probably been formed in the fostering system. I am the illegitimate son of I know not who, raised initially by my mother, who died during my first year, and then by a friend of hers who was considered too old to adopt me. I went through the dark funnels of social care and fostering before being adopted by a family that was caring and generous enough to try to make me feel at home but had its own in-built problems, including alcoholism and maternal depression. I sloped away numerous times and slept rough. Got into more than my fair share of fist fights, ran with a rabble of 'bad lads' too directionless and harmless to ever be called a gang, and was often told by my quick-to-hit adoptive mother that 'taking me in' had turned out to be 'more trouble than it was worth'.

She was probably right.

If I want to be generous to my younger self, I'd say I was a little horror. Had I come with a guarantee, they would have been well within their rights to have returned me and asked for compensation for the experience.

Like many other teenagers in my secondary school in Greater Manchester (and like Nilsen in Aberdeenshire), I'd sleep-walked through my examinations, achieved outstandingly disappointing grades and imagined my future was in either football, or more realistically the lower ranks of the army or navy.

At sixteen, I stepped through the school gates for the last time, clutching reports that essentially warned any prospective employer I was intrinsically lazy, had played truant almost more times than I'd attended school and would undoubtedly turn out to be a liability if taken on.

I'd messed up.

My only saving grace was that I knew it. And I realised if I didn't get my act together in double-quick time, then the mess would get bigger and become permanent.

Kids I'd hung around with had already become regulars down at the local police stations. Some had even graduated to being 'sent away' and several were booking bunks inside Strangeways, Manchester's architecturally chilling Victorian prison, a grim place that once hanged so many people it was one of only a few jails in the country to have permanent gallows.

I didn't want to end up there.

And it is largely down to good fortune that I didn't.

When I was twelve, my pals and I had regularly stolen sweets and food from shops and supermarkets. We worked in packs to distract staff, while palming packets of crisps and bars of chocolate out of the door. We'd done it initially because we'd been out on the streets all day and much of the night, without any money in our pockets and we'd been hungry and thirsty. Then we did it because we'd got away with it. Eventually, we did it because it had become 'the thing we did'. Without even thinking about our behaviour or the possible consequences, we had become habitual petty thieves. In mitigation, our hauls were always for our bellies, and only on one occasion exceeded what we could immediately consume.

That one occasion was when we were sheltering from the

winter cold in a nearly finished renovation of an end terrace. It had been completely gutted and still needed to be fitted with upstairs floorboards and all doors and windows. But it had a roof and walls. And that was good enough for us when it rained hard and icy winds blew, which was pretty much most of the time in Manchester from November to May.

We climbed builders' ladders, balanced our way across floor joists and ventured into the roof space so we could see out onto the street below, only to find the side of the apex had not yet been sealed off from next door. The sweet shop. Out of adventure more than anything, we clambered through the open brickwork and into the neighbouring attic, where excitedly we found a loft hatch that opened into the shop below.

Without any discussion, the piece of board was removed. Now the three of us lost our nerve. No one was brave or foolish enough to go in. But below us we could see a landing area stacked high with boxes, no doubt waiting to be unpacked and taken down to the shelves for sale. They had to be filled with something amazing. Eventually, someone (not chicken-livered me) dangled through the hatch and lifted a small box up into our space. We replaced the board and scurried away like attic rats.

Hearts pounding, we clambered back to our 'den' in the empty end house.

The haul turned out to be twelve large boxes of Black Magic chocolates, the kind that only seemed to appear at birthdays or Christmas.

We divided the spoils and started to eat as though we were in a speed contest.

Caramel. Coffee Cream. Nougat. A gooey orange. Strawberry something.

I managed only six chocolates before I felt sick.

My friends were the same.

Then fear kicked in. We were going to get caught. We'd be sent to Strangeways. Tough men would bully us, maybe even rape us in the showers. We panicked and ran out of there as fast as we could, leaving everything behind. And we never went back.

So, as a kid, I'd had an even more dysfunctional upbringing than Nilsen, and in regularly committing some form of theft (possibly even some form of burglary) I had strayed much further down the criminal side of the tracks than he had.

But I hadn't been caught.

Nothing had happened that told the world that twelve-year-old me had broken the law and should have been arrested and cautioned. Maybe even hauled before a juvenile court and punished more severely. And because of that good fortune, I was afforded the time and influence of others to straighten myself out. To get a job. To make a decent life. To have a family. To learn from my mistakes and lead a better life.

But why had I committed those criminal acts?

I'd known at the time they were wrong. Despite my young years and poor academic record, I hadn't been so stupid that I hadn't understood that there would be consequences if I got caught.

I think the answer is simple.

I just didn't care.

My life at that time seemed empty. I was emotionally dead. I felt that I had so little say about *where* I lived, *how* I lived or *what* happened to me, that grabbing some sweets and experiencing a moment's joy didn't seem so wicked. I had no affection for my adoptive mother, nor she for me. A good day for both of us was me being out of the house.

My adoptive father was a kind but weak man. He would

work far away on the other side of Manchester, return home late for his dinner, then disappear nightly to the local pub as soon as he thought it okay to say 'I'm just going out for last orders'.

My adoptive brother was a lifelong drunk who worked as a travelling salesman. On the rare occasions he returned home, he took me to the cinema – the only person who did – and bought me my first football kit (the wrong one – I was a City fan and he bought me a United kit – I only ever wore the shorts). Eventually, he moved to Canada, sobered up, got married and we sadly lost contact in my early twenties. Probably my fault. I felt closest to my adoptive sister, who was as bright as a button and always had a dream of writing a novel.

The problems that ran through my upbringing all turned out to be common themes in Nilsen's, and the more I investigated them, the more I understood both him and myself.

Like all the teenage boys I knew, sex with a girl had almost overnight become the most important thing in our lives. Fortunately, we went to a mixed-sex school, and there were girls stumbling around in a similar hormonal fog, and somehow we managed to find each other. And all of this was okay. Quite wonderful, really. Society accepted it. Even staff at our Catholic school understood it. Teachers taught us about sex, even underage sex, in classes. They told us all about condoms and other forms of contraception, they were surprisingly supportive and non-judgmental with underage girls who got pregnant.

All of this was a stark contrast to Dennis Nilsen's sexual awakening.

He was homosexual.

Homosexuality was illegal.

Imprisonable.

There were no understanding teachers at his school. No biology lessons on how to sexually interact. No understanding friends to discuss things with. No understanding family members to guide him through the maze.

Nilsen had no one he could talk to about his sexual feelings. Not a single person even told him it was okay, natural, perfectly healthy to feel the way he did.

I have no doubt that as he entered his teens, he'd been at least every bit as 'emotionally dead' as I had felt, but then on reaching puberty, instead of finding intimacy like I had, he'd received a sexual hammer-blow to his evolving identity in the form of legal condemnation.

By the time I was sixteen and leaving school, I'd already lost my virginity and was well on my way to developing a complete inability to form any meaningful, lasting relationship. But I'd discovered sex and the discovery had given me confidence and a sense that all good things came to you in the end.

For the last couple of years, I'd been working messenger shifts on weekends at the *Daily Mirror* and *Sunday Mirror* newspapers, which at the time had their northern offices at Withy Grove in central Manchester – currently the site of the Printworks. The job basically entailed doing whatever anyone on the news or sports desks wanted. I ran copies from one desk to another, made tea and coffee, went to the in-house picture library to find photographs to illustrate stories, I placed bets at local bookies, and brought photographer's films back at half and full time from local soccer grounds.

This experience made me wonder whether post-school I could be a newspaper reporter. It seemed to me to be a pretty cushy number. I reckoned I could do that.

No.

The day and night editors told me I couldn't. Worse than that, they informed me there were no more messenger shifts available, so my weekend pay was disappearing.

Youth is a wonderful thing though. You take setbacks in your stride. You have no idea of your limitations and no fear of poverty.

I lowered my sights and turned up at the offices of the *Bury Times*, a three-times-a-week regional newspaper group, head-quartered not far from the council-house home of my adoptive parents.

No.

Again, they told me I couldn't.

But this time, it had been a qualified 'No.'

The editor, Frank Thomas, wasn't there when I'd appeared at their offices so early in the day as they hadn't yet opened. I had sat in reception and waited all day for his appearance, on the chance he might see me.

He did. Just before closing time.

Very kindly, he told me, 'Even if I wanted to give you a job as a trainee journalist, I couldn't. Both this newspaper and the NUJ [National Union of Journalists] have minimum entry requirements. You must have five O Levels and two A levels, including English at both. If you had those, then I could at least have considered you.'

I had none of those. But I did have some questions. 'If I had them now, would you give me a job?'

He took a long look at me and nodded. 'Probably. The job involves a lot of turning up at places without appointments to speak to people.'

'And if I come back in a year's time with them, will you give me a job then?'

He smiled. 'I'd certainly consider it. No guarantees.'

Off I went.

I signed up, not only for the daytime curriculum at the local technical college, but also for night-school classes. I crammed the required five O levels and two A levels into a year. I worked late nights/early mornings washing glasses and cleaning tables and toilets at a local nightclub to pay my way.

One year later, Frank Thomas proved as good as his word. I stood in the same spot in the same office, and he gave me my big break.

I was a trainee journalist.

I didn't realise it then, but this was my salvation. Had I not got that job, I would have been unemployed. I had no savings. Relations with my adoptive family had deteriorated to the point where I increasingly slept on friends' sofas, so it would only have been a matter of time before I was homeless as well.

Getting the job resulted in me covering local court cases and building a network of police and legal contacts that would lead to the Nilsen interview and beyond. It also enabled me to meet my first wife and future mother of two of my three sons.

From the *Bury Times*, I moved on to work in independent local radio as a newsreader and reporter, at Piccadilly Radio in Manchester, Beacon Radio in Wolverhampton and Radio City in Liverpool.

My first job in television was at Border TV, the smallest of all ITV regions, sited in a part of the country where (no joking) there were more sheep than people, but also where *Lookaround* was the highest rating regional news programme in the country.

It wasn't long before I made my first TV documentary. It was a half-hour on alternative energy in the Lakes and Borders, beautifully filmed by hugely experienced camera crews and editors, who had during their careers worked on feature films and TV series. They'd reached the stage of their lives when they'd wanted to settle somewhere other than hotel rooms in different filming locations. They wanted real homes in a place that afforded them a slower pace of life, plus the freshest of air, mountains and hills, lakes and breathtaking countryside.

I thought they were mad.

Mad and brilliant.

I pecked at their knowledge like a winter bird feasting on a ball of fat. I learned how to frame shots, pull focus, pan, tilt and zoom. I became acquainted with dollies, tracks, cranes, redheads and blondes, Super Troupers, fills, filters, gobos, slow-motion filming, reversals, not crossing the line, multi-camera shoots, jump cuts, spot fx, Atmos tracks, music editing, sound mixing and a hundred more tricks of a hundred more trades.

In July 1982, soon after my twenty-fifth birthday, eleven-year-old Susan Maxwell went missing from her home in Cornhill-on-Tweed. A frantic manhunt involving police teams, sniffer dogs and hundreds of people was launched to find her.

By the time I reached the very isolated and beautiful village, detectives were already fearing the worst. The word on the street was that a white van had been noticed close to a bridge over the River Tweed, where Susan had last been seen as she walked home from a game of tennis with friends.

A month later, the young schoolgirl's body was found by a lorry driver. The subsequent inquest into her death concluded that she'd been sexually abused and killed within twenty-four hours of being abducted.

As I filed reports, I had no idea that I was in fact working my first serial murder case.

In April 1983, my wife Dianne gave birth in Carlisle to

Damian, the first of our two sons. We had a barely affordable mortgage on a tiny semi-detached house located in the middle of a giant new estate on the outskirts of the city. The joy of parenthood distracted me from my growing dissatisfaction at work, and distracted Dianne from the fact that she missed her parents and friends back in Manchester.

Almost exactly a year after Susan Maxwell's abduction, another young girl went missing. Caroline Hogg was only five years old when she disappeared near her home in the Portobello area of Edinburgh. The incident was way out of Border's news patch and quite firmly in that of STV's. But then came the news that Scottish police believed she'd been taken by the same man who had killed Susan Maxwell.

I headed north as fast as the tourist-jammed roads would let me. Lothian and Borders Police, two thousand volunteers and a contingent from the Royal Fusiliers were all involved in what was to become, at the time, the biggest search ever staged in Scotland.

They didn't find her.

The day before my twenty-sixth birthday, Caroline's tiny body was discovered, dumped in a ditch near the M1 motorway in Twycross in Leicestershire, some three hundred miles from where she'd been abducted.

Like all decent people, I'd felt huge sympathy for the distraught family of Susan Maxwell. But my reaction to the Caroline Hogg murder transcended that. Becoming a father in the past year had awakened innate, protective senses and opened a new range of emotions. Parenthood had made me even more empathetic. A softening experience that Dennis Nilsen never enjoyed.

What if someone had snatched my child? Had driven him away? Had bound and gagged him so his screams couldn't be heard while they sexually assaulted him? And then – after all that – they'd killed him and thrown his body away like it was garbage? I felt sick. Sick and angry. Who the hell could do such a thing? Why should someone even want to do anything like that?

Caroline's murder was national and international news, and Hector Clark, the assistant chief constable of Northumbria Police was given the task of coordinating an enquiry that now spanned four police forces.

On camera, he wouldn't say much beyond issuing a general appeal for information about the driver of a white van who had been seen near where both girls had been abducted.

Off the record, he provided what amounted to the first profile of a serial killer that I'd ever heard.

He believed the suspect to be a single man, a lorry driver or sales rep, in regular employment, probably in his thirties, who for years had travelled the country and had extensive knowledge of not only the Scottish locations but also the Leicestershire one. The nature of the attacks made him an opportunist, while the young age of his victims defined him as a paedophile. Clark suspected he'd not previously been arrested or imprisoned.

I asked the ACC why he didn't want all this information to be broadcast, and he said he feared that if he was wrong on just one of those counts, then someone who had been thinking of coming forward to give information about a specific individual would believe they were wrong and would stay quiet. His caution was a lesson to me, and I made sure that all my scripts stuck strictly to the on-camera briefing.

I persuaded my boss, Ken Devonald, that Border TV should screen a documentary on the double murder, with the focus being an appeal to the public to find the killer. He bought into the idea and acted as producer while assigning me a director called Bill Cartner. They were both patient men, and I suspect I tested that virtue to the limit while creating the unimaginatively titled half-hour *Susan and Caroline*. It was my first crime-related documentary and to my professional delight, it ended up being shown throughout Scotland in the STV and Grampian regions as well.

At the same time as the hunt for Caroline Hogg's killer gathered momentum, Central TV, a new franchise set up as part of a government sale of licenses, was opening a news operation in the East Midlands. It was clear from the trade press that they needed reporters and news presenters to be based at a state-of-the-art studio complex being built in Nottingham.

I threw my hat into the ring, quoting my experiences on the recent murder hunt, my production of the *Susan and Caroline* documentary and my reporting experiences during the Toxteth riots in Liverpool.

To my surprise, I landed one of the key jobs and ended up reporting and regularly presenting the news with another new starter, Anna Soubry, who would eventually go on to be a Conservative MP and a minister in David Cameron's government.

Central News East launched and within months we found ourselves at the centre of the biggest news story in the country.

The 1984–85 miners' strike.

After repeated clashes with the National Coal Board, Arthur Scargill, the firebrand leader of the National Union of Mineworkers called a national strike. All pits were closed. No one was to work. That was the edict. But not every coalfield fell in line – with the East Midlands and North Wales being the most rebellious, and in particular, Nottinghamshire. In many cases, this set brother against brother, and father against son. Families were split between loyalties to themselves and to their union.

In March 1986, the year following the settlement of the strike, ten-year-old Sarah Jayne Harper went missing from her home in the Leeds suburb of Morley. She'd run an errand for her parents, collecting bread and crisps from the corner shop, but had failed to return.

I was not alone in instantly linking the schoolgirl's disappearance to that of Scottish youngsters Susan Maxwell and Caroline Hogg. In the days that followed, more than three thousand properties were searched in Yorkshire and around fifteen hundred witness statements taken. Despite the lack of a link to the Midlands, I reconnected with leading members of the murder enquiry and was told that, given the age of the child and the fact she'd been abducted in such an opportunistic way, they expected the offender to be the same as the one they were already hunting.

There was also another siting of a white van near the scene.

On the 19 April, just before my son's third birthday, Sarah Jayne's semi-naked body was found, bound and gagged, floating in the River Trent in Nottingham, just a few miles from our TV studios but more than seventy from the poor girl's family home. It transpired that she had died between five and eight hours after being abducted, sexually abused, beaten unconscious and then thrown in the Trent, where she drowned.

Through my police sources, I knew the killings were being investigated by six forces, with Hector Clark, now deputy chief constable of the Lothian and Borders constabulary still coordinating the manhunt.

By the end of the month, Scotland Yard had become involved. A summit was to be held in London to discuss not only the three murders, but more than a dozen other child homicides. Public interest in the case was high and I suggested that we produced another live, special TV programme from our Nottingham studios.

The idea was turned down.

My sources were both surprised and disappointed by the decision. They'd been eager for as much publicity as they could get, because they were convinced someone, somewhere, would know something about the killer.

This experience made me decide my long-term future lay in making documentaries not news stories.

In the coming years, my experience and reputation as an investigative documentary maker grew as I directed, produced and executive produced dozens of programmes on subjects as diverse as domestic violence, juvenile offenders, car theft, child abuse and murder.

In 1988, I made my first hour-long network documentary A Shred of Evidence followed in 1989 by a regional documentary on the murder of Marie Wilkes. The twenty-two-year-old from Worcester had been seven months pregnant when her car broke down on the motorway. She walked to an emergency phone box on the M50, where she met her killer.*

As a new decade began, I was completely immersed in the daily focus of documentary making, and by the time I focused on the case of Dennis Nilsen I had become a seasoned crime journalist, with what I thought was an exemplary knowledge of how criminals behaved, what motivated them, and the many methods used by detectives to catch them.

I knew nothing.

---

* A man was arrested and jailed for Marie's murder, but his conviction was subsequently overturned.

I was a journalist, and my investigative techniques were sorely restricted by asking the five staple W's – Who, What, When, Where and Why?

Too often, I had accepted superficial responses to the Why?

If the answer made a good soundbite, then it satisfied the edit, and the needs of the edit overruled everything else.

But all that was about to change.

Nilsen and I may have shared childhood commonalities, but as adults we'd grown into entirely different people, and I was about to discover why.

5

THE VISITOR

In the early 1980s, Brian Masters was little known outside of a niche of highbrow readers who thought of him as an excellent author of books on French literature and the dukedoms of Britain. That blinkered, singular view of him as a writer was set to change.

In 1983, like most of the country, he followed the stories of Dennis Nilsen's arrest and the growing tally of his victims with great interest; one that extended further and more sensitively than the sensational stories being written in the tabloid press demonising Nilsen, not only for his monstrous crimes, but also for his sexuality. Masters noted that barely a report could pass without the killer's homosexuality being mentioned in the same way it detailed dismemberment and necrophilia.

He had rightly concluded that there was more to Nilsen's story than seen by the sexually prejudiced eyes of most reporters, and that it would need someone as open-minded and methodical as he was to tell that story.

Masters wrote to Nilsen while he was remanded in Brixton Prison awaiting trial, and made a point of visiting at least once a month. From the beginning, he declared that his intention was to write a warts-and-all biography that would afford no favours.

A number of qualities set Brian's book apart from the usual plethora of non-fiction paperbacks traditionally produced for the true crime market. It didn't sensationalise. It was well-written. It searched for perspective. It didn't condemn. It didn't condone. It didn't claim to have answers. It let readers draw their own conclusions.

In 1992, I learned from police sources that since publication in 1985, Masters had continued to visit Nilsen, and was the closest thing to a confidant that the serial killer had. There was no doubt in my mind that the author would have at least *some* say in whether the murderer would cooperate with my documentary.

In August of that year, we met at St John's College in Oxford. It was a day of brilliant sunshine and Brian was dressed smartly in a light suit, striped shirt, and plain silk tie. One of the first questions I posed was, 'Why do you still visit Nilsen, so long after completion and publication of the book?'

He laughed. An admission that he'd asked himself the same thing on more than one occasion. 'I feel I have a responsibility to visit,' he answered. 'I have no responsibility for his character or the way he is understood by the world. Whether the world likes him or loathes him is nothing to do with me. My only responsibility is to visit him because he was a great help to me in writing a book which won a prize and did me no harm at all. It would be, I think, morally reprehensible to say to him, "Well, thanks very much for all your help and now you can rot. I will never come and see you again, so goodbye". I don't think one gross immorality on his part, the killing of fifteen*men, deserves the minor immorality of me being disloyal towards the help he gave me in writing the book.'

I was struck then, and am even more struck now, by how

---

* Nilsen would later dispute the number of victims, claiming he'd killed fewer than this.

honourably Brian had behaved. In stark contrast, I never saw Nilsen again after our meetings in Albany and had harboured no desire to do so. I had wanted to cleanse him from my life as quickly as possible. By Brian Masters' standards, I was undeniably in the 'morally reprehensible' category.

Inevitably, I wondered whether Brian had struck up a friendship with Nilsen and that was what really compelled him to visit. He frowned a little as he formed his answer. 'It's not what I'd regard as a friendship,' he replied. 'Not even a "qualified" friendship, it really is more of a duty, an action of care and consideration than anything else.'

I was completely open about the TV project, explaining that I was charting the development of offender profiling in Britain and wanted to include an interview with Nilsen, done by Paul Britton. I added that the interview would be used, probably in its entirety, by the police to educate detectives, and asked if he thought Nilsen would cooperate and if he would advise him one way or another.

'He is bound to ask my opinion, and of course I am supportive of endeavours that may be of value to the police and as a consequence the public; and subject to appropriate curation, I see the value of it being in the public domain. As far as Des is concerned, the television aspect is likely to be of enormous appeal to him, the police aspect less so. My advice would be to play down their involvement. Be honest, but do not lead with this part of the proposition.'

We went on to discuss what kind of interviewee Nilsen was, whether he would be factually reliable, truthful or in the main, deceptive.

'He is, despite what many people say, human, so I have no doubt that he has at least lied to me by omission, but I have found him more reliable and more honest than not,' he replied.

THE DENNIS NILSEN TAPES

'He had no inducement to cooperate with me, yet he did, for a remarkably long period of time, and I sensed that while there were acts that he was not comfortable talking about, he did nevertheless discuss them, and I can't ever recall him saying he wasn't willing to discuss a certain thing.'

I was eager to know what Nilsen might have found embarrassing to discuss.

'There are always, with people who've done this sort of thing, aspects of the crime that they find peculiarly embarrassing. The fact that they squeezed the life out of somebody, they can talk about. They can even talk about dismemberment. But it might be a little detail that they won't talk about, something they consider to be morally repugnant. I suppose masturbating over a corpse is something that a lot of them will hide, yet Nilsen did admit to doing that.'

Masturbating over a corpse.

I asked Brian if he thought Nilsen was insane.

'I don't think so. I would say that he is mad in the soul – that's the best way I can think of putting it. He's certainly not mad in the head. Intellectually, he's perfectly able to plan, to devise things and see things through to fruition. He's working in prison. He paints. He writes. He composes. He's very articulate when he's talking. He's very funny. He can make jokes and has a very particular sense of humour. He suggested to me there should be a film about his life, listing the cast in order of *dis*appearance. He was perfectly capable, when he was on the outside, of catching a bus and going to work, of walking the dog and doing all those things that show deliberation and intellectual control. In that sense, he's certainly not mad, but there is something deeply wrong with his soul. Now, that's a word I'd never used before I started to work on this case, because it is indefinable. It's a religious word and one

74

tries to avoid such words because they are difficult to understand and pin down properly, but there is no other word I can
think of in his case.'

Mad in the soul.

It was certainly an eloquent phrase. One that filled me with
such literary envy that I did not interrogate it, or its inventor.
As a lapsed Catholic, I didn't believe in souls. If I did, then
surely I'd have to believe Nilsen's was afflicted with evil not
madness?

'Whether Des has revealed absolutely everything about his
crimes, or not, no one will ever know,' Brian continued. 'My
own opinion is that he has told everything that is of importance.
I think if he did withhold anything, it might be something
like he'd stolen a ring off one of the corpses and kept it. I
think he would probably hide that, because that is something
that is against his own morality.'

I asked Brian about a well-recorded tragedy in Nilsen's
childhood, the death of his grandfather, Andrew Whyte, and
what kind of impact he thought it had.

'Well, there's no doubt that it did have an impact. He
told me that he believed his troubles really started there,
that his grandfather's death blighted his personality forever.
Andrew Whyte had been a father substitute, someone he
spent a lot of time with, and his death at sea opened a void
in Des's young life. I think he failed to comprehend what
death was and to some degree interpreted the absence as an
example of another person, like his father, just deserting him
and his mother. He told me he often had fantasies of himself
drowning in the North Sea, where I think he was looking
for his grandfather who had been a fisherman. And then
later on, before he ever murdered anyone, he would make
himself up to look like a corpse and lie on a bed with the

mirror propped up beside him so he could see the image of death in the mirror.'

I left Oxford, grateful for Brian's time, wisdom and insight. I had gained a better sense of who Nilsen was and how he might behave once the camera was rolling. But I also had a distinct feeling that I was straying out of my comfort zone. For years I had been content and capable when called upon to comment on murder from a distance, to report on such crimes from behind the barricades of fact. But now, reasoning deeply about the act of murder, the state of mind of the murderer while committing it – well this was new to me.

The graphic image Brian had conjured up of Dennis Nilsen ejaculating over the corpse of one of his victims, lingered disturbingly. I couldn't understand how a corpse could be arousing, so could not clear it from my mind. Close behind was the equally disturbing image of a young Nilsen lying naked in front of a mirror, pretending to be dead. Our minds – *normal* minds – are not trained to think of things like these. To think the unthinkable. I had been thrown by Brian Masters' accounts of Nilsen, every bit as much as Don Dovaston had unbalanced me by asking hypothetically where I might leave the body of my young son if I had killed him.

These were things I just didn't contemplate. Hadn't wanted to imagine. But police officers had to. Sometimes for weeks, months, years on end as they tried to catch people like Nilsen. People who were 'mad in the soul'.

When I returned home, I took my confusion and edginess with me. Dianne did not come from a journalistic background and very understandably wasn't keen to hear about murder, mutilation or necrophilia. I kept it all bottled up.

Not surprisingly, I endured the first of many sleepless nights. It wasn't just that I was distressed by imaginings of corpse-like

Nilsen in front of his mirror, a drowning Nilsen or a necrophile Nilsen. I was restless because of an increasing backlog
of unanswered questions.

How could losing your grandfather make you want to kill
people and masturbate over their bodies?

What state of mind are you in when you think it's a good
idea to get a mirror and play dead in front of it?

How come no one spotted that young Des was turning out
to be a) more than just a bit weird, and b) needed some serious
help?

I was, by training, an 'investigative' journalist. I had a
compulsion to collect facts, dig dirt, figure out other people's
dark secrets, and come to solid conclusions. This shouldn't
have been difficult ground for me. But it was.

I was off work the next day, and high on the agenda was
kicking a ball with Damian. If we weren't busting bushes and
breaking flowers in the back garden, then we were at the local
fields or parks. We played in the rain, the snow, the wind.
Whatever the weather hurled at us. And it was always one of
the greatest joys of my life. But not this time. This time I was
there only in body.

'Dad. Dad, the ball!'

We were on the village park pitch, our coats down as goal-
posts because the real ones were too big for him at that time,
and me between the sticks. I'd seen him run up with grim
determination etched on his face, only to slam his shot well
wide. Then I'd switched off. My mind had no longer been in
Nottinghamshire. It had drifted to the northeast of Scotland,
meeting a Nilsen even younger than my son, a clueless child
staring out to sea, over the endless choppy grey waters where
his grandfather had journeyed and mysteriously perished.

Broken bonds. Childhood pain. Nowhere to plant your

anger. I knew all about those kinds of dangers, what it felt like to sense you were alone, how quickly you could become depressed and alienated.

Like Nilsen, I had never known my father. Or my mother for that matter. Despite being a journalist, I'd never traced them – nor attempted to. When people asked me why, I'd always brushed them off with glib answers such as, 'What's the point?' The truth is, somewhere deep down I'd felt abandoned and rejected. I didn't want to trace the man who had turned his back on an infant version of me, only for him to do it again to me as an adult. So, I compartmentalised that chapter of my life. Boxed it up. Shoved it in a dark corner of my mental attic and locked the access hatch.

'Dad!'

Momentarily, I came back into the present. Damian's leather ball was lodged in the spiky hawthorn hedge at the back of the fields. I'd warned him, *countless times*, that he shouldn't try to retrieve it from there, because he'd either get thorns in his hands or would cut his face or legs.

'I'll get it,' I shouted protectively.

I couldn't imagine life without my son. The experience of becoming a parent to him had quite unexpectedly filled the void of never having known my own parents, and had given me for the first time in my life what I didn't even know I really craved – a family. A blood bond. An emotional tie, begun during the miracle of birth and then strengthened with every bedtime story, each shoulder ride, play fight, and in our case, every game of football.

Dennis Nilsen must have forged a similar bond with his grandfather, as they watched football at the local fields, walked on the beach, bought ice creams, found golf balls and flew dragons (kites) in the blustery Fraserburgh skies. As everyone knows, it's the little things in childhood that often leave the sweetest of aftertastes in adulthood.

Or the sourest.

Increasingly, I found myself comparing my upbringing to Nilsen's. I could see that the world of the young Dennis, aged six, must have been knocked clean off its axis when *his* one and only male role model had so unexpectedly been taken from him.

I watched Damian, kitted out in his England strip, running without a worry in the world except how to strike the newly retrieved ball more accurately with his two-sizes-too- large boots. I couldn't help but think if his grandfather died, he'd be distraught. But he had loving parents who would protect him. A doting grandmother who would cover our backs and provide her own solid support.

He'd be okay.

All of us would see to that. We'd explain life and death, help him come to terms with the loss, get him through it. We'd make it our number one priority to do that.

Surely, Nilsen's mother, grandmother, sister and brother had realised what Dennis had been going through and had tried to help him? They were a religious family in a close-knit community, hadn't there been enough care to have supported Dennis in the depths of his grief?

Tired and happy at the end of our game of football, we returned home. But just as I had subconsciously drifted from the field, I now drifted from the house. Inevitably, I found myself making excuses about 'needing' to go into work, and within a few hours I was immersed in all the articles, clippings, features, books and documents that I, and now the team I had assembled for *Murder in Mind*, had gathered on Nilsen.

The Scot was born in 1945, the year the Second World War

ended. His mother, Elizabeth 'Betty' Whyte was a local, and his father, Olav Nilsen, a Norwegian soldier who had travelled to Scotland following the German occupation of Norway. By all accounts, they made a striking couple.

Olav is variously described as being tall, handsome, fair-haired and rugged, with an enigmatic meanness in his eyes. Betty was an outgoing young woman, who loved the local dances and cafes and was attractive enough to win one of the town's most prestigious beauty competitions.

They had three children. Firstly, Olav Junior, then Dennis, and finally Sylvia in 1947. All the young Nilsens lived with their mum in a room at her parents' home, with Olav Senior coming and going, either as he pleased, or as the Norwegian army dictated. It soon became apparent that he was both a poor husband and even poorer father. Aside from not providing a home or improving the lifestyle of his dependents, he would frequently be drunk and disruptive. It was no surprise when they divorced in 1948.

Following his conviction at the Old Bailey, every newspaper and media outlet in the country ran exhaustive stories on the life of Dennis Nilsen, starting with that fractured childhood in his birthplace, Fraserburgh. The fishing town is in a far-flung coastal cove of Aberdeenshire, north of Peterhead, forty miles from Aberdeen, right up on the penultimate promontory of the east of Scotland, just one bump down from John O'Groats. It is Scotland's (and one of Europe's) leading shell-fish ports, with world famous markets in the harbour that young Des Nilsen regularly visited.

Fraserburgh had a population of around twelve thousand when he was a child, and must have been a synonym for isolation. It is more than six hundred miles away from London, one hundred and seventy miles from Edinburgh, the capital city and cultural heart of Scotland, and two hundred miles from Glasgow, the vibrant, commercial pulse of the country.

It is an island within an island.

You have to physically visit places as remote as this, hike their hills, stroll their sands and shop their markets to get a true sense of how cut off from the hustle and bustle of big city life they actually are. Everything from the vast openness of the countryside, the pace of life and even the air that you breathe is remarkably different. Some people thrive in the peace and rural rhythms of these uniquely close and closed communities, others feel as though they are being suffocated.

I'm sure that the walks and sights and places he had pleasurably visited with his grandfather had after the old man's death turned into terrible reminders of his loss – things he grew to hate – things from which he had to escape.

But still, I reasoned with my sympathetic self, losing a loved one in a small town couldn't be accepted as a psychological catalyst that turned an otherwise normal young boy into an adult serial murderer and necrophile.

Over the centuries, there must have been hundreds, maybe thousands of other grief-affected children in Fraserburgh, who grew up just fine – as did his brother Olav and sister Sylvia. So, if the seeds of future deviancy were sown here – at the time that working fisherman Andrew Whyte died of a heart attack while out at sea – why did they root so deeply and flourish so dramatically in the psyche of Dennis Nilsen?

Death at sea was far from unknown in Fraserburgh. The waters around there were so notoriously treacherous that this was the place the RNLI established its first lifeboat service in Scotland. Outside of their boathouse stands a life-size bronze statue of a crewman, in honour of three lifeboat crews who lost their lives throughout the twentieth century trying to save others from drowning.

Every parent in the area made sure their children were acutely aware of the ever-present dangers of the North Sea. The potential perils of the crashing waves and the terrors of being swept out to sea by gigantic tidal pulls were drummed into young minds on a daily basis to ensure their safety. Veteran fisherman Andrew Whyte was bound to have recounted similarly harrowing tales to his grandson as they walked around the harbour and clambered among the berthed herring boats.

There's no question that many a son mourned many a father and grandfather in Fraserburgh, but Dennis Nilsen was the only son of the town to develop into a serial murderer.

Could it have been the way Andrew Whyte's death had been broken to him?

It was Halloween, Wednesday, 31 October 1951, when sixty-two-year-old Andrew Whyte was found dead in his fishing boat bunk by fellow crewmates. This was just a few weeks before Dennis Nilsen's sixth birthday.

Before the body could be returned to the family home at 47 Academy Road in Fraserburgh, there had to be a post-mortem examination and an inquest. Once held, the cause of death was identified as being a heart attack. There had been time enough for Nilsen's mother or grandmother to have slowly, carefully and considerately broken the sad news to the children.

But that didn't happen.

'No one said it like that. No one took the time to explain to me what had happened. I was completely unprepared,' he said. 'My mother asked me if I wanted to see Grandad and I still didn't know what death was, so I said I did. I was taken into this room in the house and there he was in his coffin. I didn't understand what I was seeing. It looked as though he was sleeping, but I could tell that it was a different sleep, a strange sleep. And then I was taken out again and that was it. No one explained to me what it meant or what had happened and all that had a profound effect on me.'

Bereavement experts* say you have to make sure that you use clear statements such as 'he has died' rather than 'passed away' or 'gone to the stars'. With young children of five or six, it's said to be necessary to realise that they usually do not understand that death is permanent and so may expect the person to come back. And there's a huge emphasis on ensuring that after breaking the news, they are closely monitored for stress and given constant emotional support.

In fairness to Nilsen's mother Betty, and to the rest of the adults who may have tried to care for young Dennis, the 1950s was a very different era. It was a time of bludgeoned feelings. The 1939–45 war had made death a daily occurrence and people were still in the same frame of mind. More than four hundred thousand British soldiers and civilians had been killed in WWII and few families went untouched by the burden of bereavement. It was an era of 'chin up', 'don't cry', 'mustn't moan', 'just get on with it'.

It's highly possible that everyone concerned with dealing with Andrew Whyte's death thought they were doing the right thing by underplaying the tragedy and trying to show that life went on as normal.

Today, we know better.

I recall, all too vividly, my first encounter with a dead body. It did not happen until I was an adult. Like Nilsen, I had

---

* There's excellent advice on child bereavement at www.childbereavementuk. org

been completely unprepared for the event, and as a result the image is still seared into my memory. I was a young reporter and had been sent to a funeral parlour to do a story on the rising cost of dying. I was met in a dimly lit, sombre reception area by a young woman dressed in a funereal black jacket and skirt, and asked to 'come through' to the owner's office.

I had no idea that 'through' entailed walking into a cold, tiled area, and past a naked, dead body laid out on a steel trolley.

The corpse had been that of a middle-aged man with the reddest hair and whitest skin I've ever seen. Grotesquely rough stitching zig-zagged across his chest, the legacy of a post-mortem examination.

Looking back, I'm sure the young assistant who'd taken me on this route had done it for amusement, and I imagine other professional visitors such as myself had also been subjected to similar experiences as a bit of a laugh. It's even possible the sub-editor who'd assigned me the job had been in on the joke.

I didn't find it funny.

Give me a pencil and paper, and even after all these years I could still sketch a very precise picture of what I'd seen. Had I, as a six-year-old boy with no concept of death, been surprised by the motionless, unbreathing, dead-eyed corpse of the one person in the world I had felt closest to, then I am sure it would have traumatised me.

But to what extent?

And for how long?

Would it have affected me as much as Nilsen?

I guess I would, for at least over a short period of time, have been moody, depressed, withdrawn and maybe confused. But I am fairly confident that it would not have knocked me so out of kilter that three decades later it would burst to the surface and I would start killing people and resolve to keep their corpses as flatmates.

It certainly would have been understandable to learn that following his grandfather's death, Dennis Nilsen had become extremely reclusive, frequently played truant, thrown tantrums and fought with other boys. But that does not seem to be the case. Or, more likely, no one spotted the signs of grief.

'I can't say I felt a part of a family,' he told me. 'I felt like I was an outsider, as though I shouldn't be there with them, as though they didn't want me there. Sometimes, I had the sensation that I was stood outside of the house, looking in on myself and all of them gathered around me, each of them talking and listening in their peculiar ways, all of them ignoring me. The me inside there, in front of them, that me was as invisible to them as the me stood outside.'

Alienation like this can sound alarming, but it's not unusual. I certainly felt it throughout my childhood in foster and adoption families, as I'm sure many orphaned children did. Such feelings of invisibility and detachment are also common in families with three children, so much so that it's often referred to as middle child syndrome – of which Nilsen was also one.

His mother Betty – whom he didn't speak to for many of the last years of his life – certainly didn't see him as a troubled outcast. She remembers her youngest son as 'a kind and caring child', the sort who would pick up injured birds, protect them beneath his coat and take them home to look after. After his arrest, she told News at Ten on ITV in the UK, 'I just don't understand how this could go on with nobody knowing anything,' and added, 'something must have happened to him. Because it's not my Dennis that's doing it. Not the boy I knew, that's doing these things.'

It seems a lot happened to her Dennis that she was unaware of. And there were danger signs at a very early age.

'As a young child, I strangled a cat,' he wrote in one of his letters to me. 'I was playing with a kitten and the thought just came to me that as a type of experiment I should hang it. So, I did exactly that. I strung it up with some wire that I had and watched it die. I think I was trying to explore what death meant. When it was over, I stared at the poor animal and felt not only deeply ashamed but also fascinated by the invisible presence of death.'

Although this story, or at least versions of it, has been told elsewhere, I didn't rule out the possibility that it was untrue. Nilsen was well-read enough to know that cruelty to animals is a common trait in serial killers. The account was certainly at odds with other childhood recollections of how he and his friends lovingly raised fledgling birds they'd found, and how he had been mortified when his pet rabbit died and he'd been wrongly accused of neglecting it and starving it to death.

Profiler Bob Ressler disagreed with me. He saw no difficulty in accounting for such contradictory behaviour. 'Spontaneous cruelty to an animal can be the result of anger displacement, and once done and experienced it may or may not be repeated. If the experience brings great satisfaction to the child, then it may be repeated. If it doesn't, then it's quite probable it's a one-off. The critical thing is that the child has caused a death. If this action is observed and recognised for what it is, a real danger sign, then there's a chance of behavioural correction. But the brighter kids, they cover this stuff up. They cover it up and in later life they say things like "someone should have seen what I was like. Someone should have stepped in and helped me". And in some cases, they're right. But the smarter the kid, the smarter they hide things.'

This sounds like Nilsen to a T.

Ressler went on to say that he also thought it quite possible that Nilsen had also deliberately killed his pet rabbit, but having initially denied doing so, forever felt compelled to continue with the lie. 'Serial killers are among the best liars in the world. Their very liberty depends upon daily living with their lies. Generally, when an offender introduces stories that break behavioural patterns such as denying animal cruelty, and instead they try to show themselves in a good light, they're either not telling us the truth, or they're quoting one exception to cover up a whole catalogue of bad behaviour.'

Nilsen's *catalogue* began with the taking of an animal's life and culminated in him taking the lives of at least twelve men. The reasons he gave for those murders were even more confusing than those he offered for coldly strangling the kitten.

'When I killed those young men, I was killing myself,' he said. 'The victim was me. I would imagine myself as him and imagine that what I was doing I was doing to myself – doing to a younger me.'

Bob Ressler explained, 'The "killing myself" comment chimes with necrophiles and also those with an autoerotic personality; that's the kind of person who derives sexual excitement from strangling themselves to the point of death, then saving themselves as they experience sexual climax. Seeing himself as the victim might perversely have heightened Nilsen's pleasure in killing his victims.'

6

LEARNING TO SEE

The first thing that hits you when you visit the famed FBI Academy at Quantico is that it looks exactly like it did in the movie *The Silence of the Lambs* and, for that matter, the subsequent TV series *Criminal Minds*, *Mindhunter* and of course, *Quantico*. The big 'FBI Academy' sign lies there on the roadside as you drive up. Marines man barrier gates and the building itself looks like giant brown Lego blocks dumped on a huge green baseboard that stretches more than five hundred acres.

The media liaison officer who greeted me, explained that the site was more than just a home to the famous Behavioral Science Unit and Hogan's Alley, where Agent Clarice Starling learned to shoot her way out of life-threatening scenarios in a mocked-up town.

This was where new agents were taught everything from investigation theories and federal laws to advanced driving, self-defence and survival skills. I paid polite interest and made copious notes, but the truth was, I couldn't wait for the tour to be over and for me to be left in the care of my first appointment of the day, VICAP Program Manager Terry Green.

VICAP stood for Violent Criminal Apprehension Program and it was a unique database and unit formed by the FBI in 1985 to track the country's most dangerous offenders (primarily serial murderers and rapists). Sheriffs, marshals and police departments who encountered a serious crime where they had no suspect and perhaps even no clues, filled in a special questionnaire and were able to view the VICAP database to see if there were similar offences elsewhere. If there were, then they could pool information and, if needed, also have the assistance and direct involvement of FBI profilers.

I'd managed to do some due diligence on VICAP and its manager before stepping into Terry Green's office and being met by his warm smile, inquisitive eyes and firm handshake.

Bespectacled and balding with a strikingly white walrus moustache, casually and comfortably dressed in a jumper, tieless shirt and trousers, he looked like a kindly, off-duty town sheriff. The type of guy who'd help anyone who needed it but could be as tough as an old oak tree if necessary.

Terry had distinguished himself in Oakland, where he'd set up their Special Operations Unit and led SWAT teams on numerous drugs raids. But it was as the head of homicide that he'd made his mark. He investigated more than nine hundred murders, involving several serial killers and a highly publicised case in which an eleven-year-old boy deliberately drowned a five-year-old.

Leaving Oakland, he'd joined the FBI as an analyst and instructor, then became part of the BSU team.

'Take the weight off,' he told me, motioning to a chair on the other side of a modest desk in the modest office cluttered with paperwork. 'Would you like coffee?'

'No thanks.'

As I unpacked my notepad and Slimline tape recorder, I began to give him a short recap on the documentary.

'I've been briefed. I know all about it,' he interjected, hoping to save us both time. 'Before you start with your questions –' he nodded to the recorder – 'I've one for you. In your job, you must be observant, so this should be easy. You've seen plenty of FBI seals around this place, not badges, they're different. So, tell me the colours on the seal.'

I had to take a beat to visualise the last one I'd seen. 'Blue background, gold and –' I struggled, before adding – 'red and white, I think. Yes, I'm sure, that would be red, white and blue, the colours of the American flag and the gold was at the top.'

'Very good.' He rewarded me with an approving nod. 'Now, in the centre of the seal, there are three words, beginning with the letters F, B and I. What are they?'

'Federal Bureau of Investigations,' I replied confidently.

'No.' The walrus beneath his nose shook with amusement. 'Those are *almost* the words around the outer circle of the seal, but even then, you're not right – they say "Department of Justice, Federal Bureau of Investigation" – there is no "s" on the end, it's "investigation" singular. What are the words in the middle of the seal, below the red and white stripes?'

The sheriff's kindly eyes now bored like lasers, and I realised in that moment what it must have felt like to have been a rookie agent put on the spot, in one of his classes.

'It's what some people call a backronym,' Terry hinted, growing bored. 'It says "Fidelity, Bravery and Integrity". Those are the standards that everyone here subscribes to. But that's not my point.'

He leant forward, rested forearms as huge as ham-bones on his desk. 'My point is you're looking but you're not seeing. And the first thing we teach agents is to *see* – *really see* – everything. Every detail. You saw colours and a version of the words that you expected to see. I won't ask you how many red and white stripes are on the seal – the answer's five – or how many leaves are on the laurel branches – the answer's forty two, the number of US states when the FBI was founded. I could go on, there are lots more details and every detail has meaning. It is *all* significant. And it's the same at a crime scene – every detail is important. Not only the size and type of gunshot or knife wound, but the position of the body, the clothes the victim was wearing, the colour of their hair, even the weather at the time of death. All those details are clues to who the offender is. If we observe those things accurately enough, then there's a chance we can identify the killer's signature. And if we do that, then we may be able to link that person to other offences and bring them to justice.'

Terry then walked me through to the VICAP operations room, so I could see what he called 'the nuts and bolts'. En route, he explained, 'Prior to 1985, there was nothing like this in the country. No place a homicide detective could call to find out if the type of crime he was investigating in his juris-diction had gone on elsewhere. The VICAP system's designed to do three things. Help link unsolved murders; it's important for investigators to know as early as possible that the homicide they're working is part of a serial and not a first-time crime. Secondly, it can help bring clarity to missing-persons databases, and bring some sense of closure to families not knowing the whereabouts of their loved ones. And finally, it can help identify murder victims when normal body identification systems have failed.'

Televisually, the VICAP room was a huge anticlimax. It consisted of rows of analysts hunched over desks, working phones and computers. I could have been at an accountants' office, a stockbrokers' or in an office typing pool.

It was only when I tuned into a few of the phone conver-sations that I realised I was privy to something quite exceptional and chillingly disturbing. At the other end of each line was someone not only investigating a murder somewhere in America, but they had so little to go on they had turned to the FBI and VICAP because they feared it was part of a serial killing and they needed help.

The phones rang non-stop.

Each of the analysts was taking exhaustive details of where people had been killed, what had been done to them before, during and after the murders, where the bodies had been left and literally more than a hundred other details.

Terry took me patiently through a print-out of the system's exhaustive questionnaire. I flicked to the back and saw that it consisted of close to two hundred questions about the type of crime being investigated.

Two hundred!

This was a whole universe away from my journalistic five of Who, What, Where, When and Why? And way, way ahead of any profiling system we had in the UK.

'The idea is that this form will be used throughout the country and internationally,' he explained.* 'We want everyone to ask and answer the same questions in the same way, so we have a uniformity that we can trust. That will enable us all to have the same information and track the same offenders at the same time.'

He ran a big chunky finger down a page I was examining. It was devoted purely to 'Victimology'. It detailed everything from the colour of clothes, hair, shoes, bags, make-up, to the style of dresses, jackets, blouses, underwear, scarves. 'You have to look at these things not like a beat cop but like an archaeologist,' he said. 'You're digging into someone's history. Layer

---

* In 2021 VICAP was still the heartbeat of FBI profiling and also produced the now famous Most Wanted list of national and international criminals, including terrorists.

by layer, you're unearthing the way they lived and ultimately what made them a target. You have to be meticulous. Microscopic. Miss nothing.'

Another section was devoted to 'Geography'. It asked all the questions you'd expect, and more. The basics were simple: How rural/urban was the crime scene? How far from major roads/public transport was the body found? Where was the victim's house in relation to where the body was found? That sort of thing.

'Geography is important for a whole lot of reasons,' Terry began. 'Recent research has shown us that many serial killers are compulsive drivers. Between crimes, they like to have days out cruising around, "window shopping" for victims. It helps them develop "comfort zones", places they feel they could act out their fantasies and get away with their crimes. Some offenders we've spoken to said, on occasion they just drove aimlessly for hundreds of miles because it was something to do, then a possible target would catch their eye and waken their fantasy.'

I immediately thought of the murders I'd covered and told Terry about the case of Robert Black,* the van driver who'd toured the country, killing youngsters Caroline Hogg, Susan Maxwell and Sarah Jayne Harper. He'd been caught in Stow in July 1990, when a retired postmaster spotted Black bundling a child from the pavement into the back of his van and called the police. A roadblock had been established on the outskirts of the village and the van was stopped. When one of the officers opened the back doors, he found,

---

* In August 1990, Black pleaded guilty to the Stow assault and abduction and was jailed for life. In May 1994, he was found guilty of three charges of kidnapping, murder and the unlawful burial of a body, plus an additional charge of attempting to abduct another child.

to his horror, that the abducted girl was his six-year-old daughter.

Terry Green didn't look anywhere as near surprised as I'd expected. 'I know the story,' he told me. 'In fact, we provided a psychological profile for the coordinating force. From what I recall, it turned out to be pretty accurate. In time, you'll probably find this guy killed other girls as well.* Paedophiles like to keep secrets. It's their nature.'

Having become detached from Black's case due to TV presenting and other duties, I'd been unaware of the FBI's involvement and asked when it had happened.

'Couple of years back,' said Terry, 'end of 1987, maybe start of '88. It was unusual but not unheard of to have requests from the UK, so I remember pretty much what we said – male, white, single, around forty, scruffy. Were we on the nose?'

'You were,' I said.

More of the case came back to him. 'We had this particular unsub down as a loner, didn't own his own house, rented places, moved around a lot. Most probably had a big child porn collection and –' his big eyes lit up – 'we discussed him being a necrophile. Offenders who keep the bodies of children often have sex with them. Was that the case?'

I told Terry I didn't know,† and added, 'I'm looking at another Scottish killer, Dennis Nilsen, and he most definitely *was* a necrophile. Did the FBI ever provide a profile on him?'

---

* In December 2011, Black was given a further life sentence for the murder of nine-year-old Jennifer Cardy in Northern Ireland in 1981. She is now believed to have been Black's first murder victim.

† After conviction, Robert Black admitted to post-mortem sex with some of his victims.

'Doesn't ring bells.'

'He killed twelve men – maybe more – in north London, between 1978 and 1983.'

Terry searched his encyclopaedic memory. 'We weren't consulted on that, I'm sure. And he was a necrophile?'

'He was. There's an amazing book you should read –' I realised mid-sentence how stupid I was about to sound, but finished anyway – 'it's called *Killing for Company* and explains why Nilsen killed because he didn't want people he liked to leave him.'

He gave me a sceptical look. 'I'm willing to bet it was sex with a dead body he was killing for, and not for the company.'

'It's a good book,' I protested, not knowing when to stop digging the hole I had started.

'I'm sure it is. But the guys I work with kinda wrote the *real* book on necrophilia. What type was Nilsen?'

My eyes widened. 'There are *types*?'

'Sure, there are.' The lip walrus shook some more. 'There are homosexual and heterosexual necrophiles, fetishistic necrophiles, gentle ones and violent ones. What did your offender do with his victims before and after death?'

I remembered my earlier lesson about detail and tried to be as precise as possible. 'His victims were always young men, usually poor and alone. He'd pick them up in pubs, invite them back to his place for more drink or food, then he'd strangle and kill them. Afterwards, he washed the bodies and took them to bed to fondle and caress, sometimes pretending he was seducing them. He'd have some form of sex with their corpses, often between their thighs, or he'd sit astride them and masturbate on their stomach.'

Terry nodded understandingly. 'He's what we'd call a romantic necrophile.'

'*Romantic?*' I queried. 'What he did doesn't sound that romantic to me.'

'That's because you're not a necrophile. Those actions you describe, they're gentle, they're not aggressive. They're things one lover might do for another.'

My mind reeled as I compared the 'normal' intimacy of a couple sharing a bath or shower, with the mental image of a presumably naked Nilsen bathing a naked corpse.

'Personally,' Terry continued, 'I have no doubt he killed for necrophiliac pleasures not for company. He didn't want these men alive, he wanted them dead and fully compliant, so they fit with his fantasies.'

'He said he talked to the bodies,' I added. 'Kept them until they began to decompose and he would dress and converse with them. They were his "company" then, weren't they?'

'You're seeing Bob and Roy, right?'

He meant the profilers Ressler and Hazelwood. 'Yes, I am.'

'Then see what they say. This is really Roy's field. Me – I would classify your guy as a romantic necrophile, a sexually dysfunctional individual incapable of forming relationships with the living.'

7

'SERIAL KILLER'

In the world of criminology, Robert Kenneth Ressler is legendary.

Along with fellow FBI agent John Douglas, he toured American jails interviewing serial killers about their crimes, then distilled that information into a system that better educated homicide detectives in how such offenders behaved and how they could be caught.[*]

His pioneering work, assisted and guided by others such as Anne Burgess and Harold Teten, ultimately led to the formation of the BSU.

Also well chronicled, is the accreditation of Ressler with the globally known and much feared phrase 'serial killer', emanating from a lecture he gave to senior officers at the Bramshill Police College in England in the 1970s.

In February 1992, I literally had to travel half-way across the world to Australia meet the famed FBI man. He'd only just retired from the BSU but was still providing the unit and a number of other leading law enforcement agencies with advice, consultancy and support.

We'd spoken on the phone and arranged to meet in a bar at the hotel we were both staying at in Melbourne. The timing

---

[*] In the Netflix series *Mindhunter*, the Bill Tench character played by Holt McCallany is based on Bob Ressler.

was just after he'd addressed the largest gathering of offender profilers in the world at a conference held in St Vincent's Hospital.

That afternoon, along with dozens of police officers, psychologists, psychiatrists, prison officers and pathologists, I'd watched him speak eloquently and unemotionally about how he and his colleagues used forensic and behavioural clues from crime scenes to develop psychological profiles that assisted in the capture of some of the world's worst criminals.

I was the only person in the bar sat at a table on my own, so when Ressler walked in, he clocked me straight away and headed over. As I got to my feet, I was immediately struck by his presence.

Bob had the confident walk and poise you'd expect of someone who'd served more than a decade in the military, but he also had something more. The air of celebrity. That ethereal aura that surrounds people who are globally recognizable – and know they are. It's a casual look of alertness that comes from accepting they are under constant scrutiny and must never let their guard down in public.

The man approaching me was tall and broad, with thick, silver-grey, side-parted hair, well-cut and recently combed. He was wearing a smart blue suit, white shirt and patterned red tie. Eyes that had stared into the faces of dozens of serial murderers looked out at me from behind large, gold-coloured wire-rimmed glasses.

'Bob Ressler,' he stretched out a hand, 'How you doing?' His voice chimed with an easy familiarity, measured to put decades of listeners, from detectives to killers, at ease. 'Can I get you a beer?'

A hovering waiter took our order and Bob unbuttoned his jacket and relaxed into a chair. We talked briefly about flights and jetlag and then, after our drinks came, I expanded on the outline of the documentary that I had given him when we'd chatted on the phone.

'Bottom line,' I confessed, 'is that I'm out of my depth. And listening to you and other experts lecturing here today, I realised I was even more ignorant than I thought I was.'

He raised his glass of local lager. 'It's good you spotted that turn in the road, many don't until it's too late.' He took a well-earned slug of beer and gave me a knowing so-what-do-you-want? look.

'Is there a chance,' I said, in a terribly polite English way, 'that I could engage you as a consultant to the programme? Pick your brains? Have you check over things to see that I don't make silly mistakes and maybe help me set up an interview in the US with a serial killer you think might be of benefit to the programme?'

He placed his beer on a coaster. 'There is. There's a very strong chance of you doing that. I like the idea of your project. The more people know about these offenders and how we catch them, the better. I have a kind affection for the UK, I've been a few times, and I have great respect for the law enforcement there.'

Over a second round of drinks, we settled on his fees and got down to discussing potential interviewees in both the US and UK. I mentioned that I was investigating the possibility of setting up an interview with a British serial killer, and said my first choices were either Dennis Nilsen, because he'd already been interviewed at length for a book and seemed intelligent and articulate, or Peter Sutcliffe, the so-called Yorkshire Ripper.

'I consulted on the Ripper case,' he told me. 'John Douglas and I were in the UK lecturing at a police college there and we were actually having a beer together when we met a senior detective from Yorkshire called John Domaille. I think at the time the Ripper had killed seven or eight women.'

I asked if he and Douglas had heard the famous 'I'm Jack' audiotape, in which the sender claimed to be the Yorkshire Ripper. It turned out to be a terrible hoax. However, because of the man's accent, murder squad detectives were misled into thinking the serial killer hailed from the northeast of England, and they excluded suspects who weren't from that region.

Bob nodded. 'Yeah, we heard it. Both John and I told Domaille straight off that the man on the tape was not the killer they were hunting. To us it was obvious. The tape was made by an expansive, extroverted kind of individual and the killings had been done by an introvert with some mental illnesses and a deep hatred for prostitutes.'

I asked whether they had produced a profile of either the hoaxer or the Yorkshire Ripper.

'The answer's yes and no. Domaille asked us to visit the crime scenes and sit with his teams in Yorkshire, but we couldn't do that because we had to fly straight back to Quantico. Instead, we ended up giving them an on-the-spot profile that was kinda rough, but we were sure would be in the ballpark. We said the unsub was likely to regularly go to the areas where he would kill and would fit in comfortably. We thought he'd drive a cab there, or a truck, or deliver mail. We said he wouldn't be a total loner and would have some form of ongoing relationship with a woman. And we believed, because of the extremity of the violence, that he had some mental issues.*

---

* Peter Sutcliffe was a married lorry driver coming up to his fortieth birthday when he was arrested. After being jailed for life for murdering thirteen women, he was diagnosed with paranoid schizophrenia and transferred to Broadmoor Hospital.

I asked how Domaille had reacted to the profile.

'He took it seriously and was grateful. John and I suggested he send us pictures of the crime scenes, full pathology and forensic reports, and we'd work further on it from Quantico, but the material never came, so that was the end of our involvement. I found out later that his boss had rubbished the profile and had been sold on the tape being genuine.' Bob's face told me he knew exactly how costly a mistake that had been. The Yorkshire Ripper had gone on to kill for several more years after that profile, before being caught.

'The other potential interviewee,' I continued, 'is Dennis Nilsen. He killed more than a dozen young men and—'

'I know who he is,' Bob interjected gently. 'Serial necrophile. Operated out of London. It's interesting you mention him because I've just been working on the Jeffrey Dahmer case and there are similarities. You know Dahmer?'

I did. The whole world did. When Dahmer had been arrested in the summer of 1991, he told police he'd murdered, mutilated and indulged in the cannibalism of at least fifteen men and boys.

'The defence asked me to do some work for them as an expert witness,' Bob continued. 'His lawyers knew he was going to be found guilty and put away for life. The only question was *where* he did the time – prison or a mental facility? The cops found body parts everywhere in his house, and enough forensics to convict him ten times over. What they wanted me to give was an opinion on whether he was sane or not when he killed. Under local law, he had a chance to plead "Guilty but insane", and they needed expert testimony to swing that verdict, so I went over and interviewed him for a few days.' He half shrugged. 'It was a little strange because I knew a great friend of mine, Park Deitz – he's here at this conference

– had been engaged by the prosecution and we'd never given evidence against each other before.'

'And did you think Dahmer was insane?'

'I did. At the times Jeffrey Dahmer committed those crimes I don't think he was a sane individual.'*

I asked the questions most of the world had asked. 'Do you know what made him do it? Why he was like that? I mean, I understood his father was a doctor and he had an average middle class upbringing—'

Again he interrupted, and stopped me making a fool of myself. 'The concept that every person who becomes a serial killer has come from a home where sexual abuse and physical beating and that sort of thing are rampant, is not necessarily true. Physical abuse can be bad. Sexual abuse can be bad. But psychological cruelty or emotional neglect can be as equally damaging in the child's development, as can non-intervening parents.'

'Non-intervening – what does that mean?' I asked.

'With "non-intervention" we include inconsistent discipline, allowing them to do things they oughtn't to, usually because mom and dad are just too busy to deal with them, and this can be a real problem with this type of individual. There has to be at least one pair of safe hands in a family, someone to catch a kid when they come off the emotional or disciplinary rails.'

Non-intervening parents.

This surely applied in the childhood of Dennis Nilsen? His father had been largely absent and his mother too young, too

---

* Although Dahmer was diagnosed with a number of psychological disorders, he was found to be legally sane. He was convicted of sixteen murders and sentenced to life imprisonment. In November 1984, he was beaten to death by a fellow inmate at the Columbia Correctional Institution in Wisconsin.

busy, too tired to give him all the affection, attention and consistent discipline needed to nurture him emotionally and teach him right from wrong.

'I still have connections with the Dahmer team,' Bob continued. 'Jeffrey might be a possible interviewee for you, though there are a lot of media folk chasing him, so it may be difficult. You should also try Ed Kemper; I think he's still in Vacaville.'

I said I would, then thought about a fallback if we failed to get access to either Sutcliffe or Nilsen. 'Nilsen's quoted a lot in a book called *Killing for Company*, if we can't do the interview with him for one reason or another, would you be agreeable to commenting upon what Nilsen said in the book, presuming we secured copyright permissions to do that, and get his words voiced by an actor?'

'I don't see why not.' Bob glanced at his watch and warned me he had a dinner engagement so would have to leave very shortly.

Realising my time was limited, I quickly asked what similarities he saw between Dahmer and Nilsen. Pairing them in the documentary would be perfect.

He ticked them off on his hand. 'Both were troubled children. Both repressed homosexuals who cruised bars for their victims. Both were necrophiles. Both dismembered their victims. And both – like John Wayne Gacy* – kept their victims' bodies and body parts in their homes, despite knowing that a knock on the door could easily lead to the evidence being discovered and them being jailed for the rest of their lives. There are probably a lot of other similarities as well, I'd have to look at the files.'

---

* John Wayne Gacy, 'The Killer Clown', murdered thirty-three men and young boys, keeping the bodies of more than twenty of them beneath the floorboards/ crawl space of his home.

Bob finished his beer and left.

I sat for a while in a stunned silence. It was early Sunday evening in Australia, Sunday morning back in the UK. Had I not been working, I would have been out with my wife and child, probably watching soccer-mad Damian play for a local football team, maybe looking forward to a pub lunch after the match. I'd be thinking and doing *normal* things.

Instead, my mind was filled with the sickest of thoughts and most disturbing of questions.

Why did the likes of Nilsen, Dahmer and Gacy – all intelligent men, respected at work and in their local communities – keep the bodies and body parts of their murder victims in their own homes?

Why didn't they sink this damning evidence in rivers, or bury them miles away in deep graves? Or dissolve them in acid?

Had they wanted to get caught?

Did it excite them to have had such damning evidence close by?

Or were the body parts souvenirs?

Or trophies?

In the richest aristocratic houses across the British Isles, the severed heads of antlered stags have for generations been proudly displayed on walls. Body parts of prey kept by victorious hunters.

Was this the serial killer equivalent? Were the ultimate trophies for these offenders the body parts of those they hunted and murdered? Visual reminders of their conquests, conjuring up the thrill of the chase and the rush of the kill?

Serial killer Ed Kemper* (also interviewed by Ressler),

---

* Ed Kemper was also interviewed by Bob Ressler. A dramatisation of the interview is featured at length in episode two of the Netflix series *Mindhunter* and there are trailer clips on YouTube.

when famously stopped in his car by a traffic cop, had asked the officer to check his lights for him, to ensure he wasn't inadvertently committing other offences. At that exact time, he'd had two severed heads in the trunk of his car he'd planned to keep as trophies. Like Nilsen, he'd also been a necrophile, and like Dahmer, he admitted to having had fantasies about cannibalism.

My suspicions about Nilsen's reasons for keeping bodies and body parts deepened the following day, when I watched Charles Siragusa,* an assistant district attorney, lecture on the value and accuracy of profiling, citing one of his cases – that of serial killer Arthur Shawcross.

Shawcross, known as the Genesee River Killer, had been caught and convicted in 1990. He killed at least eleven people, probably many more, sexually assaulting and raping both young boys and women. Shawcross also dismembered and kept body parts of his victims as trophies and souvenirs, including vulvas of some of the women he'd raped and murdered.

As well as being sickening, the Shawcross case was fascinating, and represented another page in offender-profiling history, once more written by the BSU's Robert Ressler and his friend Park Dietz.

The hunt for the Genesee River Killer in Rochester, New York, began after the decomposing body of a prostitute had been discovered floating in Salmon Creek, near the river gorge in 1988.

Six months later, the skeleton of another female victim was found.

---

* Charles 'Chuck' Siragusa later became a senior United States district judge in the US District Court for the Western District of New York.

Thirteen months passed, then a third was discovered – only this time she had been decapitated and her head taken from the scene.

Just a few days later, another decapitated female body was discovered. More bodies turned up throughout 1988 and 1989. Finally, the local police called in the FBI.

From the mutilation of the corpses, the type of victims targeted and the remoteness of the area in which they were taken, BSU and state profilers drew up a psychological profile.

Siragusa told the conference that the profile of the unsub would turn out to be dramatically accurate: 'A *loner, at least thirty-five years or older* – Shawcross was forty-four, right there in the ballpark. *He will have a menial occupation* – what Arthur Shawcross did for a living was cut food for salads. *Appears innocuous and unthreatening* – you can see from photographs, he was middle-aged, potbellied and balding. He certainly blended into the area where he lived. *His vehicle will be functional as opposed to stylish, a functional vehicle like ones used by the police.* Well, as it turned out, the car Shawcross was driving was an undercover police car that had been sold at auction. *Potential police buff* – Shawcross hung around a location called Dunkin' Donuts in the city of Rochester, frequented by police officers. In fact, when he was arrested and his picture was flashed all over TV, four police officers came forward and said they had actually spoken to him at that location.'

While the profile was indeed stunningly accurate, that in itself was not what was exceptional about the case. The breakthrough came when the body of the eleventh victim was found frozen in the river, just beneath a bridge. Profilers were convinced the killer was a local man and they came up with the theory that he may well return to the scenes of his crimes to rekindle his fantasies and mentally relive the murders.

Instead of removing the latest corpse, they made the controversial decision to leave it in the frozen water and keep it under covert surveillance.

Their gamble paid off.

After days of patiently waiting, a car stopped on the bridge and stayed there for an inordinately long period of time. Undercover detectives then observed a man fitting their profile gazing into the river at the body, while masturbating in his car.

He was arrested.

The conference in Melbourne played a video clip of Shawcross being interviewed by forensic psychiatrist Park Deitz (I eventually included this footage in *Murder in Mind*). Initially, Shawcross claims he only stopped to 'take a piss'. Dietz asks him on camera, 'Weren't you masturbating then?' Shawcross replies, 'No, I was urinating in a bottle.' The conversation goes on for a while, then Dietz says, 'It's just very hard to believe it's a coincidence that you happened to stop, right where your victim is, and you happened to have your penis out, and that it wasn't for masturbation . . . that's got to be the worst-luck piss a criminal has ever had.'

I spoke to both Siragusa and Dietz after the lecture and learned that this had been the first time the FBI had been able to prove their long-held theory that killers regularly returned to their crime scenes. Had Shawcross not done so, then they had no doubt he wouldn't have been caught that day and would have carried on killing. Both experts also had no doubt that the heads and body parts of the victims had been taken away as trophies. In a chilling echo of my own thoughts about Dennis Nilsen, Siragusa added, 'Shawcross was a deer hunter, an animal hunter, it was second nature for him to take and keep a body part as a trophy.'

Originally, I'd thought Nilsen's offending to be so shocking that it was unique. After talking to Terry Green, Bob Ressler, Park Deitz and Charles Siragusa I was noticing commonalities and starting to form my own investigative opinions about his offending.

Kemper, Dahmer, Shawcross – *and Nilsen* – all kept body parts.

Kemper, Dahmer, Shawcross – *and Nilsen* – all indulged in necrophilia.

Kemper, Dahmer, Shawcross – *and Nilsen* – all claimed to have suffered emotional neglect or trauma during their childhood.

Suddenly, the Scottish serial killer didn't seem unique. Far from it. But surely necrophilia was still a very limited and highly unusual offence?

The following day, I met the man who would answer that disturbing question with a wearied look formed from a lifetime of dealing with such oddities.

Just as Bob Ressler is credited with coining the term 'serial killer', Robert Roy Hazelwood is recognised as the man who decided such offenders fell into two main categories – organised and disorganised (the FBI would later develop a third 'mixed' category which is probably the one Nilsen would have fitted).

Roy's profiling specialism was that of serial sexual offending, including sexual sadism and lust murder. He is also believed to have been largely instrumental in determining the six categories of rape, criminologists use for reference – opportunistic, anger excitation, anger retaliatory, power assertive, power reassurance and gang rape.

Again, the venue for our meeting was the hotel bar, though as I recall, he drank only water. Roy didn't have Bob Ressler's physical presence, but dressed in a near-white jacket, with dark hair, tanned complexion and shades, I reckoned that on camera he could easily play the role of a very cool mafia don.

The profiler had a rich, deep voice and talked with the kind of perfect pace and dramatic stress that you'd normally hear from an out-of-vision narrator at the start of some epic Hollywood movie. Nobody could tell a story better and you hung on his every word.

'Homosexual necrophilia is very unusual,' he told me as I sought his opinions on the Nilsen case. 'Generally, we're seeing a male offender acting out on a female victim after she's deceased. While the sexual orientation has changed, the reasons for the offence largely remain the same – that being that in his everyday life the offender has extreme difficulty forming meaningful relationships with other human beings, therefore he fantasises about a relationship in which he has complete control and there won't be any difficulties. The only way he feels he can be sure of this total acceptance – the realization of his fantasy – is by killing the victim.'

'It's just so weird,' I replied, almost lost for words.

'You have to remember,' Roy continued, 'the primary sexual organs of the male and the female are not their genitals, it is their minds. What I've learned over the years is that when it comes to sex, there's no line that people won't cross. No limit to what they might do to other people or to themselves when they are in pursuit of sexual satisfaction.' He waited for me to change tapes on my recorder, then continued, 'There's certainly no limit to the type of people who will do the most deviant and illegal of things. They can be manual workers or professors, librarians or soldiers, no matter – sexual offenders come in all job categories, all lifestyles, all races, religions and income groups.'

I shared with him my intention to try to interview Nilsen, Sutcliffe, or someone like them, for the documentary.

'Good luck with that,' he said with a slight grin. 'Keep in mind that you don't always get valuable answers or insights from these guys. Often, they don't know themselves why they did what they did. They just know they did it, found they liked it, so did it again.' He paused for a moment, as though weighing up whether to tell me something or not. Then he added, 'If he talks to you, you'll need a baseline, some kind of metric to work out when he's telling the truth and when he's lying.'

'And how do I do that?' I asked.

'Methods can vary from individual to individual, but I'd suggest you ask him about things you already know are true. Indisputable facts. Take him over ground he'll feel safe on and make sure you watch and listen closely. How does he sit when he's telling the truth? What words does he use? How long are his sentences? Does he elaborate, contextualise or is he always succinct? Does he show a range of emotions, or is he monotone and impassive? When you think you've got a handle on all that, then you have your baseline. You have to be a human polygraph and notice any change to this baseline behaviour – it may – I stress *may* – be an indication he's fabricating something.'

'So how would I know if it were true or not?'

'Rather than call him a liar, which runs the risk of him quitting your interview, I'd suggest you ask him to explain things in greater detail because you're having difficulty under-standing, then watch and listen some more. See if his behaviour and language change. And you should keep in mind that his agenda might not be as academic or altruistic as yours.'

He took a beat and added, 'I mean, you're not a priest, so you're not offering absolution. You're not judiciary, so you can't cut his sentence or get him privileges, so why's he gonna do this? What's he gonna get out of it?' Roy quickly answered his own questions. 'With these guys, it's most likely that he's a narcissist, he likes being the centre of attention – not something that's good for your health when you're in prison, that's a place where you want to go unnoticed – so the thing for him will be that you and your crew are gonna scratch that terrible itch he can't reach – the itch for an audience, for people to listen to his stories, for people to be subject to his control – even if it's only a short while.'

'What, in your experience,' I asked, 'are the reasons why normal intelligent people end up like Dennis Nilsen as serial killers and necrophiles?'

The smile reappeared. 'Well, we could spend the rest of the evening just debating what a *normal* person is. We're all unique. We all have our strengths and weaknesses, our hang-ups and fantasies, our fears and excitements.' He let out a sigh, which made me think he must have been asked this question a hundred times. 'First thing, we're all the result of genetics, nature, nurture, our environments and some degrees of good and bad luck befalling us. Something that greatly excites, frightens or distresses you, might not affect me at all, and vice versa. So, we're sociologically safe in saying that no single factor is going to be instrumental in creating homicidal or seriously deviant sexual behaviour. Now, when we examine the lives of serial offenders, we usually see that they experienced a *set* of circumstances rather than one single event that threw them off the track that most of us run. Once they're off that track, they get a sense of being an outlier, a loner, not part of the crowd and they get anxious and stressed because they either don't fit in, or they *feel* they don't. This is bad enough, but then comes puberty and sex and sexual relations. We're all programmed to find a mate, it's in our genes, it's part of our needs to be with someone and enjoy intimacy and have sex. If it wasn't, then the human race would die out. So, you have these outcasts, these socially inadequate people, trying to find mates. If they do, then most likely they get back on the straight and narrow, settle down and live okay lives. If they don't, then it's possible they get further knocked off track. In latent offenders, sexual rejection, sexual repression, sexual dysfunction, coming on top of their other stresses, such as feeling isolated and inadequate, losing a job or someone close to them passing – any or all of these things can breed anger, rage and other toxic emotions. And then, very often, there's what we call a trigger. Someone does something, or something happens that is just mentally the last straw and they strike out in a way specific to their problems, and that way is quite often rape or murder.'

I thought about widening the discussion to other serial killers but decided to stay focused on Nilsen. 'One offender I'm looking to interview was a bright guy, a former policeman. He knew how evidence led to people getting caught, yet he dismembered his victims and kept their body parts – lots of them – in his flat, why would he have done that?'

'He was a necrophiliac, so he would want to keep dead flesh as long as possible. Just looking at small sections of a corpse could still have been arousing for him. We've interviewed people who kept breasts, nipples, vaginas and they did so for sexual satisfaction, they used them as masturbatory aids. Others kept heads, hands and even severed penises as trophies, so it's possible. Others kept body parts for consumption – that was a thing in their rituals.' He took a pause, then added,

'Some serial offenders just don't plan things cleverly enough, so maybe he hadn't known how long he could keep the corpses until decomposition made them joyless to him, and had no idea how he would dispose of them once they'd reached that stage.'

Mentally, I saw photographs and newsreels of the black bags full of body parts being hauled out of Nilsen's London flat by ashen-faced detectives. I no longer thought of them solely as evidence – I imagined the pleasures Nilsen had sought from each and every part of the poor men he'd butchered.

'Necrophilia,' continued Roy, oblivious to how screwed-up my mind was feeling, 'is one of the last taboos and strangest paraphilias. Some necrophiles are purely aroused by dead bodies – *any* dead bodies. Typically, they will hang around funerals, hospital mortuaries and might dig up graves to get themselves a corpse. They don't need a prior connection to the deceased and they probably won't have murder in their sexual repertoire. Others are individuals who are sexually dysfunctional with the living, and during engagement with a living partner, find they become angry at losing an erection. One day, they take their rage out on their partner and kill. They now find they are aroused enough to achieve penetration. At last, they feel potent. Powerful. In control. And that's because there is no one to judge them. No one to witness their perceived inadequacy. From that moment on, they long for this potency and power, and as a result, they find themselves fantasising about post-mortem copulation and even the fore-play to it – the killing.'

Roy kindly lingered a little longer than he'd intended that evening, and aside from making plans to film him for the documentary, he suggested interviewing a US serial killer called Robert Berdella.

'Berdella would be a real coup.' He savoured the thought. 'We've tried several times to get him to sit down with us, and all we ever got was pushback. He's a homosexual, sexual sadist who tortured his victims to death, dismembered them and left their remains in black sacks for the refuse truck to take away. He may have indulged in necrophilia as well.'

'Is he intelligent?'

The profiler smiled. 'IQ up in the 160s. This guy is dangerously smart. He was head of his neighbourhood watch, ran a number of businesses, and stayed ahead of the local cops for years. I'd be interested to see that interview if he did it.'

After paying the bill and heading to my room, I reflected on the research I'd done on Roy. Like Bob Ressler, he'd spent a good number of years in the army, in the military police. He'd reached the rank of Major by the time he left to undertake a fellowship in forensic medicine, and in 1971 was at the beginning of an exceptionally distinguished career in the FBI. From press clippings, I'd also learned he'd been born in Idaho, had three siblings and been raised by his mom and stepdad. As an infant, his biological father had taken him without his mother's consent and fairly aimlessly road-tripped the country for six months, before dropping him at his grandparents' home, only to never see the child again.

Was there better proof that traumatic circumstances in childhood needn't result in criminal behaviour? Roy had seen more military action than the likes of Nilsen and Shawcross put together. He'd faced paternal abandonment on a scale at least as traumatic as Nilsen, and like the Scot he'd had other siblings as rivals for his mother's affection. Yet, Roy Hazelwood had turned out be a saint amongst men, and Nilsen a devil.

8

I DON'T DO THAT KIND OF
THING ANYMORE

Perhaps not surprisingly, I didn't sleep that night.

The intense and disturbing conversation with Roy Hazelwood had spun the cogs of my mind so vigorously that I didn't for a second drift off.

The more I thought about Dennis Nilsen, the more I became convinced that he above all other serial killers was the one who would be of most fascination to TV viewers.

Thanks to Terry Green's short, sharp shock of a lesson in his office in Quantico, I was beginning to see details rather than just the big picture. And lying in bed in Melbourne, those details led me to examine factors that may have contributed to turning an innocent young boy into a troubled man and eventually a serial killer.

Maybe Nilsen had been unloved as a child – or at least felt he had been unloved – and this made him feel alienated.

He lacked a father figure/male role model – did this mean he became unduly attached to his grandfather?

Bob Ressler had surprised me by the amount of importance he'd given to interventional parenting. Had the absence of kindness, good guidance and fair discipline damaged Nilsen's emotional development and affected his moral compass?

Traumatised by his grandpa's death and seeing his dead

body – had this singular event at barely six years old locked in an early and unhealthy fascination with mortality?

It must have been exceptionally difficult to come out as gay in a small Scottish town in the fifties and sixties. Probably impossible for him to approach other young men whom he liked, for fear of rejection, ridicule or even being beaten up – had this been why he'd craved a 'passive' (dead) partner?

The failure to form deep friendships or intimate relationships must have led to chronic loneliness and robbed him of confidence – a factor Roy Hazelwood thought to be a commonly accepted contributor to necrophilia.

As I went through the points, I realised that although they made sense, they were based on assumptions.

These weren't facts.

They were best guesses, formed from what I'd read about Nilsen in books, magazines and newspapers.

If I was serious about pursuing him for the documentary, then I had to at least visit him in prison and do some more reliable face-to-face research. I needed double-checks. Facts. And if, as most probably was the case, it turned out that an on-screen interview wasn't possible, then at least I'd have this personal meeting to fall back on.

It was still dark when I sat up in bed, turned the light on and decided to make my first definite move. I wrote the first draft of a letter to Nilsen, outlining my background as a documentary maker, the purpose of the intended film and how valuable his cooperation would be.

I put down my pen and paper, knowing it would need revision before sending, and tried again to sleep.

No luck.

Insomnia and I were not strangers. Whenever I began a

new programme, I immersed myself so deeply in the fresh subject that I tended to overload my tiny brain, and I knew it would take at least one or two sleepless nights to process the backlog of new information.

Soon after dawn I gave up, pulled on a sweatshirt, trackpants and trainers and went for a run before breakfast. Today would be a physical hell, but if I got myself sufficiently tired, then maybe I'd sleep at night.

The hotel was in the central business district, and I soon found myself invigorated by cool, fresh air, the endorphin rush of exercise and the mentally cleansing effect of being beneath clear blue skies and out in new surroundings.

After a block or two, the scenery changed. The pavements I plodded became populated by statues of giant monkeys and overhead there were flamboyant banners, webs of multi-coloured lights and a million flags.

I was in Chinatown.

Apparently during a Chinese New Year that was celebrating the Year of the Monkey. Melbourne was known to boast the oldest Chinese settlement in Australia and one of the oldest in the Western world, and it looked like it from all the decorations.

Only a handful of people were on the streets and they were either exhausted and heading into work, or exhausted and heading home after a night's revelry.

Fun. Frivolity. Normality.

I longed for some – any – of those things.

After showering and changing, I grabbed coffee and croissants in the hotel restaurant. Everyone around me seemed to be either delegates or speakers at the conference on serial offenders. I overheard an intense conversation about a paper on rape that Roy Hazelwood had co-authored with Janet

Warren from the Institute of Psychiatry and Law at the University of Virginia.

'They interviewed this group of serial rapists, I think it was a hundred or more,' recounted a grapefruit-eating man to his cooked-breakfast companion, 'and they found in the days after the rape something like a third of them said they hit the bottle hard, to bury their guilt.'

I listened in surprise. Not because I was disturbed by the nature of the conversation, but because I knew the statistics were wrong. I was very familiar with the paper they were referring to – it was called 'The Criminal Behaviour of the Serial Rapist' and was at least two years old. I'd read a copy in an FBI bulletin in the library at Quantico, and I knew the alcohol abuse figure was actually between 20 and 27 per cent – just over a quarter – and the interview group wasn't a hundred, it was fewer than fifty, but those fifty men had been responsible for almost nine hundred rapes.

As I left for the day's lectures, I wondered how many experts like the one I'd just overheard were blithely trading wrong statistics. And did it matter? The big takeaway here was that if a detective was interviewing a suspect and there was evidence that he'd been drinking heavily over the days immediately after the offence, then he was worth a closer look.

Alcohol.

This was a new detail for me to consider.

I realised then that booze had also been a big factor in Dennis Nilsen's life. He'd picked up all his victims in pubs. He'd plied them with drinks when he'd got them into his flat. Under arrest, he'd given evidence that he'd often been drunk during the killing, and the dismembering and disposing of his victims.

Terry Green's lecturing slapped me hard.

'You're looking but you're not seeing.'

I berated myself. Alcohol had been a big detail in Nilsen's life, and I'd been so fixated on the shock headline details of necrophilia and dismemberment I'd completely overlooked the critical role alcohol might have played in his crimes.

As I sat down in the auditorium for the first lecture of the day, all the mind-clearing benefits of my early morning run through picturesque Chinatown disappeared. It was like returning from a holiday, only to face a major catastrophe during your first morning back. You feel like you've never been away.

I was being pulled under again.

During the mid-morning break, I caught up with Bob and to his dismay told him I had a couple of things on my mind. We grabbed cups of coffee, but he pointedly stayed away from chairs and tables, knowing that if we stayed standing I'd be quicker getting to the point.

'Are there any statistics or reports,' I asked, starting my tape recorder, 'detailing the role alcohol plays in serial murder?'

'Plenty,' he replied, glancing disdainfully at the recorder. 'And the serial killer is often quick to blame alcohol for his crimes. "I was drunk, I didn't know what I was doing, it just kinda happened", and BS like that. The truth is, alcohol never repeatedly strangled or shot anyone. So, in the case of serials, booze might have given them Dutch courage to act out their fantasies. It might have calmed their anxieties after the act, when they had to get rid of the bodies, but alcohol isn't responsible for serial murder, serial murderers are.'

'I'd still like to look at some statistics if possible.'

'Sure. We can fix that. Off the top of my head, I'd say

around a quarter to a third of all murderers claim alcohol played a part in their crimes. I've got information in my office.'

'That's about the same as serial rapists, isn't it?'

He nodded. 'Sounds about right. I'll get the stats for you.'

I could see he was keen to get away. 'Roy mentioned Robert Berdella as a possible interviewee, what do you think?'

He smiled in a way that made me suspect Berdella was the subject of a private joke between them.

'Would he be suitable?' I pressed.

The smile widened. 'Did Roy tell you one of the first things Berdella did when he was arrested?'

'No.'

'What d'you expect he did?'

'I guess he insisted he was innocent and asked for a lawyer?'

'No. This guy got himself a psychologist, not a lawyer.'

'Insanity plea?' I guessed.

'Wrong again. He got the psychologist to analyse the police officers dealing with him, not to analyse himself. He hired the shrink to help him work out whether the detectives had enough evidence to send him to the death chamber, or whether they were bluffing. And it worked, he beat the gas.'

'He profiled the profilers,' I quipped.

Bob shot me down. 'They were detectives not profilers. And what he did wasn't profiling, wasn't anything like profiling. Berdella is smart, but I doubt he'll talk on videotape for TV. He hasn't so far. Have you tried Kemper yet?'

I replied that I hadn't, but I was going to do so later in the day.

'California's about nineteen hours behind Melbourne.' Bob put down his coffee cup. 'I need to go.'

As he disappeared, I realised that in my enthusiasm I'd

pushed my luck. Had taken liberties. Contracts hadn't been exchanged yet, let alone signed. No payments had been made, and already I was imposing upon his time and expertise.

Instead of joining the next session, I decided to camp in my room and make calls. No sooner had I settled on my bed with the phone, notes and tape recorder than the Ambien I'd taken at 3 a.m. mischievously decided to work.

I fought off the sleep with more coffee, called my colleagues in the UK and begged them to fax contracts to Bob Ressler's office before the end of the day. I rang international directory enquiries and got a number for Vacaville Prison in California. Grateful that I wasn't personally paying the exorbitant hotel phone charges, I dialled the given number and waited for it to connect.

A male voice confirmed I'd got the right place and added, 'How can I help you?'

I explained I was a documentary maker from ITV, the leading independent broadcaster in the UK, and was producing a programme that featured offender-profiling processes run by the FBI and police forces in England. As part of it, I hoped to arrange an interview with Ed Kemper, who I understood was still an inmate at the jail.

'He is. Please hold on.' The line went dead while I was transferred to what I guessed would either be the media relations unit or, if I was lucky, the Governor's office.

Ed Kemper was one of the original offenders interviewed by Ressler for the FBI's pioneering profile programme. His stats were known the world over – he was 6 foot 9 inches tall, had an IQ of 145 and was a serial killer, rapist, cannibal and necrophile who'd murdered ten people, including his mother and grandparents. He had been labelled the Co-ed Killer because six of his victims were young college women.

After Kemper killed his mother,* he decapitated her and put the head on the mantlepiece to throw things at, and placed her torso in a closet. He told Ressler that he'd removed her larynx and pushed it into the garbage disposal machine, but it had been 'spat out', he added, 'Even when she was dead, she was still bitching at me.'

I looked at the bedside clock in my Melbourne hotel room; I'd been on hold for nearly fifteen minutes. The bill for calling the prison in Vacaville was going to be astronomic. I was on the verge of hanging up when an authoritative male voice came on the line. 'Hello?'

I explained once again who I was, what the purpose of my call was and that I wanted to speak to Ed Kemper.

'This is he.'

I was stunned into silence. Was it Kemper? Or just a guard fooling around? I needed to double check. 'I'm sorry, I've been on hold for either the media office or the governor, because I want to talk to Ed Kemper.'

'I *am* Kemper,' he stressed in a highly annoyed tone that couldn't be faked.

'Mr Kemper, Bob Ressler from the FBI suggested I call you —'

'He did? How is Mr Ressler?'

'He's fine. He's good.'

'Glad to hear it. You're from England, Great Britain, right?'

'That's right. I'm looking for a credible, articulate interviewee for this documentary, and I'd like to come to California to interview you about how you helped the FBI.'

'I don't want to do that.'

---

* Kemper told Ressler that he blamed his mother for his crimes because she always mocked him, robbed him of confidence and deprived him of affection.

I was taken aback. 'Why's that? I understood you were very helpful and Bob—'

'I just don't want to talk about my past. I don't do that kind of thing anymore.'

'That would be a real shame,' I responded. 'Your contribution would be enormously educative to a UK audience; they'd really like to hear your views.'

'I don't think so.'

I tried another tack. 'It's not a sensationalist documentary. It's focused on the psychology of offending and the psychology of detection. We're at an historic stage in the UK and—'

'It's *only* television,' he interrupted. 'TV isn't historic, or even important.'

I could feel the ground beneath me caving in. 'A lot of people regard it as visual history,' I argued. 'This would be a chance for you to explain your actions, and why you helped the FBI.'

'I was bored. That's why I talked to Mr Ressler. Forgive me, Mr Morley, I am going to go now because I believe there will soon be a ball game showing. Maybe a historic one.'

'I'm hoping you'll reconsider taking part in our documentary. I'll send you a letter with all my details on.'

'Okay. Thank you for calling.'

'One final thing –' I couldn't let him leave without asking at least one of the zillion questions in my head. 'What do you think made you start killing?'

'I guess I felt it was time.'

Then Kemper was gone.

I put the phone down and sat in a daze. I'd blown it. He'd taken the call and I'd failed to persuade him to participate. I hadn't been prepared to actually speak to him – I hadn't imagined he'd be put on the line just like that!

I'd been put on the spot and fumbled it.
Maybe Bob Ressler could pull this one out of the fire for me.
Or maybe he'd land Dahmer.
Or Berdella.
Or both.

9

LOOK WHO'S (NOT) TALKING

From Melbourne, I returned briefly to the TV studios in England to meet with the production team for *Murder in Mind* and to update the station's controller of factual programmes, Steve Clark.

A straight-talking Liverpudlian, his daily demand for originality and exclusivity had scared the life out of me when I'd joined Central TV and he'd been my news editor. Gradually, I'd got used to being professionally stretched and, as a producer, tried to coax the same qualities from my crews.

Over a canteen lunch of fish, chips and peas, we took stock of where the documentary was heading. We had ACPO access, FBI access and CATCHEM access. We had a former FBI profiler on board as consultant. We had interviews planned with current and past FBI profilers, including the manager of the VICAP offender system. In the UK, I'd sent introductory letters to Paul Britton, the head of the Home Office review, David Canter of Surrey University who'd been working with police on geographic profiling of offenders, Mike Berry, a forensic clinical psychologist who'd also assisted police in rape and murder enquiries, and top police officers such as John Stevens and Don Dovaston.

'No serial killers, though,' Steve said, putting his finger as usual on the weak spot. 'We could end up with lots of talking heads, but not the killers themselves, and that would make the programme less credible.'

'I've written a draft letter to Dennis Nilsen, but haven't sent it yet.'

'Why not?'

'Because of Brian Masters. Having thought about it, I realised Nilsen is certain to ask his opinion.'

'And you think Masters will oppose an interview?'

'Maybe. I've asked his agent to see if he'll meet me, so I can outline the documentary and see if he's supportive. If he's not, and Nilsen won't play ball, then there's US footage – videotape of serial offenders to fall back on. I'm sure we'll get some of that. I'm confident Bob Ressler will be as good as his word and, unless we run out of time, he'll help us get someone in the States. Brady and Hindley feel like no-goes, but we're going to approach the Yorkshire Ripper's wife to see if there's a way to get to Peter. Reading between the lines, I think John Stevens of ACPO will support us filming an interview with Dennis Nilsen, Sutcliffe or someone like him, if it is also being done for the purpose of educating police officers. Unless we go that route, I don't see a chance of us getting close to filming a serial murderer in a British jail.'

'Then you need to concentrate on that. Nilsen would be a coup. Forget chasing anyone else. Run with this until you get a firm yes or no, then we'll be sure where we stand.'

I outlined my Plan B of having an actor voice Nilsen's words from *Killing for Company* and then have Ressler comment off the back of the sync.

'I never like Plan Bs,' Steve replied. 'Always best you come up with a Plan A+.'

I went back to the team feeling chastened. I'd fooled myself

LOOK WHO'S (NOT) TALKING

into thinking we had enough for a good show. We hadn't. All the hard work was still ahead of us.

Over the next few days, I tried to spend as much time as I could at home, only occasionally popping into the office for brief meetings and to collect ongoing research notes that had been prepared on Nilsen, Jeffrey Dahmer and Robert Berdella.

As anyone who regularly works away from base for long periods knows, there's often a strange sensation when stepping back into family life. You feel like an intruder. Routines and patterns have been established without you being there, and suddenly you're disrupting them. Then there's the messiness factor. I'm an accidental vandal. Within minutes of being in a room, I can make it look like it's just been burgled. I don't really know how I do it. I just put things down rather than put them away, and within an hour there are books, papers, shoes, empty cups and a thousand other things littering a room. It drove my first wife mad. She was house-proud. Everything was polished and clean. Neat and tidy. Everything except me.

Damian of course was non-judgemental. I was there to playfight with. Play football with. Read stories. Just being around was good enough for him. And for me. Whenever I came back from trips abroad, we'd exhaust each other with our company, and I'd often find myself falling asleep reading bedtime stories long before he nodded off.

Returning from Melbourne, I felt more out of the family circle than I ever had. I couldn't put my finger on it, but something had either changed, or was in the process of changing. I suspect my exposure to profilers and their relentless examination of every detail of human behaviour had made me question parts of my own life.

I was frequently depressed. Often exhausted. I felt I

127

constantly had to push myself to do more than I was doing. I struggled to fall asleep. Often dreamt of the murders and murderers I'd been studying. My mind wandered during the day and would fixate on the motivations of men like Nilsen, Dahmer, Shawcross and Sutcliffe.

Peter Sutcliffe.

Despite being advised to concentrate on Dennis Nilsen, I still thought there was an outside chance of us landing an interview with the Yorkshire Ripper as well.

This was my new Plan A+.

Get both of them.

Sutcliffe had been convicted of thirteen murders and seven attempted murders, and as a result, given twenty concurrent life sentences.

Like Nilsen, he'd pleaded not guilty on the grounds of diminished responsibility.

Unlike Nilsen, he had claimed to have heard the voice of God in his head, instructing him to commit the killings.

Another similarity with the Nilsen case seemed to be the lack of importance he gave to his victims. With only one known exception, Nilsen had killed young, homeless, homo-sexual men or male prostitutes. Sutcliffe's victims were almost exclusively female prostitutes. I was fascinated to see if psycho-logical profiling would have caught either of them earlier in their offending cycles.

Don Dovaston, Derbyshire Police's ACC, had thought access to Sutcliffe the most unlikely to be forthcoming, as the Home Office and West Yorkshire Police were sensitive to the stinging public criticism that Lord Byford had handed out in his report on how the police had missed chances to arrest Sutcliffe during the biggest manhunt ever launched in Britain.

In my mind, Peter Sutcliffe was still on our target list of

LOOK WHO'S (NOT) TALKING

possible interviewees. But I figured that his consent would only be forthcoming if the filming met the approval of his only prison visitor since conviction. His wife, Sonia.

She, like Brian Masters to Nilsen, was his only real confidant, and still lived in the house she had shared with her husband throughout their married life, and throughout his life of serial crime.

Sonia was known to be friendlier to women reporters than men, so we approached her through one of our most experienced female researchers.

She struck out. We left it a few days and she tried again. No success. Worse than that, Sonia had made it perfectly plain that she'd do everything she could to ensure Peter never took part in any such interview.

The evening after the second rejection, I spoke on the phone to Bob Ressler and told him that on top of being knocked back by Ed Kemper, we'd now hit a dead end in the Yorkshire Ripper case. I asked, with crossed fingers on both hands, if he'd made any progress with securing us access to Jeffrey Dahmer.

'It's not going to happen,' Bob told me. 'Neither Jeffrey nor his legal team are in favour of television access at the moment.'

'Not even if you do the interview?' I asked.

'Not even that.' The profiler was more than one step ahead of me. 'I suggested that, and the option of handing Jeffrey a list of questions and a video camera to record his answers on his own, but that didn't fly either.'

I was despondent. There were so many similarities between Dahmer and Nilsen. It felt like I'd lost a major piece of the documentary.

'I've been thinking a little about Berdella,' he continued, 'and how you might get him to cooperate.'

I said I was open to any suggestions.

'Prison is a very angry male environment and he's been in constant conflict since he got put in there. Get a woman to make the approach to him. He won't have had any form of feminine contact for years. The letter will stand out. I'm betting he'll reply.'

Despite the Sonia Sutcliffe disappointment, I thought it worth a shot. Jill Kirby, the senior researcher working with me on *Murder in Mind*, penned a letter and sent it under her name to Berdella at the Jefferson City Correctional Centre in Kansas City, Missouri.

This was the interview the FBI had been unable to land.

One even Roy Hazelwood wanted to see.

Was there *really* a chance Berdella would break the run of bad luck and say yes?

10

WHO ARE YOU?

This very personal question was the title track of a wonderful hit album by The Who, one of the greatest and most successful rock groups of all time.

It was released in 1978, five days before my twenty-first birthday and struck a loud and vibrant chord with me as I thrashed around, sinking and resurfacing, in the deep end of life. I was trying to make a living, begging for bank loans and mortgages (and not getting either), paying off debts, just about holding down my first long-term relationship and – like most young people – trying to work out who the hell all these people were who controlled so much of my life. Or, as Roger Daltrey more precisely put it, 'Who *the fuck* are you?'

What a great question.

Go on, ask yourself. I dare you.

It's probably going to take you a bit of time and a lot of soul-searching to come up with an honest and succinct answer. There's an amusing psychological test, most probably invented by marketeers in the automotive industry, and it comprises of a similar question. 'If you were a car, what make and model would you be?'

Perhaps, like me, you think you are a sleek four-seater Roadster, speedy but sturdy, adaptable to any weather, able to race when needed and stop on a dime if required. It's very probable your family, like mine, see you differently. The consensus in my clan is that I'm a Mini – small, cramped and a bit funny to look at. For modern Mini lovers, I should add that they see me as an old-fashioned Mr Bean model.

Then there's work.

We're all different at work, aren't we?

Bosses have to cut wages, make redundancies, save costs, meet deadlines, hit targets, negotiate deals, drive growth, etc. and are bound to at least *appear* to their colleagues to be a less friendly person than they do to friends and family.

Employees have to put up with conditions, rules, regulations, controls on their behaviour, comments about their performance that they would never consider tolerating at home or in the company of friends.

So, we should probably agree that it's difficult for us to define precisely who we are – and even more difficult for others to define us.

Now, a final twist.

An international holiday/travel company found its growth had stagnated and hired an equally famous business consultancy group to help. The consultants were told that they'd tried every trick in the book – flash sales, Bank Holiday sales, Christmas sales, children go free with parents, 2-for-1 offers, buy a summer holiday and get winter holiday free. Whatever they did, growth remained stagnant.

The consultants went away and did intensive market research. Not the stop-someone-in-a-shopping-centre kind, but precise research, carried out across all target demographics, with holidaymakers invited to focus groups where they were shown a range of the company's holidays and left to comment without being fed leading questions.

They went back to the company and declared, 'You don't really know your customers.'

'Ridiculous,' came the reply. The firm had been going for more than a hundred years and had virtually created the UK's travel industry.

The consultants asked them to explain who their customers were and what holidays they wanted.

Assuredly, the executives explained that young professionals favoured action, sporting holidays, filled with events and parties. Families liked beach holidays near zoos and water parks. Pensioners liked restful escapes in milder climates near famous gardens and historic houses and places.

To the company's horror, they were then told some home truths. According to the research, pensioners said they went on holiday for excitement, for the chance to explore, and would quite like to water ski, deep-sea dive, learn to sail, rock climb and even sky-dive or bungee jump. They didn't want to rest, they wanted to be thrilled. Conversely, a lot of young professionals, especially those who were married, said they were desperate to grab a break from their busy lives and just chill out in the sun on a nice beach with a good book or some music. Thirdly, parents wanted to use the holidays to take their kids to places where they could absorb a different culture, learn about history and geography and maybe even pick up a few words of a foreign language.

Finally, they concluded, pensioners, who as teenagers had posters of biker-rebels on their walls, still, after forty years, held a passion for motorbikes and leather-clad rebels.

Fantasies didn't die.

The company took on board the comments and experimented by targeting the age groups according to the new research. Profits rose dramatically. They, and marketeers worldwide, learned three invaluable lessons:

1. Appearances are deceptive.
2. Passions endure.
3. You never really know people's needs and desires until they tell you.

The same seems to be as true in the case of serial killers.

I'd like to take credit for initially asking Dennis Nilsen the big question, 'Who are you?' but that would be a lie. At the core of FBI profiling is the equation, How + Why = Who. This is what investigators ask at every crime scene. How did the offender do that to the victim? Why did they do it that way? Those answers start to narrow down possibilities and suspects. In short, we are the sum of our actions and our desires.

Bob Ressler suggested I ask the 'Who are you?' question straight after I shared with him the first few of Nilsen's letters. 'Don't lead him,' he warned me. 'Don't say anything reporter-like, just come right out and say it straight, "Who are you?"'

So, I did.

Nilsen's written reply, as almost always, was something of a boast, a doubt, a riddle and an insight.

He said, '*It is easier for me to define who and what I am not, rather than who or what I am. I am not what people expect, not the norm, not the ordinary. I am not one of my crimes or all of them. I am not a single word, a single sentence or a single fact. I am not singular. I am certainly not only the genetic meal cooked by my parents. I am not purely the product of place or circumstance. I am not a devil, a monster or a bogeyman. I am not a cruel person or a bully. I am not disloyal or promiscuous. I am not incapable of love or loneliness or heartbreak. I am not unfeeling or unkind. In short, in answer to your somewhat prosaic question, I am not.*'

I read the reply to Ressler during one of our many late night/early morning transatlantic calls. He sounded amused as he told me: 'Nilsen's gone to some lengths to appear cleverer and more mysterious than he actually is. He knows that unanswered questions always keep a discussion going, whereas answered ones end them. This guy doesn't want closure, he wants continuation. Dennis Nilsen wants people to keep on talking about him and he's working hard to see that happens.'

I asked if there was also some truth in what he was saying.

'Sure, there is. You could apply almost all the "I am not" things that he said to almost all of us. They're the kinda things that clever orators, politicians and TV preachers say all the time. They use this technique to win over their audiences, to lead them by the nose to a common ground where they set about selling them their own brand of snake oil.'

'So, it's a sales pitch?' I asked.

'Of course. Nilsen wouldn't be talking to you if he wasn't selling.'

I was intrigued by the metaphor. 'Then what exactly is he selling, and what am I paying with?'

Ressler laughed. 'He's selling a cleaned-up image of himself. Read the letter again and you'll see how he distances himself from his murders. Having obtained notoriety, he's now attempting to manipulate public opinion into seeing him in a separate light to his crimes. He is working on his image, trying to recast himself as erudite and intellectual rather than evil.'

'And my payment?'

'You're paying with the most precious currencies of all – your time, your attention and your interest. All that is gold in the bank for this kind of guy.' He took a beat, then added,

'There are things about Nilsen that remind me of Ted Bundy – you know who he is, right?'

I said I did. Theodore Robert 'Ted' Bundy had kidnapped, raped and killed at least thirty women in Florida and Colorado back in the seventies. Ressler had interviewed him at length in prison and was on record as saying he considered Bundy, 'a master of his game' and 'one of the most difficult murderers to fully understand'.

'Bundy was very intelligent and arrogant. He worked his image so well he conned the media into thinking he was some kind of Rudolph Valentino of the serial killer world. He wasn't; he was a very dangerous pervert. He represented himself at trial and even earned some praise from the judge. I'm sort of surprised Nilsen didn't do that; he had a big spotlight on him at trial, so he must have been tempted. Bundy loved the sound of his own voice, and once he got up a head of steam there was no stopping him intellectualising. There are other similarities as well. Like Nilsen, he had sex with some of the dead bodies of his victims, penetrated dismembered limbs and decapitated heads. Sickening perversions. And like your guy, Bundy picked only on the vulnerable and easily impressionable. He was a coward. A sexual predator with some charm and guile.' Without pause, he added, 'Do you think Nilsen was charming, in a kinda English way?'

I wasn't quite sure what an 'English way' was, but guessed it implied being a little more reserved, so I replied, 'Charming? No, I don't imagine he was.' But as I spoke, I found myself reconsidering. 'Maybe I'm being unfair. I imagine if you met him when he was employed at the job centre, you could well have thought he had some genuinely attractive qualities. He wasn't afraid to criticise anyone, he was well-informed, quick to champion the underdog and socially liberal in his views and lifestyle. I guess those are all qualities that add up to a certain charm.'

'There you go,' he replied with another easy laugh. 'You're finding out these monsters are more complicated than you thought.'

I was struck by the phrase. 'Do you mean "monster" literally or figuratively?'

'Both. Nilsen did monstrous things, that makes him a monster. And "monster", by definition, is someone who does something evil and frightening. I think he fits the bill on both counts.'

Ressler's explanation had extra heft, because the thinking was clearly behind why he'd titled his first book *Whoever Fights Monsters*, an allusion to Friedrich Nietzsche's advice, 'Whoever fights monsters should see to it that in the process he does not become a monster'.

I looked over Nilsen's letters and wondered if there was enough in them to make compelling documentary content, if, when I asked the Home Office and ACPO for access to film him, they denied it.

Nilsen had written a little about almost everything – his family, films, music, photography, social injustices, his conscience, a few of his victims, a lot of his fantasies, some of the murders, some of the rituals, his life in prison, the police handling of the case, a couple of the clinicians who'd examined him, general relationships with other prisoners, his essays, his autobiography, his music, his art.

There was a lot.

But it was all mute.

Mute and faceless.

Even patched together and analysed by profilers and psychologists, the thousands of words he'd written lacked the power of seeing a single minute of him on-screen talking about just one of those things.

I was beginning to worry that Don Dovaston had been right when he'd said there'd be no way a TV reporter/journalist/presenter would be granted access to interview any of Britain's most notorious criminals. It stank of celebrity. Glorification of gore. A lack of sensitivity.

But now, after having been given exclusive access to film the police development of offender profiling in the UK, I sensed there was at least an outside chance that we might secure that interview if it was done, not by me or another journalist, but by a respected profiler or psychologist as part of a police plan to better educate murder squad detectives.

My only problem was no such plan existed.

During a meeting with John Stevens, Chairman of the ACPO Sub-Committee on Offender Profiling, he told me he hoped the review they were carrying out with the Home Office would give them a sense of what needed to be done. 'What we are trying to do now is to compile the statistical base that we've got through CATCHEM, the expertise we hope to get from detectives before they leave the police service and while they are in it. And just as importantly, what we need to do is also use the information and expertise that psychiatrists and psychologists have got. Now, where the problem has arisen, and why it has been such a difficult process, is that we are trying to combine that into one system. Once we've done that, we've got the beginning of something that looks very promising indeed.'

Those four factors suggested ACPO was considering a hybrid of the FBI's Quantico model. Instead of the VICAP database there would be the UK's CATCHEM programme and the Police National Computer, plus HOLMES – the Home Office Large Major Enquiry System. Instead of centralised FBI-agent expertise, there would be decentralised murder-squad expertise provided by British regional police forces. In place of a central core of trained FBI profilers (backed by specialist forensic psychologists and psychiatrists) there would be a decentralised UK version, made up of offender profilers from regional forces working alongside trusted regional forensic clinicians from universities and hospitals.

The missing ingredient was the FBI's famed interview programme and the data they gleaned from the serial offenders.

Britain had no equivalent.

Surely interviewing UK killers such as Nilsen, Sutcliffe, Brady or Hindley would yield similar fruits of knowledge?

John Stevens said he was open-minded about such a proposal. His more immediate concern, however, was satisfying the Home Office that profiling was of sufficient value that they would invest millions more in developing it, monitoring it and rolling it out across the UK in a much more structured way.

I took this as another small breakthrough. By my reckoning, I now had the full cooperation of Nilsen, no risk of a veto from Brian Masters, and at least an open mind from the man who held most sway in the world of profiling.

I still needed a credible interviewer. Not me. Not another journalist. Not even a US profiler like Bob Ressler. Someone the Home Office and ACPO would wholeheartedly approve.

During one of the Offender Profiling committee meetings, I mentally evaluated the clinicians gathered around the conference-room table. They had all worked with the police and provided full or partial profiles that had led to the capture of offenders.

One of them was Mike Berry, a very media savvy forensic psychologist from the north west of England. I instantly liked

Mike. Dark haired with an easy smile, he looked great on camera and, best of all, he didn't talk bullshit. He spoke confidently and without jargon and knew exactly how to chat to a TV audience. He was well suited to interview Nilsen.

Sat close to Mike was another contender, Professor David Canter from Surrey University. He'd worked closely with police on a linked series of more than twenty rapes and three murders, offences that began in 1982 and ended in 1986 with the arrest of John Francis Duffy.

Below are the main bullet points of the profile Canter produced for that investigation, and in brackets how accurate it proved to be.

- Aged 20–30 (Duffy was 28 when arrested)
- Lives in Kilburn or Cricklewood area of London (lived in Kilburn)
- Married but no children (separated)
- Loner with few friends (only two close male friends)
- Physically small (5 foot 5 inches tall)
- Interested in martial arts/bodybuilding (martial arts club member)
- Feels need to dominate women (had previously attacked his wife)
- Uses sex magazines and videos (police found hardcore bondage/porn collection)
- Keeps souvenirs of his crimes (Duffy possessed thirty-three door keys – one from each victim)
- Has semi-skilled job as plumber, carpenter or similar (was a carpenter with British Rail)

I'd been so impressed by the accuracy of the profile that I also engaged David Canter to work on the documentary as a consultant along with Bob Ressler. Unfortunately, at the time,

David had not yet been experienced enough on camera for me to consider him as a potential interviewer of Nilsen. I'd also been warned that there was some tension between him and Paul Britton.

Paul was exceptionally well thought of within both ACPO and the Home Office, and probably had the most legitimate claim to be considered as the founding father of modern day psychological profiling in the UK.

In July 1983,* the body of thirty-three-year-old Caroline Osborne had been found in a field in Leicestershire. Her hands and feet had been tightly bound and she had been stabbed multiple times in the neck and chest. However, there were no signs of robbery, sexual assault or the murder weapon.

What was found, though, was a Satanic sign. A piece of paper had been left near the body and on it a drawing of a pentagram contained within a circle.

The force conducted a huge manhunt that saw more than fifteen thousand people interviewed and more than fifty men arrested for questioning but released without charge.

The head of CID, David Baker, was a man I knew very well. He didn't have a lot of time for the media but was highly regarded as a police officer and has to be recognised as one of the most forward-thinking detectives of his era.† After months

---

* Unfortunately for Leicestershire Police, this was the same month that the body of Scottish five-year-old Caroline Hogg was discovered on a grass verge near Twycross Zoo, so they became heavily involved in the hunt for serial killer Robert Black as well as that of Caroline Osborne, which itself developed into a double homicide.

† As well as being the first head of CID to be bold enough to bring a clinical psychologist into a murder enquiry, David Baker was also the first to use genetic fingerprinting in a murder case. The technique had been invented at the nearby university by Alec Jeffreys, and Baker brought him in to help on the rape-murders of Lynda Mann and Dawn Ashworth. It led to mass blood testing of thousands of local men and the eventual arrest of bakery worker Colin Pitchfork.

of making little progress on the Osborne case, Baker remained convinced of two things. Firstly, whoever killed the beautician would kill again. Secondly, he needed a new way of thinking to make a breakthrough. He turned to Paul Britton, who was working locally as a clinical psychologist.

Britton, who'd never before even looked at a crime scene photograph, let alone helped in a murder investigation, listened to an extensive briefing, asked a number of critical questions, and then shared his thoughts with Baker. 'I felt at that stage that we were looking for a young male, probably somewhat isolated, that there was likely to be some sexual, or religious or belief disfunction, something unusual about the person in the respect that he might well have unusual hobbies or pastimes. I think we felt then that he was likely to have some sort of contact through work or pastimes that gave him access to sharp knives.'

Britton took away a stack of information on the murder and in his very precise, academic and clinical way, studied it, studied it and studied it.

In addition to the rough profile he'd already given David Baker, he was able to comment that he felt the killer was a stranger to the victim, was strong and athletic and probably still lived with his parents. Perhaps most importantly, though, he cautioned the police about reading too much into the pentagram, because aside from the drawing itself, he saw no ritualistic behaviour to suggest any serious Satanic involvement.

The profile didn't lead to an immediate arrest. Just over a year later, the killer struck again. In April 1985, the body of twenty-one-year-old nurse Amanda Weedon was found under a hedge near a local hospital, and not far from a halfway house that served as a rehabilitation home for psychiatric patients set to be returned full-time to the local community. She'd been stabbed more than thirty times, in almost an identical fashion to Caroline Osborne.

Solid police work put together a picture of Amanda's last moments – where she had been, at what time, and who might have seen her walking home that fateful day. One witness mentioned seeing an exceptionally large shadowy figure on the footpath where the young woman was killed.

The description given matched that of a local nineteen-year-old called Paul Bostock, a meat-factory worker, who stood 6 feet 5 inches tall. To David Baker's horror, he'd been interviewed (and provided alibis) several times after the first murder, but before Paul Britton had delivered his profile. When Bostock was arrested and his house searched, they found drawings of black magic symbols and women in bondage and torture scenarios. In all crucial respects, he'd been a perfect fit to Britton's profile.

Given Paul's background in assisting the police, his day job treating people with severe mental and sexual problems, plus his role in reviewing offender profiling, he was my first choice as the person to interview Dennis Nilsen.

Paul consulted privately with both ACPO and the Home Office before agreeing. I took his eventual consent as the first flickering green light for the interview to go ahead.

However, over the coming weeks, it turned out the tacit approval came with clear conditions. The main ones being that he didn't want either himself or Nilsen to be distracted by a crowd of television technicians and equipment; he demanded that *he* be the only person asking Nilsen questions, as interviewees needed a singular focus when replying; and for police purposes, he needed to be the sole pilot through Nilsen's life and crimes.

This wasn't a problem for me. I'd accepted very early on that permission would never be granted for me to interview Nilsen, much as I'd liked to have done that. Filming the first ever face-to-face between a British profiler and a British serial killer was the piece of history I craved. It would be the most valuable part of the documentary and vastly outweighed the ego boost of me playing interviewer.

There were other conditions, too. This time laid down by ACPO. A police video crew would have to be present as well, and they would take charge of the editing and processing of their tapes according to the needs of police training.

I pointed out that this was a departure from what I had led Nilsen to believe* and I felt the presence of a police crew, completely distinct from a TV crew, would be likely to either get Nilsen to withdraw his cooperation, or behave in a different manner than if there was just one crew. I promised full access to duplicate copies of the tapes that my crew would shoot. It made no difference. I was told that there was no room for negotiation here. A police crew would have to be present, but they would dress as civilians so there would be no need to tell Nilsen they weren't part of the Central TV crew.

It would be a deal breaker.

I agreed. But did so with seriously mixed feelings. Not merely because I was probably going to have to lie to Nilsen about the crew, but because it now meant an enormous amount of people would have to be in the room. Both Bob Ressler and Roy Hazelwood had warned me against this, and Paul Britton's fear of distractions by a large crew played heavily on my mind as well.

---

* I'd told Nilsen the interview would be used for the documentary *and* police training – there'd been no mention of a police crew being present.

Usually, a documentary crew for a shoot like this would be at least eight people – camera operator, camera assistant, sound recordist, lighting electrician, grip, production assistant, researcher and director.

Ideally, I'd have liked at least two camera operators (one to cover the interviewer and one the interviewee) and two sound recordists, that would have pushed it to ten people. Plus at least two from the police side (a camera operator and sound recordist, who would share our lights). So, that meant twelve. Plus Paul and myself. Fourteen.

It was too many.

Paul Britton was horrified by the thought of so large a crowd hanging over his shoulder as he tried to create a relaxed enough relationship for Nilsen to speak openly about any and all aspects of his private life, sexuality, murders and necrophilia. Bob Ressler almost laughed me off the phone when I relayed to him what the suggestions were. Bob was of the opinion that the best scenario was just Paul and Nilsen together, and a camera rolling with no one else in the room. But that was never going to happen. Firstly, Paul didn't have the expertise to operate the equipment, secondly, it would be hugely distracting for him to monitor lighting levels, camera exposure and focus, plus sound levels. And thirdly, there was no way Nilsen would agree to the interview if I wasn't in the room with him.

The only solution would be working with a greatly slimmed-down crew.

But that was much harder than it sounded.

Back in 1992, there were strict union rules that governed the minimum number of people that could work on news, documentaries and dramas. It was set in stone. Stone that could result in a strike if you broke it.

According to the rulebook, the minimum I could take to Albany would be six – camera operator, sound recordist, electrician, grip, director and myself (as producer). I would probably still have to pay day rates for others, such as a production assistant, even though they wouldn't attend.

It was still too many.

I discussed the dilemma with Steve, who, as always, cut straight to the point. 'Why don't you do what you did on the *Murder* documentary?' He gave me a knowing look. *It's better to apologise than ask permission.*

While producing the fly-on-the-wall documentary *Murder*, I had personally shot film and recorded sound because we hadn't had the time to physically get film crews to the crime scene or to the homes of some of the men being arrested for murder. It had been a case of either I did it or we didn't get the footage. The unions had very reluctantly accepted the argument and allowed the documentary to be broadcast.

Having mentally crossed the staffing hurdle, I talked to Paul and John Stevens, explaining that I would be the only person attending the filming from Central TV, but would bring professional equipment and would help the police camera team with theirs to ensure they also got good footage.

We had a deal. The green light glowed brightly. Everyone was relieved.

All that remained was for the Home Office to make the practical arrangements for our visit to the prison and then confirm the dates.

It was now a waiting game. The Home Office was notorious for moving at a glacial pace, so I informed both Brian Masters and Dennis Nilsen that the necessary separate permissions had been secured with the police and Home Office, but as yet we had no fixed dates for the recording.

In his role as programme consultant, Ressler reminded me that I was now not only going to have to accept that Nilsen would come to the interview table with his own agenda, but Paul Britton would as well. 'Sometimes clinicians get fascinated with aspects of an offender's behaviour that are of no real interest to anyone other than another clinician,' he warned, adding that it would be a good idea to send Nilsen a letter detailing areas that would be of most interest to the TV audience. 'If you do that, you're sure to get some of the things you want, even if you're not personally asking the questions.'

There was nothing unusual about sending an interviewee the kind of outline briefing that Bob suggested. It was a standard courtesy in documentary making. And a very useful one. It often identified personal areas that an interviewee wouldn't answer questions on, or, on the contrary, would give you the strongest replies.

Nilsen was no exception.

He replied promptly and politely, making it clear that *'Nothing is out of bounds. There is no part of my life, my mind, my memories or fantasies that I seek to censor or shield from scrutiny. I ask only that you listen and understand and that if you edit, then you do so with style and integrity, not with ham-fisted butchery that bludgeons my facts into meaningless sentences.'*

What followed was a very thick dossier of Nilsen's own thoughts about himself, covering in explicit detail all the areas of interest I had outlined in my correspondence. As he drew to a close, he wrote, *'I have long been aware of the popular and academic interest in me and to that end have been working on my autobiography, after all, who better to shine a light into this very, very dark darkness? I am hoping that our upcoming*

*encounter will warrant inclusion in those pages as one of my
better experiences with strangers.'*

I rang Bob Ressler and told him about the book and the
excerpts he had sent.

'Now you know his agenda,' the profiler told me, deadpan.
'He sees TV as good publicity for his book.'

11

THE INTERVIEW – PART II

Tuesday 8th September 1992 seemed to be an unremarkable day as I showered and dressed in my hotel.

But I knew it wouldn't be.

The TV news said it was twelve degrees Celcius and sunny on the Isle of Wight.

Downstairs, in the crammed breakfast room, families ferried food from a white-clothed buffet bar groaning with cereals, croissants and stainless steel trays of scrambled eggs, crispy bacon and grilled tomatoes.

The air zinged with holiday talk – where to go, what to do, when to eat.

This was not what I wanted to hear.

I had barely slept and had slumped out of bed physically tired and mentally exhausted. I needed peace and quiet, not giggling, happy kids and overloud parents.

I should have stayed in my room and had something sent in.

My mind was crammed with details of Nilsen's crimes and the chronology of his life. That morning I could have breezed through an MA in Nilsenology.

Off the top of my head, I could list the names, ages and deaths of all his identified victims, the methods used to kill them, the addresses he'd occupied at the time of their deaths, how long their bodies had been retained, how and when he'd disposed of their remains, and even which victims' body parts had been recovered by police when he was arrested (plus, of course, the distressing details of which victims' remains had most likely blocked the drains and led to his arrest).

I'd followed the advice of Bob Ressler and created separate background files on the following categories: Childhood Incidents, Puberty, Adolescence, Sexuality, Relationships, Occupations, Victimology, Offending, Necrophilia, Present-Day Fantasies – and Contradictions.

'Contradictions and omissions are among the most important things you can identify,' he had told me. 'They can indicate when someone has lied to you – in which case, they are most probably trying to conceal something that's of great psychological or evidentiary importance. A contradiction or omission can show you the exact moment in time, the exact geographical place and circumstance, in which an offender's behaviour changed. It could be the moment they turned their fantasy into a criminal reality. The moment a sexual fantasist became a rapist, or a rapist became a killer, or a killer became a necrophile. Contradictions and omissions can indicate shame and guilt, or just as easily a lack of shame or guilt. Before you decide on any of those things, you've got to spot them, and that means knowing their history better than they do. It means staying 100 per cent alert 100 per cent of the time they are speaking to you or writing to you.'

In a bid to feel normal, I'd left all my Nilsen files upstairs in a locked briefcase in my room and had chosen instead to read the daily newspapers over coffee and toast. I didn't have the stomach for anything more than normal.

In one of the papers, I noticed a 'This Day in History' column. It disclosed that back in 1974, on this very date, Gerald Ford had pardoned Richard Nixon for his Watergate crimes, and in London on 8th September 1888, the mutilated body of Jack the Ripper's second victim, Annie Chapman, had been found in Hanbury Street in the Spitalfields area. The serial killer had just been warming up. He would go on to claim at least another three lives.

Like all crime journalists, I had a reasonable knowledge of the Ripper case, including the fact that the police surgeon Thomas Bond had given officers, at their request, what many people now believe to be one of the earliest psychological profiles.

He'd told them that he thought they were looking for a man of solitary habits who suffered from periodical attacks of homicidal and erotic mania, with the character of the mutilations possibly indicating satyriasis, a condition of hypersexuality where a person's libido is suddenly or frequently raised above what is generally regarded as normal.

Bond said, in a letter to one of the chief investigators, '*All five murders no doubt were committed by the same hand. In the first four, the throats appear to have been cut from left to right, in the last case owing to the extensive mutilation it is impossible to say in what direction the fatal cut was made, but arterial blood was found on the wall in splashes close to where the woman's head must have been lying . . . all the circumstances surrounding the murders lead me to form the opinion that the women must have been lying down when murdered and in every case the throat was first cut.*' He went on to discount theories that the killer might have been a doctor or vet, saying the mutilation and disembowelment showed no real medical expertise or knowledge.

There are several reasons Bond isn't hailed more vocally as a latter-day profiler. Firstly, the Ripper has never been caught, therefore his 'profile' hasn't been substantiated.

Secondly, most of his observations, especially those about the nature of the wounds, type of weapon used, and which hand the perpetrator may have used to hold the weapon, are thought to be standard contributions for a police surgeon or pathologist to make. Though to be fair to Bond, he did bravely step out of his remit and add, 'The homicidal impulse may have developed from a revengeful or brooding condition of the mind.'

Is that what had happened in Dennis Nilsen's case?

Had a homicidal impulse developed from a revengeful or brooding condition of the mind?

He was certainly a brooder, his letters testified to that.

More than a century after Bond's profile, on the anniversary of the death of Jack the Ripper's second victim, I left the breakfast table to interview London's second most notorious serial killer, Dennis Andrew Nilsen. A man who had killed his final victim just over six miles from where Annie Chapman had been slain.

I made the most of the fresh air and cool breeze as I stood outside Albany Prison and waited for Paul Britton. Like myself, he was a not a great sleeper, and when he turned up he looked as though he'd spent as restless a night as I had.

After a short time, we were joined by Superintendent Wilf Laidler and Chief Inspector Dennis Cleugh from Northumbria Police. This was the police video crew. Both men quickly confessed to 'not really being experts' in this field and I told them not to worry, I'd make sure all the equipment worked properly and they got a good recording.

Wilf Laidler was about as far removed from TV as one could be. He was actually the staff officer of Chief Constable John Stevens, and it was apparent that he had been sent along to make sure everything went as planned and that there were no nasty surprises to report to his boss.

Dennis Cleugh was a different kettle of fish. You knew from just speaking to the avuncular Geordie that he was one of those wonderfully practical men who could turn their hand to anything, from fixing a broken washing machine to building a greenhouse. Putting a camera on a tripod and pressing a start button was well within his capabilities.

As we lugged our equipment into reception, I took a final breath of prison-free air and couldn't help but smile at the way they marched in, dressed in matching blue jeans and Pringle T-shirts.

'I like your gear,' I said, still fighting my smile.

'Thank you very much. Now, do you want this interview to happen or not, man?' quipped Cleugh, with an even bigger grin.

There followed an arduous, arm-lengthening haul of lights, cameras, tripods and other equipment through numerous internal perimeter fences and at least nine (I lost count) locked iron gates.

The ideal location for an interview is a quiet, cosy room that has comfortable chairs and thick curtains and carpets that soak up sound and kill echoes. Think of your lounge, with a sofa and chair, curtains dressing the windows, maybe a tall green pot plant or two. That would be perfect. Put your interviewee in that kind of environment and they'll relax, and you'll have a chance of getting the best out of them.

I had been fearing that our destination today, despite my request for something depicting the above, would once again turn out to be the closet of an old office that we'd shoehorned into the previous day for our initial meeting with Nilsen.

It wasn't.

Instead, we were led through to the back of the prison training unit, and into a large, virtually empty room. It seemed like an abandoned hall. Beneath a ceiling flaking plaster were barely whitewashed, breeze-block walls and a patchy, faded cord carpet that may perhaps have been brown back in the distant century when it had been first purchased. Thick heating pipes grumbled, groaned and hissed as they snaked like boa constrictors around old, tall skirting boards and finally sank their plumbing fangs into the bellies of huge hippo-sized radiators that made the place as hot as a sauna.

My heart sank.

Once we rigged lights in here and they added their not inconsiderable kilowatts of heat, then there was a serious danger Nilsen would burst into flames like a vampire doused in holy water.

This, we were told, was a prison-officer conference room and the only available free space.

I found such a declaration hard to believe. It had the acoustics of a subway tunnel and the charm of a soccer stadium toilet block. My guess was that once more, some careful thought had been put into finding the most uncomfortable and unsuitable place for us.

Having complained that yesterday's room was too small, it followed that today's would be too big.

Aside from acoustics, light is always a problem for TV crews. Even outside, in full sun, you have to contend with sharp shadows and squinting interviewees, so you end up bouncing light from giant reflectors and creating 'flags' – giant panels of fabric to blot, soften and direct it. Filming inside was often better, in the sense that the only real way of getting good lighting is to turn off all the lights, blackout any windows to stop any inward bleed of daylight and then build your own perfect lighting set.

This was what we had to do in Albany.

And it was a major job.

Paul Britton watched patiently as I clapped my hands in every square metre of the room until I found the least acoustically objectionable spot. We then hauled in a wobbly, dirty table and two matching chairs, before gradually adding lights, tripods and cameras.

Dennis Cleugh and I did some final technical checks and declared we were ready.

I asked Paul if he was comfortable with the setting and he politely said, 'It's fine.' It plainly wasn't anything like the relaxed surroundings he normally interviewed people in, but I was grateful for his understanding. A professional TV host would have had a prima-donna tantrum by now, but Paul just stayed calm and focused.

I'd been told to go into the adjoining room when we were ready, and Dennis Nilsen would be brought to us 'in due time'. As I walked in, I was surprised to see that he was already there.

He was dressed in prison-issue white T-shirt, faded blue and white overshirt with sleeves rolled up to his biceps, jeans and trainers. He was also wearing a very angry expression. 'I've been waiting here for twenty minutes,' he said as indignantly as a CEO might to an Uber driver who'd left him shivering on a street corner in a snowstorm. 'Is this the way we're going to do things today?'

All the words of wisdom from Terry Green, Bob Ressler and Roy Hazelwood came back to me. Nilsen was setting the agenda. Showing me who was in charge. The use of 'we' was a manipulative attempt to subjugate me. Now he was expecting an apology for us being about twenty minutes behind schedule. He was clean-shaven, and his mop of hair had been freshly combed for the big day. Clearly, he'd been looking forward to this, at least as much as I had, meaning I could seize control of the agenda without any fear of him refusing to cooperate.

'Listen –' I said confrontationally – ' we've had to overcome a lot of technical problems this morning, with no help from anyone in the prison – in fact, we've been put in a room that was almost entirely unsuitable – but we've made it okay. More than okay. Now, given that you've told me in your letters that you used to be a keen photographer and shot a lot of films yourself, I'd appreciate some understanding of our situation, and why we're running a little late. Now, let's go in.'

I didn't wait for a reply, I just turned and led the way into the room, trusting that he'd follow.

Fortunately, he did.

As we approached the three other men, I peeled back a little and readied myself to make the introductions. Paul Britton was already at the table, my 'crew' were loitering further back near the cameras and lights.

'Paul you already know,' I gestured to the clinical psychologist.

'Good morning,' he replied, with notably less warmth than yesterday.

I turned to the police officers and said, 'And this is Wilf, and Dennis.'

Both managed 'hello' and 'morning' but neither moved forward. There'd been either a conscious or subconscious agreement that they were not going to shake his hand. Everyone it seemed, had their own agenda.

Nilsen sat without being asked.

What I witnessed next, is something I've only seen a few times in my career.

He settled in the glow of lights, cosied down like he'd eased into a deckchair on the first day of a long-awaited holiday.

Nilsen relaxed.

Soaked up the experience.

I handed over our payment – a couple of packets of Marlboro Lights – and his eyes danced from one camera to the other, from one light to the other, and finally from one person to another. I could hear Ressler's voice in my head. *He sees TV as good publicity for his book.*

Well, if that were true, he was going to have to earn it. I'd learned enough about Paul Britton to know that he truly was a 'forensic' psychologist, and that meant he was going to turn over every stone of Nilsen's life, then microscopically examine every grub and worm that came crawling out.

Everyone was eager to get going, but first I needed to fit a personal microphone on our interviewee.

'You're right about the room,' Nilsen said to me, noticing he wasn't having any luck in engaging Paul in small talk. 'It's awful in here.'

I wasn't looking at his face as I answered, 'It'll be okay.' My eyes were fixed on his plain white T-shirt, because circumstances now dictated that I needed to put my hands beneath it in order to conceal and fasten down the long, black microphone wire that connected into a battery pack. If I didn't, then the cable would show up on camera and would move about and cause microphone noise.

This could be very awkward, I admitted to myself.

I needed to put myself into Des's very personal space and put my arms around him. It's a routinely intimate and awkward act that most sound recordists make a joke of when they do it; often saying something like, 'Forgive me, I'm going to have to partially undress you now . . . ', but my stupid imagination had magnified the level of discomfort at least a hundredfold.

Nilsen had embraced those he'd killed.

He'd embraced their dead bodies.

He'd embraced the corpses and had sex with them.

Now, I needed to embrace him.

'Des, I have to fit you with this microphone. Would you mind standing up for me?'

Army Nilsen, Policeman Nilsen, shot obediently to his feet.

Instead of fitting it to the front of his T-shirt, I clipped the bulbous black top of the microphone to the open edge of his blue shirt and told him, 'I need this cable to go under your outer shirt. It has to pass around your body, maybe tuck it into the top of your jeans, and then this slim electronic battery pack has to fit into your back pocket.'

I was holding it up and hoping he'd do it himself.

'Go ahead,' he said.

I think I hesitated a beat too long. Or else I let out a disappointed sigh, because I saw in his eyes a recognition that I was uncertain about what to do.

He knows I don't want to do this.

Still holding my gaze, Nilsen lifted his arms to shoulder height and stood disturbingly straight legged, heels together, as though he'd been nailed to a cross.

Be professional. Just do it, I told myself.

I tore pieces of sticky black gaffer tape from a roll, checked the microphone clipped to the outside left edge of his blue shirt and then looped it round to the inside and taped it to the reverse. I put my hand on the outside of the shirt and rubbed the tape to make sure it had stuck properly and wouldn't peel off due to the heat of the lights.

I became aware that the room had gone silent.

This just magnified my discomfort.

Now, perversely, I was feeling bad about how I was feeling. I didn't want Nilsen to be offended by what he might perceive as prejudiced behaviour. I didn't want him to think I found him so reprehensible that I considered him untouchable.

'I won't be a minute,' I said as I traced the cable back to his left side and added more tape.

He stinks of cigarettes, I noted.

And of prison.

Not just the current air of this part of the Vulnerable Prisoners Unit, but of ten years of constant confinement

My arms were now stretched around him, my head almost resting on his shoulder. I was slightly bent forward and could feel the warmth of his breath on my neck as I secured the cable with more gaffer tape. I knocked him accidentally and shifted his balance as I rubbed more tape to the cloth to make sure it had adhered. He put a hand on my shoulder to steady himself.

The hand now touching me has strangled people to death.
It has held someone's head under water as they drowned.
It has held his penis as he masturbated on their corpses.

I berated myself for being distracted.

Clear your mind. Be professional. Focus.

'Can you turn, please?' I asked.

He did. I switched on the battery pack then slipped it into a saggy, back pocket of his jeans, and taped it down again.

'That's it, thanks.' I backed away, making sure I didn't catch his gaze. 'Paul, if you and Des can just chat for a moment, then that would help us to check sound levels.'

Paul Britton nodded, but it was Nilsen who took the verbal cue. 'I see everything just like a camera. Sometimes in close-up. Sometimes in wide-shot, depending how much I want to take in.' His right hand moved slowly, like he was panning to the right. 'I was a camera passing through people's lives, they were just images flickering before me or behind me, and I'd see them like that – as images – not people. I'd know they were people – if they interacted with me; if they asked me for a light, or for a cigarette or something – but they were still always images. The image was always the most important bit.'

This disturbed me. He was describing the same peculiar detachment that camera operators experience when they are so focused on filming an event, such as a death in a war zone or a trauma centre, that they don't *emotionally* experience it in real time. Like oil and water, they glide over the moment rather than become absorbed in it.

I'd felt exactly that detachment when I'd filmed the pathologist in Derby turning over the body of Mohammed Rafia, the middle-aged man who'd been stabbed to death. I'd focused on the lacerations, the blood, the victim's face, the defence wounds on his hands, and the technical processes of adjusting focus, widening and narrowing the shot, shifting the frame and capturing the sound. All those actions had in those moments insulated me from what would have been the correct emotional reaction (sadness, shock, surprise, fear) to what I was seeing.

But in Nilsen's case, what he was claiming was that he felt detachment *all* the time. That he had passed through life constantly feeling like that. Feeling removed, even when he was left with no choice but to interact with people in the moment. Worse still, he was so emotionally separated from people, he saw them only as images.

Disturbingly, however, this also resonated with me.

As an orphan, I'd felt I was just passing through certain people's lives. Social workers, teachers, foster parents, other children in homes I'd stayed or visited, they were more images on walls than meaningful relationships. There's a good reason why when we've been arguing with someone we love that we turn away and say 'Oh, for God's sake, just leave me alone!' During times of pressure, we detach.

Isolation, we sense, is necessary to 'gather our thoughts', or, to be more prosaic, 'get our shit together'. It gives us an internal refuge from external pressure. But when it's extended, when it's a daily retreat from reality, then it becomes emotionally corrosive.

I watched Nilsen settling into position as Dennis Cleugh and I tweaked the lights, checked the sound and camera equipment. He was no longer sitting. He was posing. He'd opened his overshirt and slouched back, conveying an image of being entirely relaxed.

Around his neck was some sort of handmade lanyard, fashioned from twisted soft cloth. I presumed it could be easily snapped, or else it surely presented a threat of strangulation, at least for himself, if no one else. Within touching distance of his left hand was a pouch of rolling tobacco. A fallback, in case visitors didn't bring free cigarettes. In front of him lay a large, shallow ashtray that he would very quickly fill with scrubbed-out butts of chain-smoked cigarettes. His right hand toyed with his makeshift lighter.

These were his props.

This image of the very self-assured, laid-back Nilsen has now been seen millions of times on the internet, and his style of dress and the relaxed, monotone manner of his delivery of answers became, I am sure, the template for David Tennant's chillingly realistic portrayal of him in the ITV three-part drama *Des* shown in the UK.

Paul Britton struck an entirely different figure in his smart, dark business suit and neat notes. Directly across the table from Nilsen, he had positioned himself in a fully attentive posture, leaning slightly forward, but not so much so that it gave a hint of aggression or threat. All it conveyed was interest, a keenness to listen and learn. It was designed to make the interviewee feel at ease and comfortable enough to speak. Unnecessarily generous in Nilsen's case – the problem wouldn't be getting him to talk, it would be shutting him up.

Paul had the kind of honey-coated voice that could comfortably narrate a bestselling meditation app. He spoke at a gentle pace and in a tone warmer than an Eskimo's coat. Once I'd checked the framing of the shots, set my own personal tape recorder rolling and given the technical all-clear to start the interview, Paul explained that he wanted Nilsen to begin by telling us his personal history, his earliest memories.

And off our interviewee went. No tentative steps into the chilly waters of his childhood, just straight into the heart-stopping, icy deep end of his formative years.

'One of my earliest childhood memories is as a toddler at my grandparents' home in Academy Road in Fraserburgh. I would be down the road and off down the street. I would scramble under the gate, get caught and be brought back, then I'd scramble under the gate again at any opportunity. I'd always be toddling off down the road, looking for something.'

It's highly unusual, but not impossible, for adults to have memories of themselves younger than three years old, but Nilsen seemed to have strong recollections of not only feeling alone but wanting to be on his own. 'I didn't want to feel loneliness, I don't think any child would want that, but I wanted freedom and that meant getting out. I was a free spirit that needed not to be held in one place.'

As he spoke, I recalled him writing in a letter to me, '*I find prison both restraining and liberating. Most days my mind moves more easily beyond these walls than it did beyond those of everyday existence prior to my arrest, that was a time when the shackles around my spirit were unbearably tight.'*

Nilsen had moved on. Now he was talking about his mother, one finger jabbing his chest. 'I was the least person and last thing she was interested in. I can't say we had a loving, mother–son bond, or anything like that. I don't remember a lot of affection or comfort from her.'

For a second, his eyes left Paul Britton's and strayed to the table. I wondered if he was feeling some discomfort at the questioning. Then he touched the cigarettes and thought better of lighting one. It wouldn't look good on camera and I'm sure he realised that.

'In 1983 when I was arrested,' he continued, 'journalists started digging around in Scotland and found my father had divorced my mother on grounds of adultery, and I can believe that. I used to look at my brother Olav and think he looked nothing like me. I remember my mother had this picture taken of her and Olav. It must have cost her a lot of money – it was a proper studio portrait. There she was, with her hair nicely done, and this blonde baby, sitting proudly on her lap, and she was smiling away. When I came along, there was no such picture of me. The only photograph ever taken of me was a snapshot, by an aunty with a Brownie box camera.'

In stark contrast to his meandering writings, Nilsen was sharp and straight to the point. He was also a TV natural; completely at ease in front of camera, with no hint of self-consciousness or nerves – unlike many of the police officers and psychologists I'd interviewed.

'Developmentally, my mother did nothing for my confidence,' he continued, 'no one really did. I was surrounded by a crowd of emotional vandals who hacked away at my emerging self, driving parts of my personality back into a witheringly cold darkness that stunted growth and propagated shame, guilt and self-loathing.'

Casually, Paul Britton asked him the most pointed of questions, 'Did you love your mother?'

Unhesitatingly, the reply came back in an equally casual manner. 'No, I didn't love my mother.' He took a slight beat, then added, 'I was always trying to please her, but as a kid there wasn't much you could do. Clean the place up, wash the pots, get a pat on the head. I wanted to be close to her, but she was always too busy. I remember her as a dominating presence. She was left with three children and had to work part-time as a cleaner. She was strong-willed, a very stubborn woman. I think I have a lot of her characteristics. We're very similar in ways.'

For a second he seemed to reflect on their times together. There was no nostalgic look in his eyes. Just a rare moment in which he wasn't speaking quickly and dominating the conversation, then he continued, 'I wanted my mother to approve of me. I wanted her to praise me, to notice me, but at times it was as if I wasn't there.'

I suspect every mother of a young child will understand the full meaning of his comment. Young boys (especially under seven), constantly demand, 'Mum, watch me do this.' 'Mum, watch how high I can swing.' 'Mum, look how fast I can run.' The list of actions they want maternal approval for is almost endless. They *need* to be regularly reassured that they are brilliant, wonderful little warriors. They crave their mother's love. And that attachment lasts until *they* feel strong enough to shake it off themselves and instead begin seeking fatherly approval as they step towards puberty and beyond.

In total contrast to the psychologist's softly spoken questions came Nilsen's brutal answers. 'If someone walked in here,' he told us, 'and said to me, "Des, your mother's dead in Scotland," I wouldn't cry. I wouldn't shed a tear.'

More shocking than what Nilsen said was the way he said it. Cold. Calm. No trace of anger. No emotion. Just a bland statement. Delivered in the same tone in which you might mundanely comment, 'I think we'll need to get some more milk before tomorrow, there's only a little left.'

'I find it hard to cry,' Nilsen told us. 'I find it *very* difficult to cry.'

There was no flicker of reaction or judgment upon Paul Britton's face. Just clinical interest. But I could see from their eyes that Wilf Laidler and Dennis Cleugh, both family men who I am sure thought the world of their mothers, shared my shock.

I remembered Bob Ressler's advice to keep notes about contradictions and this area was surely one. Within minutes, Nilsen had gone from sympathising with his mother's lot in life, saying how much he was like her, detailing how he had craved her attention, to saying how he wouldn't shed a tear if he was told she was dead. Even to my psychiatrically untrained mind, it seemed obvious that he'd been a troubled child, very probably far more troubled than his stressed and overworked mother, Betty, could ever have detected and dealt with, had she had either the time or inclination.

Paul Britton moved the conversation on.

What about his grandparents – Lily and Andrew? Nilsen had grown up under their watchful eyes. Hadn't they supplied a safety net of additional emotional support? After all, aren't grandparents the world over notorious for spoiling their grand-children with companionship, gifts and affection?

'There was no love or tenderness with Grandmother,' he

told us. 'It wasn't that kind of relationship at all. She was very strict, very religious, not the warm and gentle granny figure.'

Both Paul and I had done enough research to know that Nilsen was telling the truth. Lily Whyte had tried her best to live up to her name of having a pure, *lily white* character. She'd believed her grandchildren should grow up in the same way. Attend church every Sunday. Avoid the corrupting influence of modern music. Don't smoke, drink or swear. Instead of being the archetypal, soft-touch, overindulgent grandma, Lily had striven to be an even more domineering matriarch than Nilsen's own mother.

'Let's move on to your relationship with your grandfather,' Paul said. 'What memories do you have of him?'

'We spent a lot of time together. We'd go for long walks. He'd spend time with me.'

The answers were surprisingly short. More clipped. Less expansive than we'd expected them to be. In a pre-interview letter to me, Nilsen mentioned Andrew Whyte *'telling fascinatingly terrible stories about the mysteries and savagery of the sea'*. He'd almost nostalgically talked about the *'pure pleasantries of perambulations in the park, along the beach or the local golf course, punctuated with treats of an ice cream or drink'*.

Now though, it seemed like he didn't want to discuss him at all.

'I remember falling asleep in his arms at the end of a long walk along the beach or on the golf course,' he added, realising more comment had been expected of him. 'He noticed me and gave me the attention I wanted.'

Paul asked him to try to sum up what feelings he had for his grandfather at that time.

'I wouldn't quantify it as love. I wouldn't say Grandfather gave me love, more attention.'

This was our first hint that either the relationship hadn't been as strong as we'd previously understood it to be, or possibly that Nilsen was beginning to revise his views on the relationship and the influence it had on his life.

Paul gently moved the conversation to the day Nilsen had been told of his grandad's sad demise.

'I wasn't really *told*,' he insisted. 'I was asked if I wanted to see Grandad and taken into this room where he was laid out in a coffin, and I thought, "What's he doing in there?" You know, I thought it was some crazy kind of stunt or something. Everyone seemed sad but it just didn't make sense to me.'

Again, the usually expansive Scot had no more to say. He interlocked his fingers defensively. For the first time since taking his seat, he looked vulnerable. Even slightly confused.

In his letters, Nilsen had said that not only had he not understood what viewing his grandfather in the coffin had meant to him, but he'd struggled for perspective long after the death. Now he continued. 'I asked my mother, "Where's Grandad? Why doesn't he come for me any more?" and I was told, "You won't be seeing him again. Your Grandad's gone." I asked, "Where?" and my mother said, "He's gone to a better place." And I wondered where that was, and why hadn't he taken me? We went lots of places together. What had I done to make him not want to take me to the "better place"?'

Paul Britton gently asked Nilsen if, when he realised his grandfather was dead, he missed him.

His answer took us all by surprise.

'I missed the influence of somebody who took an interest in me,' he said. 'Did I weep for him? No. No. Never.'

At first, I found this an ever more shocking statement than his claim that he wouldn't shed a tear if he was told his mother had died. I even read it as somewhat undermining all the claims that his grandfather's death had been so traumatic for him. Then I realised it was necessary to take a number of other factors into account.

The entire decade following the end of World War II was unquestionably the golden age of 'boys don't cry'. No one wanted to be branded 'a cry baby'. No blubberingly, emotional raw child wanted to hear the phrase, 'Shut up, or I'll give you something worth crying about'.

Secondly, when depressed, lonely children – and some adults – are already feeling so emotionally low, enduring such strong feelings of detachment, they simply withdraw further into themselves instead of crying. The feelings of sadness that others are suddenly experiencing after a loss are feelings that they have every day. I know this from personal experience, both as an adult and child. It wasn't until my second marriage and after my third child that I didn't feel crying was a shameful weakness. Now, as a grandfather myself, barely a week goes by without something wonderfully generous and kind reducing me to tears.

Reflecting on his own grandfather's passing, Nilsen summed up, 'If anything, it perhaps demonstrated to me the power of life and death. One day my grandad had been in my life and then he was gone, and the sea had apparently done that.' For the first time, his face registered an emotion. It wasn't sadness. It was the raised eyebrows and slightly tightened lips of surprise. Like he'd just been baffled by a card trick, performed up close and personal.

Nilsen told us that after his grandfather's death he would retrace the happy walks they'd taken together but had felt markedly different. 'Sometimes, if I was on my own on the rocks and cliffs, I would think about death all the time. I would look out at this innocent stuff called water and wonder how it could kill. I would court the sea like crazy and I couldn't even swim. The thrill was seducing it, surviving it.'

He explained that he would while away 'long, lonely hours' at the cove and on the shores of Broadsea, or out at Kinnaird Head near the ancient lighthouse where he'd paddle in the crashing water, venturing out until he reached the point where he would feel unsafe, and then he'd stay there, 'courting fear' until he either got frightened or bored.

'When I was about eight years old, I waded out in the water at Inverallochy, looking back toward the golf course where I went with Granddad, and I don't know how, but I suddenly got out of my depth and couldn't get back. The pull of the waves was too strong and I went under. An older boy dragged me out of the water and probably saved my life.'

When Nilsen had told this same story to Brian Masters, he'd added that when he'd sat up on the sand, coughing water, he'd found his shorts had been removed and his rescuer had masturbated over his body.

But there was no such assertion during our interview.* It fell into Bob Ressler's categories of inconsistencies and contradictions. It hid something else.

Perhaps it had been a minor scare blown up into a melodrama as an extension of his 'flirting with death' thrill-seeking in the water. Or, more likely, as an eight-year-old, he'd just frightened himself by taking a step too far out and seen the older kid who'd pulled him back in as his hero. Let's face it, if that were the case, then it would have stood out as a rare act of male kindness in that bleak period of his life.

---

* In his autobiography, Nilsen said the account of the hero masturbating on him after saving him from drowning hadn't happened, but had been a fantasy he'd experienced at the time.

One thing was incontestable though. In Nilsen's impression-able young mind there were now the parallel dark impressions of death and water. A fusion of fascination, fact and fantasy. In his letters and essays, he occasionally referred to himself as 'The Drowning Boy', and subsequently *History of a Drowning Boy* became the title of the autobiography he penned but was unable to get published during his lifetime.

It's also an inescapable fact that Nilsen either drowned or attempted to drown several of his victims, and that, post-mortem, his sexual rituals involved bathing and washing the bodies – not just out of hygienic necessity.

The journalist inside me was now anxious for the Q&A session to move on to Nilsen's fantasies, his selection of victims, the murders and post-mortem rituals, but Paul was far from finished with the serial killer's early years. We went back to when he was seven years old and had killed a cat.

'I was playing on my own, in a disused toilet block, and I came across this kitten, a stray, I think. And I hung it up on a piece of wire to see how it died, to see how long it took to die. I hadn't planned it beforehand or fantasised about it. It just sort of occurred to me that I was going to put this wire around its head, pull it tight and hang it. I did it to see what the process of death was. I thought, "What is death? What is it?" I was afraid of death, but I thought if you could rationalise it and expose it, then it would be less frightening. If you fear the power of death then you examine the power to see what it is.'

Nilsen went on to say that when he looked at the silent, lifeless kitten dangling from the old toilet cistern he didn't feel any thrill or excitement, he only felt ashamed and disgusted with himself and never repeated it.

A *shame he hadn't felt after strangling his first victim*, I thought.

Paul Britton wanted to know about young Des's relationship with his older brother.

'I felt that Olav could always out-do me. I had this feeling that there was something odd there. I looked at the photograph of him with Betty and thought "Who is this guy? He looks nothing like me." I felt Olav was destined to succeed. When I was in the C stream [at school], he was in the A stream. He took Latin and that kind of thing, while I was still struggling with mathematics. He was tall and strong, and I was a weak, shy, introverted individual. I wouldn't say boo to a goose. Olav was nothing like that. Nothing like me.'

Sibling rivalry, of course, is as old as Cain and Abel, the sons of Adam and Eve. Most parents of multiple children have had to devise ways to get their kids to become friends as well as relatives. No such formula for fraternal friendship seems to have been found in the Fraserburgh family home of the Nilsens.

'He'd tease and ridicule me at school. He'd mock me. Call me names like "Hen" and "Sissy". He'd never stick up for me, protect me, or anything like that.'

Remembering how Kemper had been mocked by his mother, I wondered for a moment if Nilsen had been psychologically killing his brother when he murdered young men he'd been attracted to and had lured back to his London flat.

He went on to confess that when he was about ten years old, he had been so intrigued by the differences between himself and Olav, that "sometimes when he was asleep in the bed we shared, I would explore his body with my hands, being careful not to wake him. I'd look at his penis and I would stroke it, handle it, masturbate it I suppose. And I think on at least one occasion Olav was aware of what I was doing because he got an erection, but he never woke, never opened his eyes, and he never spoke about what I had done".

Paul Britton asked Nilsen if he had found the experience of 'exploring' his brother to be arousing.

A slight frown creased his forehead. 'I think I found it more interesting than exciting. Here was big, strapping Olav and I had some control of him, some power over him.'

Nilsen's nocturnal molestations were not limited to his brother. He confessed, 'I would explore my sister's sleeping body as well. I'd stroke Sylvia's private parts as she slept in her bed. I think I did it out of curiosity, just to see what a girl's naked body looked and felt like.'

Again, this recollection was a shortened version of an account he'd given me in a letter, when he'd explained that, '. . . part of the explorations of their bodies was to discover if they had a secret, whether there was something they kept hidden that made them more loveable than I was, more worthy of attention than I was.'

We were now deep in the interview and it was becoming apparent that the nature of his responses was changing. When the cameras first started rolling, Nilsen had gushed. Words had flowed like water from a burst dam. That wasn't the case now. Now there was no urgency. There was control, like a tap momentarily turned on to dispense just the right amount. He was consciously editing himself. Holding back. Being careful not to say too much. It's something I had become very experienced at spotting through decades of interviewing politicians and police officers. It's what isn't said that is truly interesting. That's usually where the stories and the uncomfortable truths are hidden.

'I really need a smoke.' Nilsen reached for his cigarettes and makeshift lighter and we stopped filming. He'd taken control and shut us down. These days, a crew would have kept the camera rolling and included the footage, but back in the nineties you respected an interviewee's right for a break, even if the interviewee was a serial killer and necrophile.

12

THE INTERVIEW – PART III

Smoking break over, Paul tried to pick up where we had left off – part way through dealing with Nilsen's relationship with his sister, Sylvia, who was three years younger than him.*

'Things were different with her,' he said. 'I was different with her, I felt I could impress Sylvia. I wanted her to feel proud of me, like I wanted my mother to feel proud of me.'

By this time in his life, Betty, who had been divorced in 1948, had met and married Andrew Scott, a local builder, whom Nilsen described as 'a semi-literate labourer. A weak man. Totally under my mother's thumb. But at least he was there, he had the decency to be present'.

The family had moved to a council home in Strichen, about eight miles inland from Fraserburgh and the children went to Strichen School, where Dennis stayed until he was fifteen. He said the school was very strict and he'd often get 'belted' by the teachers for not paying attention or 'slacking' in class. Behaviour he put down to not being fed properly at home before being packed off for the day, plus being forced to work morning milk and paper rounds to 'earn his keep' and 'a little spending money'.

'I'd regularly get thrashed at school,' he told us. 'Mr Shanks,

---

* Some criminologists have speculated that Nilsen was attracted to men who facially resembled his sister when they were growing up together, and that many of his victims bore more than a passing likeness to her.

174

the history teacher, would have this test of history dates, and if you got any wrong, you got strapped three times. It wasn't the pain that hurt, it was the humiliation. My whole life was a humiliation, the way I was treated at school, the way I dressed, the poverty of the family. I was shabby and under-nourished – you were certainly made to feel that you knew your place in society.'

I felt some sympathy for the young Des. I'd gone to a similarly barbaric Catholic primary school, run by nuns. Every Friday morning, Sister Mary Antony seemed to positively glow with excitement as she presided over her weekly spelling test of twenty words given to us at the beginning of the week. Score less than last week and you were 'in for the whack'. In front of the whole class, you were called to the front and made to stand there, hand extended, while she expertly administered a blistering whipcrack of a thin wooden cane across the palm or fingers for every number you scored below your previous week's total. If you moved your hand, you got double. You also got double for selling your free dinner tickets (given to poor kids like me coming from low-income families living in council housing) and triple canings for fighting or accidentally kicking a football through the maths room window. It's a wonder I still have any fingers.

Summing up his relationship with his family as 'very shallow', Nilsen told us, perhaps surprisingly, that he had made 'friends of a sort' at his new school, boys he would hang around with at break times, or even after school and play pretty much anything except sports. With a couple of classmates, he'd frequently visit abandoned air-raid shelters where they'd make dens for themselves and nests for fledgling birds that settled there. 'I'd say they were friendships built on some shared interests, that's all.'

Once more I noted that he was heavily censoring and editing this period of his life. I think Paul Britton knew why, because he soon moved the discussion on to Nilsen's recognition of his own sexuality.

'I've always known I was gay, right from the age when you start to think about those kind of things, from about seven years old,' he said, as though it bore no consequence on his life. And then he dried up and waited for the next question.

Again, I noted the short reply. Garrulous Nilsen was once again cautious Nilsen. He was either deliberately making Paul fish for psychological insights from this period of his life, or perhaps, far more interestingly, he was experiencing genuine difficulties in talking about things. Unlike myself, Paul wasn't at all thrown by the interview suddenly becoming more staccato. He knew from professional experiences with countless offenders that we were now entering 'a difficult to talk about' phase of life, the point when childhood fantasies take on sexual dimensions.

'From early childhood,' Nilsen began, 'I'd created this person, he was an observer, he had a passive role, and he was a predator. He was two people in one and both people were me. I was the predator and the victim as well. I could oscillate between the two roles. Life is real to me, but it is not real. All my life has been a fantasy on a theme.'

Paul urged him to expand on his comments.

'I had dreams and daydreams. In my daydreams I was the hero, and everything revolved around me. It was a way, I suppose, for me to get the attention I wanted. I was Robin Hood. I was the leader. I was the top dog. I was the really important person in that scenario.'

I thought it painfully ironic that the boy who fantasised about being a hero, in reality, had to become a villain to get the attention he so desperately wanted. The conversation was moving on, but I was still absorbing the substance of his comment.

Was the keeping of the bodies his way of forcing them to 'pay attention' even after they had been killed?

I was reminded of Ed Kemper keeping his mother's head after murdering her and throwing things at it as the ultimate revenge for the years she'd humiliated him. For centuries, the deprivation 'of a decent burial' has been considered amongst the worst of moral offences.

The arrangement I had with Paul, and with the Home Office and ACPO, was that only Paul would ask the questions, and I respected that, but I was bursting to intervene and blurt out my unprofessional, non-clinical theory.

'I was a benevolent hero though,' Nilsen continued, 'like Gary Cooper in *High Noon*, a firm dictator, firm but fair, the type other people looked up to but respected.'

Wow.

Bells clanged in my head.

Nilsen had just likened himself to Gary Cooper – one of Hollywood's biggest ever stars – a man with a secret life so sleazy and contrary to his squeaky clean public image that studio executives employed a battalion of publicists to cover it up. Gary Cooper, the man who famously told a scriptwriter who wanted to fine-tune his character, 'Just make me the hero.'

And *High Noon*?

This isn't just any old western movie.

This film is all about honour and duty. Its central theme is how a community wrongly and unfairly isolates an individual it should be backing. It shows an ageing marshal abandoning his personal plans to leave town and start a new life with his wife because the noon train is arriving, and on it is a killer he'd once jailed and his gang, all seeking revenge. The hero prevails (of course) and in the final shots throws his marshal tin badge in the dirt to show his contempt for the society that had deserted him (none of them would raise guns against the gang) but he'd still defended.

The movie won four out of the seven Academy Awards it had been nominated for and four Golden Globes. Bill Clinton is reported to have shown it a record seventeen times in the White House's cinema, and said of it, 'It's no accident that politicians see themselves as Gary Cooper in *High Noon*. Not just politicians, but anyone who's forced to go against the popular will. Any time you're alone and feel you're not getting the support you need, Cooper's Will Kane perfects the perfect metaphor.' It was little wonder that this character had so appealed to our interviewee.

Nilsen was an avid movie-goer right up until his arrest. As a child, he spent as much time there as his meagre pocket money and strict mother and grandmother would allow. 'It was much needed escapism,' he'd told me. 'I'd step off the narrow, narrow-minded streets that I hated so much, and step straight into some completely different world, one that filled me with excitement and awoke my dulled imagination. For the short time that I sat there in that darkness I'd be totally immersed in whatever fantasy existence was being played out in the picture. I'd be there. I'd be right alongside the actors. That world on the big screen was as real, sometimes more real to me, than anything that waited outside for me once the picture finished.'

Paul Britton and I were soon to find out that as well as Gary Cooper, there was another universally known leading man that captured Dennis Nilsen's attention and featured in his fantasies.

Dracula.

'I would have nightmares about Dracula,' Nilsen confessed. 'But beforehand, I would prepare myself. I would set the scene, so that when Dracula appeared, I would attack him and pull his head off. I'd decided that I was going to stalk him, that he was going to be the one frightened of me, not the other way round.'

As Nilsen told the story, I realised Dracula was portrayed as neither dead nor alive, and slept in a casket. Wasn't that how Nilsen had seen his grandfather, when he'd struggled to understand what death was and thought Andrew Whyte was just sleeping?

Dracula's mission was to kill people, with the intention of raising them from the dead and then keeping them around to worship and follow him. Uncannily close to Nilsen's fantasies and his re-enactment of them. And then of course, there was the sexual component. The deadly love bite. An act that crossed the discriminatory divide and embraced boys as well as girls.

In his letters, Nilsen spoke of his forbidden feelings, his awakening homosexuality during his teenage years. Playfighting at school, he'd found himself excited while overpowering a weaker, younger boy and he'd developed soft sexual fantasies about young male figures he'd seen pictured in non-pornographic books and magazines. '*I was romantically attracted to a certain type,*' he wrote, '*they would have a gentleness to them, a desirable kind of peace.*'

Now, in Albany Prison, he made further confessions about his teenage fantasies. 'I would think about undressing young boys as they slept. I had a passive image of them in my mind, because I knew the only way I could get near to them was for them to be asleep. It was very important for them to be passive and for me to explore that passivity.'

At this point, I was wondering why Nilsen's sexual aspirations all seemed to involve creeping up on unsuspecting, powerless people and then basically abusing them while they were unconscious. And then I realised something. Nilsen had been born in 1945 and throughout his adolescence, say from 1954 (when he was ten) to 1964 (when he was twenty), homosexuality wasn't merely frowned upon in the UK, it was a criminal act, punishable by imprisonment. Indeed, there had been a sharp rise in the prosecution and persecution of homosexuals in the 1950s, as the government had sought to assert post-war authority through strict law and order controls.

In 1952 (when Nilsen was seven and, according to him, becoming sexually aware) the brilliant British mathematician and scientist Alan Turing was national news. Not because he was finally recognised for his wartime success in cracking German Enigma codes while at Bletchley Park,* or for his pioneering work in advancing computer science. He was news because he was being prosecuted for 'gross indecency', legal code for homosexual acts, and had accepted the court's offer of (I'm ashamed to even write this) chemical castration instead of imprisonment.

Yes, in twentieth-century England, our society castrated or imprisoned men just because they were gay.

No wonder Nilsen's fantasies were so repressed and his imagined conquests so furtive. He could hardly have talked openly about how he felt, could he? He couldn't for one moment have contemplated confiding in his mocking brother

---

* Turing's codebreaking has been credited with shortening the war in Europe by at least two years and saving more than 14 million lives, and, of course, was immortalised in many books and films, including the Hollywood blockbuster, *The Imitation Game*. He is also featured on the back of the £50 note.

– the risk would have been far too great. And I'm sure he would have been scared to death of approaching another boy and expressing his attraction to him. Given that national war heroes were being publicly shamed and tortured by the courts for their sexual identity, how could *he*, an anonymous child in a rigidly religious corner of Scotland, begin to feel free and confident about his emerging sexuality?

In 1954, Alan Turing, now considered one of the greatest heroes of modern times, committed suicide. Again, his homosexuality was all over the newspapers – papers that Nilsen delivered. Amazingly, and shockingly, homosexuality wouldn't be legalised in England and Wales until 1967 (when he was twenty-three), and even then it was only permissible if it was consensual between two men over the age of twenty-one and in private.

At fifteen, Nilsen left school, like many of us did, with unremarkable reports. The only thing he'd been above average in was art, and that didn't count for much in the nearby fishing villages or farming communities. His family thought there was a chance he might get a job at the Consolidated Pneumatic Tool Company where his uncle worked. But Nilsen had more adventurous ideas.

The skinny, weak boy, mocked by his bother as 'effeminate', signed on for nine years' service in the British Army.

'I had to get away from there, from Strichen, from Fraserburgh and that small corner of the world. I needed to make something of myself and I thought the army would give me the opportunity to do that and to learn a trade that would help me make my way in life.'

Paul Britton rightly wondered aloud, how, given his self-recognised homosexuality, Nilsen was able to reconcile that with the very macho life of soldiering.

'Every time there was talk or jokes about "queers" and "poofters" I had to bite my tongue, and sometimes I had no choice but to laugh along. I found it utterly humiliating and painful.'

Nilsen trained in Aldershot, picked up some academic qualifications that were the equivalent of O levels, and also, more importantly, he passed key catering examinations. As a private, he was posted with the 1st Battalion of the Royal Fusiliers to Germany.

In 1967, when he was twenty-one years old, he received a posting to Aden, now known as Yemen, that would result in what he cited as his first consensual homosexual act. He told us that he was in charge of catering at a military prison in Sharjah that housed Arab terrorists, when he found a young rent boy who slept with some of the officers.

'I think he was about twelve years old, somewhere between twelve and fifteen. This was the first intercourse that I'd had, but it wasn't anything other than that. The boy would hang around begging everyone to take him back to England, which of course couldn't happen.'

The significance of the statement wasn't lost on Paul or me. This was a sexual landmark. A young man, desperate for love and affection, hadn't lost his virginity until he was twenty-one, and it had been to a paid rent boy who might have been as young as twelve. As he'd said the age, we noted how Nilsen had almost immediately realised how shameful it would be seen, and had quickly suggested he might have been older, maybe thirteen or fourteen - still at least seven years younger than him.

By his own account, 'the sex' – and even more importantly, 'the boy' – had meant nothing to him. This Nilsen certainly wasn't *High Noon* Hero Nilsen. This was not the moral-minded champion of the underdog that Nilsen had painted himself as being in many of his letters.

This was the birth of the predator he had described to us earlier that morning. *From early childhood I'd created this person, he was an observer, he had a passive role and he was a predator. He was two people in one and both people were me. I was the predator and the victim as well.*

In Aden, fantasy had become reality.

Nilsen as a man, as a twenty-one-year-old soldier, seen by a young foreign boy as a uniformed figure of power and authority, someone with the whole weight and reputation of the British Army behind him, had claimed his first victim.

He'd paid for sex and carried out an act that in most countries would be criminal and classified as child abuse. Had he been caught, it would have resulted in prosecution, possibly imprisonment.

But he'd got away with it.

He'd no doubt emboldened himself and mitigated the abuse with thoughts that others – including army officers (if we are to believe him) – were doing the same. Therefore, it was acceptable. Justifiable. Not reprehensible. Because Nilsen, as he would frequently insist, had moral codes.

As these thoughts crossed my mind, I was reminded of what every FBI profiler I'd met had said – you have to force yourself to think of the offence, not from your moral viewpoint, but from the standpoint of the offender – why did they do what they did in the way they did it?

The simple answers were because he wanted to, and he thought he could get away with it. And while these are true, the other reasons, the ones leading up to the act, are more uncomfortable to consider. Pre-puberty, he had been a child with a level of such low esteem that it had become ingrained in his developing personality. As he became sexually aware, he felt even more isolated and lonely. More than ever, he craved attention and respect, certainly not the further ostracisation that he knew would come from saying he'd love to find a male partner and have an honest and open, meaningful relationship with him that included all the pleasure and emotional reassurance that came from sexual intercourse and intimacy.

Throughout his childhood, adolescence and then early twenties, Nilsen had been acutely aware that British society felt his feelings were so wrong that they were criminal. In other words, in his mind, he *was* a criminal. Everything he heard from every bigot around him will have confirmed to him that he had already crossed society's line between right and wrong, and despite all his inner thoughts, he knew there was no way he could see himself crossing back again.

Now, at twenty-one, here he was as man in the respected ranks of the army, discovering that he, and similarly minded others, could vent their closeted sexual frustrations. He could have real sex, not fantasy sex. And he could even break the law and get away with it. In short, he'd been aware of losing his criminal virginity as much as his sexual virginity.

Also notable, was that Nilsen couldn't recall the young rent boy's name. It's possible he never even asked it or knew it. Just as in later years, he wouldn't be able to recall many of his victims' names. He didn't care about such things. Such people. They were merely his prey.

Paul Britton must have had similar thoughts to mine, probably far more astute, and I suspect he noted the similarities of 'compliance', 'passivity' and 'silence' between a rent boy and a corpse. I'm certain, had he been given the chance, he would have very willingly explored this area in greater depth, but the interview was now spinning like a whirlwind into even darker aspects of Nilsen's sexual acts and fantasies, and there was no way of reigning the storyteller back without fear of curtailing some vital disclosure.

Nilsen told us that as an NCO (non-commissioned officer), he had his own room and would use the privacy to frequently indulge in a variety of chilling rituals. These included covering himself in talcum powder, so he was a deathly white colour, then masturbating in front of a mirror while pretending to be dead.

'I'd angle the mirror so I couldn't see my head and then I could imagine that the hands acting upon me were another person and yet they were still me.'

Death had now made his grand entrance – naked and powdered white, posing in a mirror.

'I've had a rabid love affair with a mirror for years,' Nilsen continued, 'a form of narcissism if you like, the oblong frame is always more powerful for me.'

I began to feel like some shattered pieces of Nilsen's life were being stuck together. To him, the mirror frame, like the camera frame, not only reflected real life but it also distorted it and gave him a feeling of detachment – a position of safety from which he could act out his sexual fantasies.

It was at this point that a prison officer surprisingly appeared with mugs of tea for all of us, including Nilsen. (If you do an online search of Dennis Nilsen images, you'll see his white mug left of frame in the camera shot.)

As we all took our drinks, and Nilsen lit another cigarette, I had the distinct feeling we'd just identified another landmark on his road to murder and necrophilia. The moment when fantasy became concreted into the foundations of his development and deviancy.

By powdering himself white, Nilsen had effectively (for himself at least) become more than another person – he'd become another person who approved of him and who gave him attention. Someone who wouldn't rob him of confidence, would be in full agreement with whatever he wanted to say or do and be an eager, consensual and fully compliant person for him to have sex with. As he was in total privacy, and in total control of this entire sexual ritual, it was certain to always end in his satisfaction. The person he had created as his mirror partner not only looked dead; he was so passive he *played* dead. The repetition of this ritual must have subconsciously fostered thoughts about manipulating real dead bodies as sexual partners.

The wide-eyed teenager, fantasising about homosexual coupling hadn't imagined his first encounter would be with an Arab child whom he'd have to pay. The twenty-one-year-old NCO covering himself in powder and masturbating in front of a mirror hadn't imagined he'd one day be regularly ejaculating over white-fleshed corpses. As Roy Hazelwood very eloquently said, 'Seeds of fantasy grow in unpredictable ways when nourished by opportunity.'

Even before we'd finished the disturbingly grey tea that the guard had brought us, Nilsen had continued talking about his army days. He told us how he had got so drunk one night when posted to Germany, that he woke the following morning naked and in bed with another naked man. I managed to turn a camera on just in time to catch him saying, 'I felt really annoyed. Not that it had happened, but that I hadn't "been around" to witness it, to enjoy having been in that situation.'

Nilsen said he couldn't remember the man's name, and I wondered if the incident had been real or imagined. It seemed unlikely to me that he would have got this close to having a consensual partner without having either known his name beforehand or discovered it afterward, along with whether the man had any future interest in him.

Instead of the nine years of service he'd signed up for, Nilsen completed eleven, leaving the army in the early seventies, when he was almost twenty-seven years old. It's fair to imagine that he hoped for a fresh start, that the decriminalisation of homosexuality almost half a decade earlier had created a more tolerant society than the one he'd escaped from in his mid-teens. One in which he might find happiness. 'At that point, I had only one thing on my mind,' he stated. 'To find a partner to share my life with, socially and sexually.'

Nilsen said that like many ex-soldiers, he 'fell into' a job in London's Metropolitan Police,* expecting it to give him the same camaraderie and comfort of structure and routine that he'd enjoyed in the military. He soon found out that he'd been mistaken. 'The Met was even more homophobic than the army, it really was a case of out of the frying pan and into the fire.'

PC Q287 Nilsen did not like his new life. This was most apparent when once, on night duty, he shone his torch into a parked car and illuminated two men having sex. The law compelled him to make arrests, but of course he couldn't. He told Paul Britton, 'Being a policeman insulted my sense of morality, I had to leave.'

The comment chimed with a more vitriolic passage penned in a letter to me, when he said, '*I have scant regard for the*

---

* Nilsen isn't the only recorded necrophile to have been a police officer. From 1980–2005, Ukrainian police criminal investigator Serhiy Tkach, known as the Pologovsky Maniac, murdered and raped the dead bodies of at least thirty-seven girls and women. In 2015 he married a prison pen pal and, following a number of conjugal visits, she bore him a daughter.

police service in general and the Metropolitan Police in particular. It was supposed to be the envy of the world, but I found it to be rife with prejudice, hypocrisy and corruption.'

Nilsen said that in 1973, soon after passing his probationary exams and being posted to Willesden Green station, he reached a breaking point: 'I'd had enough. Even though I didn't have another job to go to, I knew I had to resign.'

Alone in London, unemployed and unsure of where his next pay cheque might come from, he said he had been very aware that his life was in a downward spiral. 'I was experiencing increasing desperation. There was that nagging feeling that you are becoming isolated from everybody. The feelings had started as a child but had got increasingly worse.'

What Nilsen had described was his awareness of the reoccurrence and further advancement of his emotional detachment from society. What he was *unaware* of, was that such detachment, if not abated, results in a numbing of emotions and ultimately a condition where extreme sufferers might lose the ability to feel anything significant, such as love or sympathy, towards anyone else.

I was reminded of his comment just a few hours earlier, when he said that he hadn't seen people as people, just images.

In this deteriorating emotional state, Nilsen flitted from the police force into unemployment, comparative poverty and temporary homelessness. His confidence slumped when he had to sell personal belongings, including the much-treasured single army medal he'd been awarded, to raise money for rent.

It was hard not to feel empathy toward Nilsen as he undramatically detailed his soul-destroying months of unemployment. Losing your job is a grief that scars anyone unfortunate enough to suffer it. It raises terrible self-doubts and erodes confidence in the strongest of people. Nilsen, the former army corporal, was now job hunting with barely enough money to feed himself. His fall from grace haunted him.

After a brief spell as a security guard, he found himself 'suffering the humiliation and indignity' of having to sign on for unemployment benefit. Ironically, because of his catering background, he eventually landed the position of clerical officer at a Manpower Services Commission job centre in Denmark Street, a branch kept busy filling vacancies in London's kitchens, cafes and restaurants. Nilsen would remain in the job, building a reputation as a good employee, until he was arrested in 1983.

By coincidence, and fortuitously for him, his office stood less than a five-minute walk from the vibrant heart of Soho, the sexual heartbeat of London and home of the capital's growing LGBT community. He soon became a frequent visitor to the pubs and clubs of Old Compton Street, Endell Street and Dean Street.

'I became very sexually active then. Promiscuous. It was easy to find someone for sex but not for anything else. That was all that was on offer. I could secure a quick fuck but not anything that meant anything. Certainly not a relationship.'

Superficially, Nilsen's luck took a turn for the better.

In the summer of 1975, when the average wage was about £50 ($72) per week in London, he received the news that his estranged father Olav had died back in Norway and left him £1,000 ($1,450). In 2021 currency, that's about £8,000 ($11,600). He was also told that his dad's real name had been Olav Magnus *Moksheim* – the surname 'Nilsen' had apparently been an alias the soldier adopted when landing on Scottish shores and mixing with the local ladies.

Flush with cash, Dennis Nilsen's drinking began escalating. In the army, he'd looked forward to sharing beers or spirits with fellow soldiers at the end of the day. This was a form of socialising he missed in the police force, a job where everyone seemed to scatter as soon as shifts ended. Now he was renewing his love of alcohol and the fleeting bar-room companionship of fellow drinkers.

Nilsen told us that around the time of his thirtieth birthday, in November 1975, he'd been out drinking when he met a small, good-looking young man in the Bayswater area of London, who all but advertised his gayness by wearing earrings and make-up. 'I virtually kidnapped David Gallichan,' he said, smiling for the first time during our interview. 'Very quickly I knew I wanted more than sex from him.' He moved the makeshift lighter and seemed to reflect, before adding, 'With David it wasn't love. It wasn't *love*. I had probably been *in love* with the idea of being in love when I moved him in, but it didn't turn out to be that.'

Gallichan had been at least ten years younger than Nilsen, a good four inches smaller, much slighter in build and meeker in character. Unemployed, living in a hostel, without much experience of life outside his hometown of Weston-Super-Mare in Somerset, he would have instantly fitted the bill as someone Nilsen thought he could dominate.

Like Nilsen, he'd been brought up by the coast and his childhood had been one of boats, beaches, long walks and closeted homosexuality. It's not hard to imagine that their mutual interests and inclinations made them feel safe and attracted to each other. The Scot needed someone who wouldn't challenge or criticise him, and Gallichan needed an older father figure, a protector.

After just one night, they pledged to try to build a life together and went flat hunting.

The two men settled on a ground-floor property in an old

Victorian house that also came with access to a rear garden: 195 Melrose Avenue in Cricklewood. The place where the former army corporal would start killing.

The flat was about seven miles and half an hour away from Nilsen's workplace. He used some of his inheritance money to furnish it and added a small black-and-white mongrel puppy they named Bleep.

For the first time in his life, Dennis Nilsen looked to be on the road to domestic bliss.

He and Gallichan, whom he nicknamed Twinkle (as though he were another pet under his control), overhauled the hugely neglected garden that lay beyond their French windows. They created paved pathways, put in a pond stocked with fish, and did such a good job that they were able to persuade the landlord to allow them exclusive access to the space – a concession that would become chillingly convenient in the not too distant future.

Nilsen said he'd felt secure enough to take Twinkle to his work's Christmas party, boldly introducing him to everyone as his partner. But behind closed doors, the relationship was more one of a bully and the bullied, rather than any partnership.*

---

* Home-movie clips, viewed more than a million times on YouTube, give damning insight into Nilsen's relationship with David Gallichan. At the start of the footage, Nilsen is beneath some sheets, bare chested, cigarette in his left hand, glass of beer in his right hand. He is facing the camera and is jabbering angrily at Gallichan, mocking him for not operating it properly: 'I can't understand you. I asked you to start filming from the feet, slowly up to the head – and you go zip! You zip pan. Bloody hell, don't you ever watch movies?' You must've seen thousands of movies; you must know what it is like. They are training chimpanzees at Cape Canaveral to operate a camera, anyone can do it.' Later he is recorded, unlit cigarette in mouth as he strips to his black Y-fronts and says, 'What are you doing switching the bloody thing on and off for? You'll never make a cameraman you know.' And outside in the garden, in a scene where Gallichan is digging – and where Nilsen would later burn corpses – he calls him 'a big nincompoop' and says, 'Don't stand there with your hand on your hip, you look like a big poof'.

Ex-Corporal Nilsen constantly barked orders at his under-ling, chiding and mocking Twinkle for being stupid and effeminate in what seems to be a sad repetition of the way his brother Olav had belittled him.

By 1976, Nilsen had bored and bullied Gallichan into staying out late and seeking relationships with other men.

'The affair had become one-sided,' he told us. 'I was dependent upon Dave to live up to his responsibilities and he didn't do that. I wanted him to come back in the evenings. I needed that security, a sense of belonging, the feeling of having someone.'

Nilsen had felt most let down in June of that year, when he'd needed surgery to remove a painful gallstone, and Twinkle only visited him once during more than a week of confine-ment.

After that incident, which Nilsen interpreted as a lack of caring, the relationship headed irrevocably downhill. Sleeping in separate beds, both men started bringing new lovers back for sex at their Melrose Avenue home. Nilsen claimed that Twinkle turned up with a fifteen-year-old boy whom he ended up 'having sex'* with before returning to Gallichan's bed.

He'd told me in a letter, *The relationship, if you can call it that, had vapourised. It was still in the air but the heart and soul of it were gone. I could see no future in it.*

And apparently neither could Twinkle.

In the summer of '77 he walked out and never returned.

Nilsen said he found it a relief that he had gone. Disturbingly, he said he had 'been thinking of ways to get rid of him'.

---

* If true, then this recollection of Nilsen's is admission of another illegal sexual act. Even if not forced, the fifteen-year-old would have been below the age of sexual consent, which at the time was twenty-one for consenting homosexuals.

The door to our interview room opened and we were informed by a prison guard that it was 11.30 and time for lunch. Nilsen offered to skip it, and so did we. It didn't matter, we were told, he would still have to go back to his wing for the designated duration.

Paul, Wilf, Dennis and I left the jail and headed a few minutes up Horsebridge Road to a family pub recommended to us by one of the officers. It was sunny, and the beer garden was frothing with Isle of Wight holidaymakers. I was grateful for the fresh air and change of scenery.

We ordered food and drinks and reflected on the morning. 'I've never seen animals behave like that man,' said Laidler, who'd told us he used to work as a shepherd in Northumberland before joining the police. 'No animal would do anything like the things he did.'

No one argued with that.

Our lunches came, a mix of baked potatoes and sandwiches. As I ate, I thought as much about what Nilsen *hadn't* said as what he'd told us. He'd omitted well-documented accounts of being taken to a mortuary during his time as a PC and being more fascinated than frightened when confronted with a variety of male and female corpses, some of which had been mutilated and others opened up during post-mortem examinations.

He'd excluded a critically heated and final row with his brother Olav during a visit home to Scotland. It had come about over the ground-breaking black-and-white film *Victim*, starring Dirk Bogarde as married lawyer Melville Farr, who, back in the fifties, had to disclose his closeted homosexuality in order to expose a gang that had been blackmailing homosexuals and had caused one young gay man to hang himself. Olav apparently ridiculed an iconic scene, in which Farr's wife confronts him about his feelings for the dead man, and the lawyer passionately confesses he'd 'wanted' him. This mockery enraged Nilsen to the point that he vowed never to see his brother again.

In our pub garden, happy, laughing children left their tables and were squatting to peer through wire mesh at rabbits in a hutch. This idyllic distraction reminded me that Nilsen had also skipped stories of how, with friends, he used to kill rabbits 'because they had myxomatosis and I couldn't bear to see them suffer'.

I had no chance of getting Nilsen out of my head. My mind was sifting through every aspect of his life. I'd given Paul lengthy notes, press clippings, books and copies of some of Nilsen's correspondence with me to prepare him, but I was still afraid that something might be missed. The whole morning had gone by and we still hadn't got to Nilsen's first victim. The documentary maker inside of me was worried that we would run out of time before we got to any of the criminal acts that had seen him jailed for life.

I spoke briefly to Paul in private, and he told me not to be concerned. He said he was very pleased with the way it had progressed, particularly that Nilsen had kept his answers to the time period he was being questioned about. Progressing chronologically was apparently very important. Paul said he'd been well aware that Nilsen had been 'self-editing' and 'censoring' and thought the reasons why he had excluded certain things would become apparent, reassuring me that there was a lot more revealing material to come.

Within the hour, he would be proved right.

We were back in position and ready to roll long before Nilsen was escorted back to us. To our surprise, he returned from his break carrying a very small battery-operated Casio keyboard, which I guessed was the one Brian Masters had given him as a birthday present. 'Instead of lunch, I composed something that I'd like you to hear,' he announced, excitedly. 'It's called "Themes on a Childhood".'

Once again, I feared time being lost on trivia, but we all sat politely and listened while he played.

Nilsen was a fan of the likes of Rick Wakeman, Yes and Mike Oldfield, and their influences were instantly recognisable in the short, soaring, progressive pop that he performed in an almost trance-like state. I'm no musician, but to me it wasn't bad. Not great, but not awful. It had structure, a beginning, middle and end, and it was evocative of waves coming out of nowhere, rolling gently and then crashing to a climax.

There was an awkwardness as he lifted his murderous fingers from the keys and looked around the room for applause or words of approval. None was forthcoming. As he slid the keyboard off the table and glared angrily at Paul, I wondered if he really had created it over lunch or had composed it some time ago and simply sought to impress or distract us.

The interview picked up where it had left off, in the summer of '77, after David 'Twinkle' Gallichan had packed his meagre belongings and walked out of Melrose Avenue and his partner's life. Of the following months, Nilsen said, 'I drank a lot and worked a lot. I immersed myself in my work, especially union activities, as these seemed the most important things in the world to me.'

Nilsen had taken on a role in the CPSA, the Civil and Public Services Association, as the organiser of the Denmark Street branch, and went on to become branch secretary. He would regularly attend rallies, protests and picket lines, not surprisingly flourishing in the spotlight. By the autumn of 1978, he'd become noticed as a local firebrand. He worked hard to pass the exams that gave him entrance to the elite CPSA Branch Chairman's School at Surrey University. Over lunch tables and in bars after class, he rubbed shoulders with national officials and said he felt important and valued. 'I was in my element when I was a union official. I liked helping people who had trouble helping themselves. I hated the injustices that fellow workers were made to suffer and I knew I could speak out for them, give them a voice.'*

Union work was a perfect fit. He had people on his side and there were visible common enemies – bosses and the government – to be raged at. He had weapons – the union rulebook, industrial action and most of all, the power of his own voice and personality.

Management came to dread the torrent of letters he sent, the nit-picking over rules and regulations, the face-to-face meetings he would demand. With his feet planted on the moral high ground, Nilsen became the *High Noon* hero he worshiped, fighting for everyone, even those he didn't like, even those he knew to be homophobic.

Work, drink and sleep became the trifecta of his existence. The latter occasionally being replaced with casual sex hook-ups in the gay bars notorious for their no-questions-asked, one-night stands.

'My personal life had become shallow and unsatisfying, a shadow of the brightness I'd hoped for. I was entrenched in despair, and at times the loneliness took on levels of unbearable physical pain.'

---

* When he was arrested, Nilsen is reported to have told one of the detectives, 'The killer's not here. The killer's in Number 10.' He was alluding to 10 Downing Street, home of the British prime minister, Margaret Thatcher, and by inference was blaming her government for creating the society of poor, unemployed and homeless from which he picked his victims.

Christmas did not provide Dennis Nilsen with the much longed for festive break that everyone around him seemed hell-bent on enjoying. He spent it with only his dog Bleep as company. Gone were the healthy distractions of work and union activities. All he had left was drink.

One of his favoured watering holes was the Cricklewood Arms, about a mile away from his flat. He said that on the night of 30 December, with New Year's Eve rapidly approaching, he 'went out with the intention of getting blind drunk. I needed to get out and be with people. I was going mad sitting in that flat on my own'.

In the pub, he sank pints of Guinness like it was going out of fashion, then either inside or outside – he couldn't remember – he fell into the company of a young Irish lad who, like him, had been on his own. He took him back to Melrose Avenue where they carried on drinking throughout the early hours of the morning.

Nilsen told us he couldn't recall much about the young man, what he looked like, or even what his name was, which seemed somewhat untrue, given that when he was eventually arrested and questioned by the police, he told them, 'He was much shorter than I was. About five foot six inches. He was southern Irish and had short, dark brown, curly hair. His hands were rough. At closing time, he indicated to me that he had too far to travel. We went back to Melrose Avenue and started drinking. We had a damned good old drink and, later on, I remember thinking, "He'll probably be going soon – another ship passing in the night".'

All he could remember, he claimed to us, was that he woke up in bed with him the following morning and wanted to explore the young man's sleeping body in the way he had done with his brother and sister.

'On the spur of the moment, I picked up a tie that was nearby and I started to strangle him.'

For the first time since we had started filming, Nilsen shifted uncomfortably on his seat. He partially covered his cheek and mouth by leaning lazily into his hand, a gesture often seen as a sign of lying, and insisted that his recollection was 'hazy'. I had read his extensive account of this moment, given to Brian Masters for *Killing for Company*, so I knew he was either lying now, or had lied to Brian. I presumed the issue of premeditation was what made Nilsen uncomfortable. If he admitted to having had the forethought to seek out a tie from, say, inside his wardrobe,* and work out exactly how best to strangle a sleeping person, which presumably someone in the army would know, then the claim of this being a 'spur of the moment' action would be rendered a falsehood.

Nilsen told us he remembered that when the man woke and began to struggle, 'I pulled him choking from the bed, straining until he became unconscious'. Uncertain whether his victim was dead or not, he says he then filled a bucket with water and held his victim's head in it, 'until bubbles stopped rising to the surface' and he was certain he was dead.

The Ressler rule about contradictions told me that Nilsen was lying about this first murder, but I would have to wait more than a decade to discover what he was concealing. In 2005, when interviewed by detectives, he formally identified this man as Stephen Dean Holmes – in fact, not a man at all, but a fourteen-year-old boy.

The teenager had not been a rent boy, a runaway, a homeless man, or a drunken down-and-out. He'd been a happy kid

---

* Nilsen claimed the blue tie he used to strangle his first victim had been one close at hand, left on the floor.

who'd had a great time at a local rock concert and had wanted to finish the evening with the excitement of buying an underage beer in the Cricklewood pub.

The thirty-three-year-old, six-foot-tall former soldier had seen the much smaller, baby-faced teenager with dark bushy hair as easy prey.

It can also have been no coincidence that this slightly built, very young-looking youth had been disturbingly close in age to the Arab child that Nilsen admitted paying for sex during his time in the army.

Nilsen's lack of detail about his first victim (obviously a memorable event) had most probably not been because of a hazy memory. Nor his desire to avoid the issue of premeditation. But had been because he didn't want to be seen for what he really was – a coward and a paedophile. These were the two categories that he believed carried even more stigma than being a murderer or necrophile.

Across the prison table, Paul Britton looked on the verge of questioning the veracity of his account, when Nilsen gave us a telling perspective on how he had regarded his victim as he looked down on the boy's dead body.

'After the killing, there was this buzzing, buzzing in my mind. The image of him was buzzing all the time.' He said he lifted the corpse and carried it over his shoulder, 'in a fireman's lift', catching a glimpse of himself in a mirror. 'It was such a powerful sight, so powerful, seeing myself like that.'

This act of dominance, his carrying of a small, dead, teenage boy, someone less than half his age, signified that a subconscious sexual narrative was being played out in distinct stages. Once completed, it would form a ritual to which Nilsen would become addicted.

Stage One had been the selection of his victim – a weaker, younger, more vulnerable male.

Stage Two had been luring his victim back to the flat with the offer of something he wanted – in this case, drink.

Stage Three had been the murder. Planned. Premeditated. Organised.

Now, we were to hear about Stage Four – the washing.

Nilsen ran water in his bath and immersed the small, naked boy in it.

'I don't really know why I washed him, perhaps it was just cleanliness. I think I wanted him at his best for my fantasy.'

Pathologists will tell you strangulation – asphyxiation – is not a quick and mentally or physically painless way to die. The victim is conscious, choking and panicking for quite a while, and very often, during death, they soil themselves and require bathing afterwards.

When Nilsen looked at the naked, newly dried teenager, he saw something way beyond his first victim. He saw himself. And also the passive image he'd created in the mirror, when he'd masturbated during his sexual fantasies. 'Funnily enough, at this point, I was him. In my mind, I was him as well as me,' he explained.

The baptismal act had created a miraculous change.

'He was now me,' Nilsen insisted. 'He was now my body in the fantasies.'

Profilers say the act of strangling affords the murderer an almost godlike sense of power, as they literally have some-one's life in their hands. More pressure and the victim dies. Less, and they live. It's possible this provided an extra sexual dimension to Nilsen's actions and further enhanced and embedded his complex fantasy of being both the predator and the prey.

As Nilsen recounted his post-mortem actions, I watched him closely. He was now at his most relaxed. Gone were the awkward hand-to-face signs of lying, the uncomfortable shifting in his seat, the defensive crossing of his arms and discomfort that he'd exhibited while glossing over details that showed him to be morally reprehensible.

His voice remained monotone as he told us how he'd put the dead body under the floorboards because it had become stiff with rigor mortis. The following day, he'd gone shopping for new underpants for his victim and was excited by the prospect of returning to him.

The body was removed from its dusty resting place, bathed again and prepared for sex.

'I had a frisson of excitement. I imagined him doing to me what I was doing to him. I wanted him to be me. The Y-fronts were brand new; a flawlessness was necessary.' He went on. 'Because of the lighting in Melrose Avenue, there was always a gentle red glow in the room and this fell on his body making him look warm and alive.'

As Nilsen told us that he found the site of the body arousing (this would now be about four hours after death), I noticed that I had stopped breathing. I was literally holding my breath.

'I started to have anal sex,' Nilsen continued, 'but I lost my erection because of the coldness of his flesh. It seemed wrong anyway, it spoilt the image of him. It was the visuals that produced the erection.'

The two police officers in the room were now glaring at the casual storyteller. Neither of them blinked. Their focus was intense. Their feelings of repulsion no longer hidden.

Nilsen continued talking, describing how he withdrew his limp penis and resorted to masturbation in order to ejaculate and gain the 'biological release' that he said he needed. He told us he then slept soundly that night, his body satiated, his mind apparently already coming to terms with what he'd done and what he was.

I could no longer look directly at him. No longer concentrate on the meaning of what he was saying. I dropped my gaze into the viewfinder of the locked-off camera directly in front of me. I checked the focus, the framing, the sound levels, the battery metre, the amount of tape that was left, everything I could so that I focused on anything except the images being described by the man less than a metre from me, the murderer who was recounting his first kill as coolly as someone recalling their first day at school.

'The most exciting part of the little conundrum was when I lifted the body,' he continued, ' when I carried it. It was an expression of my power to lift and to carry and to have control, and the dangling element of limp limbs was an expression of his passivity. There were these two opposite things. There was my power and his passivity, the more passive he could be the more powerful I was.'

After sexually satisfying himself, he returned the corpse to the dusty space he'd cleared beneath the flat's floorboards. He said that he'd then intermittently bring it out of hiding, to repeat the washing, dressing, undressing and sexual activity. He'd position the dead teenager in multiple poses around the flat, usually masturbating over his stomach while sat astride him, staring down at his blank, expressionless eyes and putrefied flesh.

The instinctive revulsion, fear and respect that most of us feel when encountering a dead body was not there for Nilsen. To the contrary. It *aroused* him.

What was now in place was the complete ritual of a serial killer:

- Select a victim.
- Seduce intended victim into coming back to the flat.
- Strangle him.
- Bathe the body.
- Dress the body.
- Abuse the body.
- Hide the body.
- Repeat abuse until the body is too biologically decomposed to be kept any longer.

The winter of '78 passed into the spring and summer of '79, during which Nilsen shuffled the body of his first victim in and out of its resting place beneath his feet, for almost eight months. Then he reached a critical moment.

'There came a point when he became ugly,' he recounted emotionlessly. 'It was the dead meat syndrome and I had to get rid of him.'

Nilsen's first thoughts were to cut up the cadaver. 'I bought an electric knife and a big cooking pot. I paid twelve pounds for the knife and it was useless. I eventually gave it away to a girl in the office. I said: "Here, have this to cut the turkey up with at Christmas".'

I knew exactly the type of knife to which he was referring. I'd carved our own family turkey with a similar gadget and it had failed part-way through the white meat. I found myself uncomfortably thinking about how the thin, sliding blades of steel would have even more quickly clogged and jammed while cutting through putrefied human skin, hair and bone.

Surely, I thought, *after more than a decade in the army and all those years of mass food preparation in the catering corps, Nilsen would have used butchering machetes and boning knives*

on pigs, cows, lambs and poultry, and been able to make a
better choice for this grizzly task?

If what he said was true, and not an invention to amuse himself at our expense, was it strange that he could remember exactly how much he'd paid for the knife, but couldn't remember the name, age or many of the features of his very first victim – something that surely was of far more significance to him?

Apparently not.

The body of the fourteen-year-old boy, which by now must have been infested with all manner of insects, was kept until mid-August '79, when temperatures were around twenty degrees Celsius (sixty-eight Fahrenheit). He put what remained of young Stephen Holmes on a bonfire in the back garden.

To disguise what he presumed would be the disturbing smell of burning human flesh, he added old rubber tyres, knowing that they would emit their own pungent odours and a cover of thick black smoke. Additionally, he banked on the tall fence ringing the rear of the property to give him the privacy he needed for the disposal.

When the fire died out, he checked the ashes, deciding to either pick the bones out, crush them and dispose of them, or simply grind, dig and rake them into the earth.

To the naked eye, Stephen Holmes had vanished.

By the time the first leaves of autumn began to fall from the trees down Melrose Avenue, Dennis Andrew Nilsen had been transformed.

Gone was the cherubic child of the Scottish schoolyard, the introverted teenager who showed promise at art, the determined explorer who set off for the army and adventures abroad, the police probationer who pounded the beat looking to build a new career for himself, the union official willing to champion the cause of the underdog.

His destiny had been decided.

There was no going back.

Publicly, Dennis Nilsen was a respectable civil servant, a fervent trade unionist, a moral member of society.

Privately, he was a child-abusing predator, a murderer and a necrophile.

He told us that in those days, as he realised what he'd become, he'd had thoughts about killing himself, about turning himself in, about never killing anyone ever again. 'I'd lacked the courage to do either,' he confessed, adding that there was the extra complication of his love for his dog, Bleep, and his belief that if he was gone then the dog might perish or be put down.

Nilsen said he'd felt anxiety after the first killing, 'a fear of being caught' and what he called 'a basic guilt', but he made no statement of remorse, sorrow or regret. 'Such feelings are private,' he told me, 'they're between me and those I wronged.'

Before the interview, Paul Britton had drawn for me a basic diagram that charted the upward and downward curve of an offender's anxiety about being caught. It had been plotted against the upward and downward curve of his desire to experience the thrill of offending again.

Anxiety peaks immediately after the attack, when the fear of being caught is strongest. It plateaus months later, when the offender realises they are not suspected of the crime. It then dips and carries on dipping with every day of freedom – growing more confident each day that they are not going to be arrested and punished for what they've done.

Desire to reoffend – to once more experience all the satisfaction of making their fantasies become reality – is at the lowest when anxiety is at the highest. Then, as the fear of apprehension subsides, the desire grows.

With each day of freedom, the fantasy strengthens and the desire to reoffend slowly climbs.

The desire curve continues to kick upwards a little during the months that anxiety plateaus. It then rises sharply when the offender becomes completely convinced that they have got away with the crime and will never be brought to justice. At this point, they are mentally back to the state they were before they committed the first offence. After each subsequent offence, the duration between each crime often becomes shorter because of sharper falls in anxiety levels and increasingly rapid restoration of desires.

What Paul could have added was that the more intelligent of offenders will, by this stage, have learned from their first experience how to avoid making evidential mistakes, and will be confident in taking that learning into each subsequent offence.

Nilsen hit that critical rise in desire in October 1979, just a few weeks after disposing of his first victim.

After drinking in a local pub, he'd invited a young Chinese student called Andrew Ho back to his flat. The alcohol continued to flow until Nilsen attempted but failed to strangle him with a tie. Ho rushed straight from the flat to the local police, and within the hour they were questioning the former soldier about the incident.

Nilsen bluffed his way to freedom. He told the officers it was all just bondage play between two consensual gay lovers. Sensing a lack of support, Ho became reluctant to press charges and investigations stopped there. Had they not been, the Scot would surely have been arrested, and his murder count may have stopped at only one.

But that was not the case.

Two months later, Nilsen killed again.

Once more, his victim was not a homeless, unemployed gay man, but just someone unfortunate enough to cross his predatory path.

Twenty-three-year-old Kenneth Ockenden was slightly built and outgoing with shoulder-length dark hair and an easy smile. Confident and friendly, he liked to explore new pastures. He was in London visiting relatives and photographing landmarks. He was a day away from flying back to his native Canada and sharing his latest memories with his doting parents.

On the afternoon of December 3rd, Kenneth had the misfortune to take a break from his morning's sightseeing to grab lunch in a West End pub. Dennis Nilsen had some time off from work and was already drinking there.

Across the bar, the Scot spotted the good-looking man with a camera.

He moved in.

Nilsen struck up a conversation, they bought drinks for each other, and then, out of kindness, Nilsen offered to show him the sights so he could get the best possible photographs in the shortest possible time.

After playing the role of friendly, personal guide, he lured the drunken young man back to his flat where he cooked them both a meal and plied him with more drinks.

Nilsen described to us how there came a moment during the evening when his mind turned to murder. 'He was sitting on the sofa and I was thinking, he'll be gone tomorrow; he'll be flying back to Canada tomorrow. And I just wanted him to stay.'

In hindsight, it's more likely that Nilsen's mind had been made up hours ago in the pub, the moment Ken Ockenden told him he was flying out of Heathrow the following day. Here was a potential victim who was already set to disappear from British soil. To a sexual predator like him, this would have been an opportunity too good to turn down.

Midnight came and went. Music played and drinks flowed. Nilsen's fantasies churned in his mind.

'I had thought about having sex with him. I wanted a sexual relationship with him, but we hadn't talked about it.'

Oblivious to his host's growing urges, the drunken young Canadian donned the headphones he'd been given, closed his eyes and tuned into the music the killer had invited him to hear.

And then Nilsen struck.

He strangled him with the cable running from the headphones to the stereo unit.

Nilsen's ritual was playing out.

Kill. Bathe. Abuse.

Ken Ockenden had defecated while asphyxiating and needed extra bathing. Nilsen said he'd been exhausted by the time he'd done all the washing and cleaning. 'I listened to some music in order to compose myself, to stop the buzzing.' He then carried the washed corpse to his bed and slept with it for what remained of the night.

If we replay the events of the day, we can see that Nilsen must indeed have been exhausted right after the murder, and probably in no state to play out the sexual side of his fantasies. Aside from the exertion of murdering someone, he had spent at least twelve hours drinking and walking around London. The lack of immediate post-mortem sex was most probably a result of him being simply too tired rather than any other psychological reason.

But the following day was to be a different matter.

Nilsen had to rush off to work, and away from the corpse he'd craved, his fantasies deepened. He took time out to purchase a Polaroid camera, the type that has a self-developing film in its chunky body and instantly provides the user with the peel-and-reveal pleasure of seeing the shot they've just taken develop right in front of them. The kind that means if you are a serial killer, you don't have to take the incriminating film of your victim somewhere to be developed and in doing so put your liberty at risk.

'I got a camera and took photographs of Ken lying flat out on the carpet. It was something that I had to do. I had to put him in the oblong frame,' Nilsen informed us. As shocking as this first sounds, photography of the dead used to be common in Victorian England. They were accepted as a comforting part of the grieving process, and, after death, relatives would call a photographer and be pictured with the deceased, often propped up on custom stands, in numerous favourite places around the home.

Like the Victorians, Nilsen moved the corpse of Kenneth Ockenden around his small flat, posing the dead man in a variety of positions.

Ressler had told me that Dahmer and other serial killers had done the same. They'd learned that victims never looked as good as they did in the first moments after death. The blunt reality was that their bodies decomposed. Or, as Nilsen crudely put it, they turned into 'dead meat'.

Photography was a necrophile's way of uniquely capturing the object of their desires at the exact moment they had triumphed in turning fantasy into reality.

'I placed a tissue over his sexual parts to add some mystery to the shots,' Nilsen recalled with relish, reliving his post-mortem abuse of the Canadian.

The only genuine regret that he seemed to have was that he'd wished he'd been able to use better photographic equipment, like his much-loved home-movie camera. 'They were good pictures but there's not much you can do with those types of camera – they're just the flash and take type.'

Such photographs, I knew from the likes of Roy Hazelwood, would be used for masturbation, either when the victim's body had reached such a stage of decomposition that it was no longer visually arousing, or when it had been disposed of.

But Dennis Nilsen was doing more than taking photographs.

More than creating his own pornography.

More than feeding future fantasies and pushing them to new levels.

He was, for the first time, taking trophies.

What bigger trophy can there be than capturing the very image of the person as they were during the first day of their death?

Keeping their bodies, perhaps?

'Eventually, I gave the camera away,' he told us. 'I gave it to a guy in the office. I said, "Here, I've got a Polaroid camera, I've got no use for it, you might as well have it".'

The story had the same ring to it as the gifting of the electric knife, and I couldn't help but think Nilsen might have derived some weird frisson of ironic pleasure from knowing that his grateful colleagues would innocently be using articles that had been centrally involved in his darkest post-mortem acts of mutilation and masturbation.

In the months following Kenneth Ockenden's death, Nilsen used the young man's corpse as a life-size sex toy. He pulled it out from under the floorboards whenever the urge took him. Pushed it back into the dusty darkness once he was done.

Occasionally, he kept his Ken doll up for a while and talked to it. 'Nothing special,' he said, 'just chit chat.'*

Psychologists and profilers have long known that serial murderers dehumanise their victims, thinking of them not as people, but as objects. Disposing of an object is mentally a much easier a task to deal with than the thought of terminating a human life and causing a ripple of endless sorrow through the existence of all the victim's loved ones.

It didn't come as a surprise to learn that Nilsen objectified those whom he killed in exactly this way. He said, 'The depersonalisation was necessary to keep my sanity.'

But there was a major departure from the norm. 'Once they were dead, they came alive again for me, I saw them then as people not objects. I had to see them like that for my fantasies to have meaning. They were people I talked to. People I showed my own peculiar respects to.'

Nilsen said his 'peculiar respect' extended to a most surprising form of sexual fidelity, something I can only describe as necrophilic monogamy.

'I never had sex with anybody when there was someone under the floor,' he declared. 'I couldn't get my rocks off like that. I just couldn't do it.'

Again, my mind had trouble understanding – and processing – his latest set of standards. By 'anybody' he meant a living person. And by 'someone' he meant a corpse. Was this evidence that he had developed a unique set of 'morals', which meant it was wrong to have sex with the living in the presence of the dead?

I knew from his own admissions that he had no problem

---

* Decades later, in his autobiography, Nilsen would claim he never talked to his dead victims, but would place them in his flat and 'think' to them, while he stroked and caressed them.

sexually interacting with the corpses months after death. Despite their various degrees of putrification and insect infestation, the corpses still excited him. Apparently during this period, the living could not arouse him – or couldn't if the dead were close by.

This is even harder to understand, given Nilsen's mirror fantasies and his claims that during post-mortem sex he was both the dead victim and the live aggressor.

Looking at the blackened, marbled flesh of a decomposing young man, did he still see himself?

The simplest conclusion was that Nilsen had reached the point where he was more excited and motivated to have a dead sexual companion than he was to give up his murderous ways and seek out only living partners.

But if that were true, then it wasn't something he either recognised or was willing to admit.

Nilsen said he felt 'sexually regenerated' when he burned the bodies in his garden. 'I put this putrid bundle on the pyre and it was like a cleansing operation. I knew then that I could go out and have sex. It was one-night-stand sex, transient and unrewarding. The predominate objective was still to have a real relationship.'

Goodness knows what Nilsen considered to be a 'real relationship'.

Paul Britton valiantly resumed the task of having Nilsen chronologically account for all his victims – those he killed, those he attempted to kill, those he could remember the names of and those whose identities he'd either forgotten or claimed to have never known.

A full year had passed between the murder of Stephen Holmes in December 1978 and that of Ken Ockenden in December 1979. If the aborted strangulation of student Andrew

Ho was factored in (October 1979), then it became apparent that Nilsen's attempts to control his murderous urges had lasted less than twelve months.

True to the pattern long-ago identified by profilers at the FBI's BSU, the gap between Ockenden and his next victim was considerably shorter.

In May 1980, less than five months after the murder of the Canadian tourist, Nilsen killed again.

Once more, his victim was a vulnerable, young teenager.

Martyn Duffey was a dark-haired, troubled and vulnerable gay youth, who looked younger than his sixteen years. Growing up in Birkenhead, he'd been in care, had needed help from psychiatrists and social workers and had a history of drug dependency and petty theft. Like millions of others down on their luck, Martyn had run away to London, hoping to start a new life. Instead, a chance meeting with Dennis Nilsen would end it.

The civil servant was returning home from a union conference in the north west of England when he spotted the teenager in an area near Euston train station that was notorious for rough sleepers, sex pick-ups and drug deals.

Martyn Duffey willingly returned to Melrose Avenue with him, and after a few cans of beer said he was tired and went to the bed he'd been told was his for the night.

Nilsen's ritual was in play for the third time.

Kill. Bathe. Abuse.

He strangled the young man. Hauled him to the kitchen sink. Drowned him to be certain he was dead. Nilsen stripped off Martyn's soiled clothes, bathed him and then, as in previous post-mortem defilements, sat astride his naked corpse and masturbated until he ejaculated on his stomach.

Kill. Bathe. Abuse.

I glanced across the room and noticed Wilf Laidler and Dennis Cleugh looking every bit as revolted and mentally drained as I felt. There is a limit to how much even hardened police officers can listen to someone talking unemotionally about such abhorrent acts, without becoming overwhelmed and desensitised. And we had reached it. I was no longer capable of 'walking in the shoes' of the offender as I'd been so sure I would. I didn't want to be within a thousand miles of such footwear.

Only Paul Britton had the resolve and skills to stay in that zone with Nilsen. To psychologically remain in the civil servant's small flat, with its two-bar electric fire, its dead teenagers, bath taps running, floorboards being lifted, murdered flesh and murderer's soul decaying in harmony.

Nilsen told us that between the killings, on more than half a dozen nights he'd brought drunken young men back to Melrose Avenue and entertained thoughts about killing them. Andrew Ho was only one of many who narrowly escaped with their lives.*

'One man woke up when I was taking his trousers off. I had a tie around his neck and was starting to strangle him when he woke. He thought it was all part of some kinky game and said, "Fuck me! Fuck me!" I just lifted up his legs and had intercourse with him. He thought it was all part of it. He left the next morning.'†

Dates and days and times, names and faces, ages and precise locations, now all seemed to momentarily or permanently

---

* This admission seems to contradict his claims that he couldn't have sex with living people while there were corpses in the house, but without precise dates of when all the bodies were disposed of, it's hard to prove.

† Given the dark dexterity involved in simultaneously strangling and undressing a victim, this recollection is either mistakenly recalled by Nilsen or has been invented.

elude Nilsen. Either that, or he'd grown weary with Paul's very structured timeline interviewing and simply wanted to wreck it.

He needed another cigarette break and wanted the cameras to stop rolling for a few minutes.

No one argued. I almost wanted the interview to end completely and head for fresh air and home. The hours of content we'd already recorded were so graphic I knew much of it would have to be cut to satisfy TV watchdogs at the IBA (Independent Broadcasting Authority), who could fine TV stations or seek to remove their licenses if they breached decency standards.

But Nilsen scrubbed out his dogend and was ready to go again.

Once more he seemed unable, or unwilling, to progress chronologically as Paul wished. With hindsight, it's little wonder. This was the period where his mental state was most quickly deteriorating, his drinking increasing, and his offending accelerating.

Only four months would elapse before Nilsen took the life of his fourth victim.

He met fellow Scot, Billy Sutherland in August 1980, in a pub near Piccadilly Circus, and claimed to remember nothing about the killing. Nilsen said he simply woke to find 'another dead body' in his flat.

After this murder, the gap between killings contracted to just a month.

In September 1980, he claimed his fifth victim, a man he could only remember as 'an Irish labourer with rough hands'.

In October, he killed his sixth victim. Another unidentified man, whom he described as a 'slim prostitute, either Filipino or Mexican'. Another chance meeting in a pub.

In November 1980, Nilsen murdered his seventh victim, a vagrant he'd picked up in Charing Cross Road.

Nilsen claimed the life of his eighth victim at the end of November/start of December*; 'a long haired hippy' he met in a pub after closing time in the West End.

All the men had been subject to the same murderous acts and post-mortem rituals.

In Melrose Avenue, the bodies had quite literally begun to stack up, and Paul Britton wanted to focus on how and when Nilsen came to the decision that a victim's body should be moved from the flat, and the method he used for doing it.

I braced myself.

'When there were, say, two or three bodies under the floorboards, come the summer it got hot and I knew there would be a smell problem, and I knew I would have to deal with the smell problem. I thought what would cause the smell more than anything else? And I came to the conclusion that it was the innards, the soft parts of the organs and stuff like that. So, on a weekend, I would sort of pull up the floorboards, and I found it totally unpleasant, and I would get blinding drunk so I could face it, and I'd start dissection on the kitchen floor.' He shrugged. 'I'd go out and be sick in the garden because it was really repulsive.'

'What sort of preparation would you have to make for that?' Paul asked.

'What do you mean, preparation?' Nilsen queried.

'Well, if you were to bring these young men's bodies into your kitchen and start to dismember them, then that's going to leave an awful mess,' Paul suggested.

---

* Dates relating to victims are those Nilsen gave to Police, and are often his best estimates, occasionally altered over time in his letters and other writings.

'Why should it leave a mess?'

'Well, it could, couldn't it?'

'No, it didn't. It didn't leave a mess.' As Bob Ressler had predicted, Nilsen now adopted the air of a learned lecturer passing on his life experiences to naive students. 'In death situations - where a knife is involved - there's a lot of blood flying around. If I were to stab you right now, your heart is pumping away there, there would be blood splattering all over the place.' Nilsen's left arm lifted and he flicked his hand backward and upward to the wall behind him to indicate the spatter. 'But in a dead body, there are no blood spurts or anything like that. It congeals inside, becomes part of the flesh and becomes like anything you'd see in a butcher's shop. There's little or no blood.'

Nilsen, I noticed, was totally relaxed, no tense hunching of the shoulders, his fingers gently interlocked, his thumbs flicking up and down with each emphasis in his sentences.

'You know these plastic bags that you would have, these bin liners, you'd get one of those,' he continued, 'you slit one of those so it forms a kind of a sheet, you haul the body out from under the floorboards, you put it on the sheet, and then you cut it up.'

By the end of 1980, Nilsen was accumulating corpses quicker than he could dispose of them. Flies and insects were so attracted to the growing smells of rotting flesh that he had to regularly disinfect the entire flat, hunt the flies with aerosol sprays, and sprinkle salt on the corpses to kill off the maggots.

Trained in butchery during his days in the Army Catering Corps, Nilsen had become adept at dismembering bodies, and this process, including the breaking of chest bones and decanting of organs into plastic bags, apparently created no deep trauma for him. Once more, his victims had become objects. He was simply disposing of the 'dead meat'. When he couldn't burn or bury body parts in the garden, he stored their heads, limbs and bones in bin bags, carrier bags and suitcases that he stacked in the garden shed and around his flat.

Just before Christmas, he had a clear out. A bonfire that raged all day. A mass cremation that excited neighbourhood kids so much they crept through gaps in the garden fence to try to warm themselves by the fire.

Christmas also heralded a brief sexual encounter with a man he met in a pub and brought back to his newly cleansed home. After staying the night, the stranger was allowed to leave and they never met again.

If Nilsen had intended the big clean out and the brief human encounter to be a new start for the new year, then it all went very wrong, very quickly.

Four days into January '81, he brought home an unidentified eighteen-year-old Scottish youth he'd met in a Soho pub. After a night's heavy drinking, the teenager became his ninth victim. Nilsen dismembered this body, along with the hippy victim claimed in December.

Nilsen's tenth victim came in February. He was a Northern Irish lad in his early twenties, whom he nicknamed 'Belfast Boy', because he couldn't remember his name.

A little over a month passed until victim eleven was killed in April 1981. He was understood to be a tough, English skin-head Nilsen met in Leicester Square. Again, he couldn't remember his name but recalled a tattoo around his neck with the inky invitation CUT HERE.

The regular rhythm of monthly offending that had been fairly consistent since August 1980 changed after this murder (or at least statistically it looks as though it did), and Nilsen wouldn't reoffend until September, a gap of four months.

This was a difficult period, during which he was overlooked for promotion at work, robbed of his wages in the street and had his flat broken into and vandalised, including the theft of his precious stereo. Such was Nilsen's depression, colleagues at work organised a collection for him to replace his damaged furniture and personal belongings.

By August 1981, he was back in the dangerously awkward position of the previous summer. Temperatures were rising and the smell of bodies beneath the boards was becoming unbearable. No amount of disinfectant and fly spray could combat the stench and threat to human health.

Once more, he tried to have a clear out; cutting up corpses, bagging organs, burying what he could in the garden or back under the boards. But it barely made a difference. By now, his relationship with his landlord had deteriorated and it seems the short cut solution of a bonfire of body parts was simply out of the question.

In September 1981, Nilsen broke his murderous fast, claiming the life of Malcolm Barlow, his twelfth victim. The twenty-three-year-old from the north of England had collapsed outside a property a few houses down on Melrose Avenue. Nilsen spotted him and, after discovering he was an epileptic, helped him into his flat and called an ambulance.

After being treated in hospital, Barlow returned the next day, ostensibly to thank his Good Samaritan and perhaps also beg a bed for the night. Nilsen invited him in and said he made them both a meal and they had more drinks. Afterward, the young northerner made the fatal mistake of falling asleep.

Malcolm was the last man to be strangled to death at Melrose Avenue.

In October, Nilsen was persuaded by his landlord and a letting agent to move out. They induced him with the offer of cash compensation and an attic flat in a tall, Edwardian house, about five miles away, at 23 Cranley Gardens. They also consented to his request to stage a goodbye bonfire, ostensibly so he could dispose of old belongings and rubbish he didn't want to take to the new abode.

This neat arrangement enabled him to dispose of the human remains that were now packed to bursting point beneath the floorboards.

After the fire, he scoured the ashes, raked away any remaining bones and dug into the ground anything that might arouse suspicions or prove incriminating.

The slate was clean again.

The move to Muswell Hill brought another cessation in the murders. But it only lasted until March 1982. A gap of about five months. The same 'cooling off' period as between his second victim Ken Ockenden and his third, Martyn Duffey, in May 1980.

In a West End pub, not far from the Leicester Square tube station, he bumped into a man in his twenties called John Howlett, whom he had briefly met before. Howlett said because he'd served in the Grenadier Guards, friends called him 'The Guardsman'. From the pub, he and Nilsen headed back to Cranley Gardens via the off-licence.

The former chef cooked and they drank until Howlett invited himself to stay the night by crashing out in his host's bed. It was there that Nilsen claimed what's recorded as his thirteenth victim, strangling him to death after a violent struggle that he later told police he'd almost lost.

'Summoning up all my strength, I forced him back down and his head struck the rim of the headrest on the bed. He still struggled fiercely so that now he was half off the bed. In about a minute, he had gone limp. There was blood on the bedding. I assumed it was from his head. I checked and he was still breathing deep, rasping breaths. I tightened my grip on him again around his neck for another minute or so. I let go of my grip again, and he appeared to be dead. I stood up. The dog was barking in the next room. I went through to pacify it. I was shaking all over with the stress of the struggle. I really thought he was going to get the better of me. I returned and was shocked to see that he had started breathing again. I looped the material round his neck again, pulled it as tight as I could and held on for what must have been two or three minutes. When I released my grip, he had stopped breathing.'

The same old ritual was playing out, but Nilsen faced a fresh problem. His new attic flat had little space beneath the boarded floor and no rear garden. If he intended to keep the corpse, it would have to be concealed in cupboards or wardrobes. And if he was going to dispose of it, then he had to devise a method other than burning it on a bonfire.

Three days after he'd killed Howlett, he decided he'd clean house.

At Melrose Avenue, Nilsen had dissected corpses on split bin-liner sheets laid out on the stone floor in the kitchen. In his new attic abode, the bath seemed the best bet. Predictably, he fell back on his Catering Corps cooking skills. He dismembered the corpse, removed the organs, chopped them up, then flushed them down the lavatory. It was so laborious he realised that this was not a viable option for the severed limbs, torso and head.

He fired up the stove and started cooking.

His hope was that he could boil flesh from bone, then smash the bones into small pieces that could be dumped in his dustbin or on waste ground near the flat. The human soup that he created poured more easily down the toilet. He boiled the man's head in a large cooking pot that would later be photographed on the stove by police teams and become infamous across the world.

Did he taste that 'soup'?

Did he cook any of those organs?

Devour any of that flesh?

During my meeting with Brian Masters in Oxford, I asked if he thought Nilsen had ever consumed any of his victims.

Apparently, it was a question he'd asked Nilsen and had received the glib reply, 'Oh no, I'm strictly a bacon and eggs man.' Masters added, 'I did laugh. It was a funny response to a serious question and it probably shows that he might have tried it once and didn't want to admit it, but I don't think he did it habitually. The idea of experimentation, even, if you'll forgive the word, "spiritual" experimentation – of taking the spirit of somebody else into your body and making them re-live in your flesh, is something they [necrophiles] do find attractive. So, it wouldn't surprise me at all to learn that he had attempted it, but I don't think he made a habit of it. He wasn't cannibalistic by nature.'*

I wasn't convinced and had put the question of human consumption to Nilsen in a letter but received no reply to it, while he had answered every other query. It's hard to think that this was an oversight by the notoriously fastidious clerical officer.

In Albany Prison, Paul Britton asked again.

Once more, Nilsen gave a less than forthright answer. 'It didn't interest me. It wasn't part of the fantasies.'

I noted that it wasn't a complete denial. A little later, in a

---

* Masters also wrote a book about self-confessed cannibal Jeffrey Dahmer, so is probably better placed than most to comment on this.

chilling echo of what Brian Masters had said about the like-
lihood that Nilsen had at least tried cannibalism, he told us,
'The bodies are all gone, everything's gone, there's nothing
left, but yes, I still feel a spiritual communion with these
people.'

It was a strange choice of words for an ardent atheist, one
who'd asserted, 'God didn't make Man, Man made God', to
come up with. Hundreds of millions of people have for centuries believed that when a priest blesses the communion wafer
during Catholic mass, an act of 'transubstantiation' takes place
– that is, the wafer, without changing appearance, becomes
the body and blood of Jesus Christ, so that when the recipient
swallows it, God is literally within them.

Was this Nilsen having fun at our expense? Alluding to a
final taboo, but not admitting it? Attempting to keep this dark
secret for his own personal enjoyment? Or were we all wrong
to assume that human soup was the only dish the former chef
created and never tasted?

By mid-afternoon in Albany Prison, a frown had etched its
way into Nilsen's forehead and much as he relished the sound
of his own voice and the rarity of an audience other than those
locked up with him, it looked like he too was beginning to
show the strain of being interviewed. But Paul Britton was
determined to complete the psychological journey through
the final victims up to Nilsen's arrest and the murderer's
personal reflections going to trial.

June 1982 marked the end of more than half a decade of
work in Denmark Street and Nilsen's promotion to the super-
visory grade of executive officer in Kentish Town, just a few
miles south of his new home.

If the extra responsibility he had taken on, the increase in
salary, and the good relationship he had struck up with his

supervisor Janet Leaman* provided settling feelings of well-being that muted his urges to murder, then the effect had run out by the end of summer.

In September 1982 (another gap of about five months since his last killing), Nilsen came across fellow Scot Graham Allen worse for wear in Piccadilly in central London.

The Glaswegian, in his late twenties, accepted the kind offer of a meal and a bed for the night. After making him an omelette, on which Nilsen claimed his guest almost choked, he strangled him to death.

This time, the corpse of victim fourteen was left in the bath and covered, as much as possible, in cold water.

Nilsen said that he kept Allen's body in there for about three days before he dismembered it then disposed of the innards in exactly the same cooking-and-flushing way he had done with John Howlett.

Almost another five months would pass, until, on 26 January 1983, Dennis Nilsen took the life of what detectives believe was his fifteenth and final victim.

Like many of the other murdered men, twenty-year-old Stephen Sinclair was small and vulnerable, standing only about 5 feet 5 inches tall. The young Scot had bleached blond hair and a lengthy history of juvenile crime, including drugs.

According to Nilsen, the familiar hunting part of the ritual played out. He spotted Sinclair in a pub, promised him food and drink, and ended up strangling him to death with a homemade ligature after the youngster fell asleep in a chair.

As usual, he bathed the corpse, but this time he needed to enhance the fantasy he generally played out, so he laid the

---

* Janet Leaman is believed to be the only colleague who visited Nilsen while he was on remand in Brixton Prison.

young man's body on his double bed, then, reverting to old masturbatory rituals, he first positioned a mirror so he could watch both himself and the corpse and then covered himself in talcum powder so he could look as dead as his companion. Profilers would identify this as a disturbing alteration of behaviour, as it signified he had grown bored with his usual ritual of murder and abuse and might have needed to kill more often in order to satisfy his cravings.

Once Nilsen's sexual appetite for abusing Sinclair's cadaver waned, he set about the laborious tasks of dismemberment and disposal. By now, he had become inured to the process.

'It was simply something that had to be done. Man can get used to some disturbing things if you are exposed to them for long enough. People got used to being in the trenches in the First World War and seeing a friend's brains blown all over them. The remains had no significance to me, they were something untoward and were simply awkward to get rid of.'

They were indeed awkward.

Dismemberment was relatively easy compared to the crucial task of disposal, upon which his liberty always depended. For the third time, Nilsen cut, cooked, crushed and flushed as many body parts as he could manage. Only on this occasion, he came unstuck. Or to be more precise, flesh and bones of his victims stuck in the communal drains.

The events that unfolded next, and the time span they covered, spoke volumes for the serial killer's state of mind during his final days of freedom.

Thursday, 3 February 1983 – another tenant in the building found his toilet wouldn't flush so he reported the problem to the letting agents.

Friday, 4 February – when it still hadn't been fixed, the

tenant's girlfriend toured the building and asked other renters, including Nilsen, if they had been experiencing problems.

He told her he hadn't.

When Nilsen shut the door on the woman, he knew his crimes were close to being discovered. He says he spent all day drinking and dismembering. Trying to make the evidence against him as small and disposable as possible. It really was a case of too little too late.

Saturday, 5th February – a plumber turned up and tried, unsuccessfully, to unblock the drains. The letting agents called Dyno-Rod, a firm specialising in large-scale drainage clearance. They said they couldn't send anyone until the start of the week. Nilsen was informed and advised not to use his toilet if at all possible.

Time was running out for the murderer.

Monday, 7th February – everyone went to work. Nilsen to his job in Kentish Town. Dyno-Rod to the problem drains at Cranley Gardens. The roulette wheel of discovery was now in full spin, and the studious executive officer working at his desk was well aware of it.

'I thought of getting out my passport, buying a plane ticket and going to live in a flat under Ronnie Biggs,* but I couldn't be bothered. I knew the police would come.'

It's highly debatable whether Nilsen did believe his arrest was inevitable, or whether he was arrogant enough to think he could, after years of burning bodies in gardens, once more get away with his crimes.

When he returned home from Kentish Town, he found the Dyno-Rod engineer hard at work, and true to his character,

---

* Ronnie Biggs was an infamous British criminal who had eluded Scotland Yard and fled to Brazil after robbing the Glasgow–London mail train of more than £2.5m ($3.4m) in 1963.

duly set about writing a letter of complaint to his landlords about the parlous state of the property he'd rented from them.

After penning the missive, he went back outside and heard the engineer, a former beach lifeguard who'd pulled rotting bodies from the sea, say, 'It looks like one for the Old Bill.'

Nilsen said he told him, 'It looks more to me like someone has been flushing their KFC.' He then returned to his flat and began drinking. Thinking. Worrying.

Later that night, around midnight, when he was satisfied everyone had gone to bed and that he wasn't likely to be seen (in fact, he was, by several neighbours), he crept down from his attic bolthole and did his best to clean the drain of all the visible flesh.

Tuesday, 8th February – Nilsen once more went to work. And so too did the Dyno-Rod man. During the day, the murderer's mind drifted from his job centre chores to Cranley Gardens.

'I thought to myself, "Well, Des, you can still pull this off." I had cleared much of the flesh from the sewer and there were only a few bits left to move. I thought of going down the road and buying some Kentucky Fried Chicken, then I'd break it into similar sized pieces and scatter them down the drain, leaving some of the wings and tips to be found. It was fifty per cent certain they'd go down the following day, and I decided to do nothing. It was a case of heads or tails. If they found the pieces, I was through. If not, I was free.'

The Dyno-Rod man noticed that the suspect blockage from the day before had been cleared. He called out his supervisor to inspect what remained. After examining what seemed like part of a human hand, they finally rang the police.

The officers that turned up took samples away to the mortuary for forensic analysis. A pathologist soon confirmed that the 'waste matter' was human flesh.

Wednesday, 9th February – Nilsen went to work for what he feared could be the last time. Paranoid that he might be arrested and killed in a police holding cell, he left a note saying that if anyone heard he had committed suicide they shouldn't believe it.

When Nilsen arrived back home, detectives from the Metropolitan Police CID were waiting to question him about the flesh and bone discovered in the drains.

Initially, he argued the contents could have come from any of the self-contained flats in the big old house, but then under pressure from Detective Chief Inspector Peter Jay, he admitted the remains were human and had come from his flat.

The game was up.

Numerous accounts in newspapers, books and court reports state that on the way to Hornsey police station from Cranley Gardens, Jay then asked Nilsen had he killed one man, two, or more? And Nilsen supposedly replied, 'Fifteen or sixteen.' It was a death toll that would, at the time, have made him the most prolific serial killer in British history.

'That's untrue,' he told us, fidgeting with his makeshift lighter on the prison table. Indignantly, he insisted, 'There were twelve. There weren't fifteen or sixteen. I was at the back of the police car heading to the police station, and at that moment of my arrest they'd asked me how many there were, and I didn't realise, I just gave them a figure. And because I was cooperating with the police, I decided I'd stick with it, you know. Three of those victims were invented just to complement the continuity of evidence of the police, just to keep them happy.'*

---

* Nilsen would continue to claim that the unidentified victims proved that his count of twelve was correct, rather than the fifteen recorded by detectives.

'Right at the end,' he continued, 'the pressure was getting worse and worse and I could see it all accelerating. If I hadn't been caught there could have been one a week, there could have been hundreds.'

As equally confusing as the number of people he killed, was the fact that he also spared the lives of several other men that he had begun to kill. At his trial, Nilsen faced six charges of murder and two of attempted murder. Those two men, Douglas Stewart and Paul Nobbs, gave evidence of how Nilsen tried to strangle them but ultimately let them go. A third survivor, Carl Stottor, appeared as a prosecution witness and said Nilsen had both strangled and drowned him then left him for dead. Bleep, the killer's dog, had detected human life and started licking and nuzzling him, and this had alerted Nilsen. Surprisingly, instead of finishing him off, he'd revived him. Looked after him all night. Even walked Stottor to the train station the next day, to make sure he got home okay.

Nilsen had no explanation for why he'd let any of these men go, other than to say, 'At those moments I felt something toward them, some form of humanity.'

I supposed that in those vital seconds, those men, for some reason – such as the dog's intervention – had stopped being only objects to Nilsen and had become people again, and that had broken his will to kill.

Paul Britton asked him how he had felt, when finally he'd been arrested, his secrets exposed, and he was publicly exposed as a serial murderer.

'I was relieved. All my demons were exorcised. I wallowed in it.'

His comment reminded me of the photograph I had seen of him in the back of the police van, an intrigued look in his eyes, the hint of a smile on his lips, as the national and international press photographers crowded around the vehicle, trying to snatch a glimpse of him.

Paul drew the interview to a close, 'Tell me who you are. Who is Dennis Nilsen?'

I remembered the long written reply he'd sent me when I'd asked the same question. The self-serving list of who and what he wasn't.

This time, he was a little more direct. Only a little.

'I did some terrible things, but there is some mitigation. I'm ordinary but unique in places. I don't fit in with the herd. I don't do what other people do. I'm different from everyone else. I have a uniqueness but that doesn't make me better than the herd. In some ways, I'm definitely more moral. I couldn't be bribed, for example. I don't bully people and I don't pick on people.'

Paul thanked him and said we were done.

Done?

I was almost as surprised as Nilsen.

As mentally exhausted as we all were, I thought we should continue. Surely we needed to revisit some of the inconsistencies? Press him on points that hadn't quite rung true? Get him to expand on those short, evasive statements and clarify his contradictions?

No.

Paul insisted that the interview was over. To put the matter beyond doubt, he had taken to standing up and shaking Nilsen's hand, who plainly did not want to leave. Leaving meant he was no longer the centre of attention. Leaving meant returning to 'the herd'.

From this moment, until we departed, he blanked Paul. He looked only at me and quickly asked again about the documentary – when was it intended to go to air, how long it might be in duration, how much of his interview would be seen?

When he ran out of questions, he babbled about a brief affair he'd had with someone 'in London's film circles' and how he'd missed his true calling.

'I should have gone into TV, or film,' he told me as I began to pack away the equipment. 'The only thing I could have been good at was making films. I think at the end of the day, I could have made it in movies, if only I'd had the guts to leave the civil service.'

13

AFTERMATH

I came away from Albany Prison elated and confused.

Elated that Nilsen had taken part and been so forthcoming.

Confused by the way Paul Britton had unilaterally finished the interview, followed by a demand from the two policemen that they took away all copies of the tapes, including the ones from the Central TV camera.

It was possible, I feared, that I had just recorded the first ever TV interview with a British serial killer and now, for reasons beyond my control, it might never get broadcast. Worse still, it might get lost, destroyed or never used to inform detectives about how offenders like Nilsen really think and act.

Once I was back in our Nottingham studios, I called John Stevens and left a message asking for a call back.

My worries were heightened sometime later when I spoke to Paul. He said he had obtained the tapes I'd shot and was still supportive of me using extracts for the documentary, but the decision on whether that was possible lay with the Home Office, not him.

That hadn't been the deal. He knew it. And so did I. My cooperation had been on the assurance that I would be able to show not only Paul conducting the interview, but some of the interview as well.

The rules of the game had been changed.

Paul said that he now had custody of the broadcast tapes

I'd shot on the Central TV camera and needed domestic standard copies to play on his office VHS video machine.

I suggested he bring them into our studios so we could make copies.

He agreed, but stressed he would have to take both the copies and the originals away with him.

I promised him he could do exactly that.

When Paul arrived at our studios in Lenton Lane, I met him downstairs and we chatted briefly, walking through to the VT suite where I'd arranged for the copying to take place. He was guarded and a little aloof. Very business-like. If I'd had any doubts that something out of my control was in play, they disappeared as he settled in a chair, and I left him to vigilantly watch the tapes being copied.

The transfer took close to four hours and I'm told he never left the room for a minute.

When it was completed, we shook hands and he left.

Unbeknown to Paul, I had arranged for the VT suite he'd been using to be linked to one down the corridor, where I'd instructed a technician to make another set of high-resolution copies of the tapes. In my mind, I now had what was rightfully ours – the full interview with Dennis Nilsen – the interview that I had envisaged, instigated, arranged and recorded.

All that was left was for me to update my boss, Steve Clark, on what I'd done, and prepare us for the inevitable complaints that would follow from the Home Office, the Association of Chief Police Officers, Chief Constable John Stevens and, of course, Paul Britton.

After briefing our lawyers, I was instructed by them to inform both Paul and John Stevens that we had copies of our tapes and intended to use them in the documentary as originally planned.

This I did.

I felt awful telling Paul that I had lied to him.

Always calm and polite, he characteristically took the news very coolly and professionally.

At the time, I was simply relieved that he hadn't thrown an entirely justifiable tantrum and threatened recriminations, such as complaining to the TV watchdogs of the era. Later, I'd wondered whether the expert profiler had profiled me, and fully anticipated I would sneak a copy of the tapes if given the chance to do so. Perhaps he'd even discussed such a possibility with John Stevens and they'd agreed to give me that opportunity?

The rest of September passed without much legal development and I spent the time working on the programme and consulting with Bob Ressler and Roy Hazelwood.

At the start of October, I received a letter from a Home Office press officer, saying:

Thank you for your assistance in the interview between Paul Britton and Dennis Nilsen at Albany Prison. You should know that it did leak out in some of the national newspapers. But we have attempted to minimise the interest so as to keep the story under wraps for Central TV. Of course, you will not be using the film, sound or written extracts from the interview because it was undertaken for police research use only and not for broadcasting. Inspector Laidler of Northumbria Constabulary was required to give the prison authorities a written undertaking to this effect.

I had never agreed that none of the interview would be used for broadcasting. To the contrary – I'd *only* consented to facilitate it on the understanding that some of it would be broadcast. It seemed the Home Office were completely unaware that the approach to Nilsen had entirely been my idea.

No matter.

Everything would probably be okay in the end.

Or so I thought.

As far as I was concerned, I had been dealing directly with ACPO, on the understanding that they dealt with everyone else (the Home Office, the Prison Authority, etc.), and the verbal agreement, as I understood it, had been that I arranged the interview with Nilsen, Paul Britton asked the questions because he was a profiler and the intention was that the interview would be of use to other profilers and detectives, and I would get to use extracts.

I had fully understood and willingly agreed to rule out broadcasting anything from the interview (or any other interviews granted by ACPO) that would be 'instructional'* to any possible offenders in helping them evade capture or commit crimes.

I showed the letter to Steve and his take was that matters were now becoming politically charged. He thought it likely that all permissions had been granted, but then, when the politicians (Home Secretary, Home Office ministers, etc.) had found out that the interview had taken place, they'd 'wanted to shut the stable door after the horse had bolted'.

A little later, I attended an official and somewhat awkward ACPO/Home Office Offender Profiling meeting called by John Stevens. After I updated everyone on the progress of the

---

* A big ACPO concern had been that Nilsen would disclose a forensic practice that allowed him to evade capture, and if details of this were broadcast they would be seen by other serial offenders who might adjust their behaviour and stay free to kill again.

documentary, it became apparent that the real purpose of the gathering was to discuss what was now referred to as 'The Dennis Nilsen Tapes'.

I stated in no uncertain terms that I considered the recordings that I'd made to belong to Central TV, and while I intended to honour our original agreement about excluding sensitive content if necessary, Central would go to court to assert its right to broadcast the material.

John Stevens was every bit as cool, polite and professional as Paul Britton had been when I'd told him about the copied tapes. It was in stark contrast to the Home Office press officer who was also present. The expression of rage on his face spoke volumes. He'd clearly been instructed to shut everything down, take custody of the copied tapes, and bury this file deep in a dusty Whitehall basement.

Once more, I returned to the studios and the machinations of documentary making.

As I began to edit and started to write the script, I could see that ACPO had given me an enormous amount of exclusive access. As well as the Nilsen interview, I'd been allowed to film how CATCHEM worked, record meetings between ACPO and the Home Office discussing offender profiling, and had, with ACPO consent, carried out several interviews with profilers such as David Canter, Mike Berry and Paul Britton.

To my surprise, I was invited by John Stevens to accompany him, Paul and other profilers to Russia to meet psychologists, psychiatrists and detectives working on similar projects, to see if an information and cooperation exchange was viable.

It seemed to me that my own personal Cold War, if not over, was at least thawing.

We filmed at the Serbsky Institute in Moscow, the country's

top mental assessment centre for murderers, rapists and child offenders. A team of psychologists had drawn up a lengthy psychological profile that had recently proved instrumental in helping catch schoolteacher Andrei Chikatilo, the so-called Rostov Ripper. He was a sexual sadist, who over a period of about a decade, had murdered fifty-three men, women and children. He'd raped and mutilated his victims during and after stabbing them to death, sometimes even eating body parts as they lay dying.

I was given exclusive access to the team who'd drawn up the profile and also police footage of Chikatilo. In it, he uses a plastic knife and various human dolls to re-enact how he carried out his heinous crimes.

During the visit, the delegation also discovered that Russian profilers had carried out the world's largest interview programme of serial murderers and rapists, even dwarfing the FBI project started by Bob Ressler and John Douglas.

On camera, John Stevens told me, 'What we found extremely interesting and extremely valuable is, of course, they have done interviews with three hundred offenders, in depth, sometimes taking place over a month. Now, we haven't had the ability to do that in the United Kingdom, because of the restrictions that we place in terms of convicted prisoners; and that's tremendous value in terms of what we've found out. Because of the Chikatilo murders, which have been a catalyst, they've put all their efforts in, all their eminent psychiatrists and psychologists in, into interviewing these people, to come up with trends and find out what actually makes these people act in the way that they do.'

Over the next few days, Stevens brokered an agreement to get access to the Russian data for British use. On camera, Paul Britton told me that he felt it would prove to be vital. 'I think it will help us to be very clear about the detailed motivation of offenders. In details such as their life history, family circumstances, it would give us the opportunity to add full flesh to the bones that we have from statistical material, and that of course will enable our investigating officers to bring these sort of offences to a conclusion very much more quickly than they otherwise would.'

I saw the access I'd been given and the two interviews I'd recorded as hugely significant. They reinforced my belief that the Nilsen interview was important and that police in the UK wanted to embark upon a larger scale programme of interviewing serial offenders.

On returning to the UK, I was somewhat horrified to discover that Central TV's legal department had written to the Home Office, essentially demanding that it showed its hand. Our lawyers wrote:

As Central do wish to avoid litigation and, in particular, any eleventh-hour interlocutory applications to the courts, I am writing to you to request that the Home Office state their position on use of the film to Central in writing. I trust that that position accords with Central's own.

Basically, the TV station was hoping to avoid any last-minute attempts by the Home Office to get a court order that would ban the broadcast, now planned for 26th January 1993. It also, I imagined, wanted to avoid all the costs of hiring top barristers to fight our corner.

A response came from the Treasury solicitor not only claiming that it wanted to block the broadcast, but stating that the Home Office now considered *it* owned the copyright of the interview and would not grant us permission to use any footage.

A big, public battle was now almost inevitable. And distracting.

To the best of my abilities, I forgot about the external issues and focused on the Nilsen interview. Listening to it over and over again was both darkly depressing and frustrating. The programme I was making was about offender profiling, not *only* about Dennis Nilsen. Nevertheless, his interview had been so rich in content that it undoubtedly warranted an hour on its own.

Maybe more.

If I added analysis from the likes of Paul Britton, Bob Ressler, Roy Hazelwood, David Canter and Mike Berry, it could make four sixty-minute episodes.

Because of the government opposition to the filming, I knew the time wasn't right to suggest anything other than using short sections of it in *Murder in Mind*. I needed to stick to the deal that the filming had been done to show Paul Britton, a Home Office accredited profiler, interviewing a British serial killer for the first time.

Steve Clark thought we'd have a big enough battle doing that, let alone arguing for extra programming on the serial killer.

We both knew there was a distinct possibility that Central TV's owners or its board might cave to political pressure and instruct us not to include any footage of Nilsen, which would have left us with no alternative but to resign.

There was also a chance that the Treasury solicitor and our lawyers might get tangled up in out-of-court discussions, and as a result we would face the dilemma of pushing back the transmission, or broadcasting as planned but without the Nilsen interview.

And of course, there was a possibility of the Home Office

seeking and winning a High Court injunction to stop the entire programme *ever* being broadcast.

In the end, we came up with strong alternative strategies.

The first, was to cut an hour-long documentary that contained a proportionate amount of Nilsen footage – i.e., treating the interview with no greater importance and no longer duration than the other sections such as CATCHEM, Chikatilo, VICAP, etc.

The second, was to cut Nilsen and all references to him out of the documentary completely.

The third, based on the potential of a ban applying only to transmission of the *recorded* interview, was to have an actor voice everything Nilsen had said, with Ressler and Hazelwood adding reactions and analysis.

Steve valiantly shouldered all the internal politics, legal discussions and the growing concerns of commissioners at the ITV Network Centre* about the programme contents. He took on the burden of liaising with all the external lawyers and the intended handling of the media once the story broke. It would only be a matter of time before news got out that the interview had been done, and once it did, there would be an explosion of interest. As a former journalist, I knew exactly what that would entail. It would mean reporters and photographers outside our homes, cars, anywhere we ate or visited, until they got enough on the story to satisfy their news desks. And that treatment wouldn't just be for the two of us. It would be the same for anyone who'd worked on the programme, including lawyers, researchers, cameramen – in short, anyone who might have

---

* ITV is a network of regional TV franchises in the UK, sharing a common schedule of programmes, coordinated by a London-based HQ known as the ITV Network Centre.

had a glimpse of the Nilsen material and could comment on it.

As well as having multiple back-up copies of all tapes and transcripts kept in multiple locations, we knew we'd have to request double security measures at our Nottingham and Birmingham studios. Journalists would try to get jobs as cleaners or site managers so they could go through the offices at night. Or they'd turn up pretending to be actors or guests appearing on other programmes being recorded there, such as dramas and game shows, and they'd sit around in the canteens asking questions. And if they got a bite, then they'd throw money at anyone who they thought could give them a quote about the documentary.

Christmas 1992 saw me spend little time at home and even less time sleeping. Preparing three hour-long documentaries for possible broadcast inside a month was taking its toll, but not nearly as much as Nilsen was. He was in my head all the time.

It would be overdramatic to say I was suffering PTSD from the interview – I wasn't. But I was deeply depressed, barely slept, and even during the day I struggled to clear my mind of images of what Nilsen had done and how he'd done it.

Being in the room with the serial killer, shaking his hand, fitting his microphone, feeling his breath on my neck, hearing his voice, seeing expressions on his face and certain looks in his eyes – all those things had changed how I viewed what he'd done.

His crimes were now much more vivid in my mind.

Seeing and hearing him so casually recount more than a dozen acts of murder and necrophilia had been troubling enough, but then I had taken that material away and replayed it over and over again in order to decide which sections might fit best into the documentary. I'd had to discuss each and every one of his most disturbing comments with Bob Ressler and Roy Hazelwood to understand them and to decide what quotes we'd use. I'd had to write scripts incorporating our research and explaining Nilsen's fantasies.

And once I stopped considering the Nilsen material, then the rest of the programme was as equally dark – child murders in the UK, serial rape in the US, cannibalism in Russia. Every frame of this whole damned documentary was a deep-dive into the minds and actions of the most appalling individuals known to mankind. To paraphrase Ted Bundy's death row words to Bill Hagmaier, the big fish had dragged me under.

Now I wanted out.

I wanted it all to stop.

As tiredness and depression mounted, I reminded myself that in the USA, I'd interviewed an FBI profiler called Larry McCann. Witty, smart and kind, his desk had been stacked with active cases, many as bad as the ones I had detailed in the documentary. He'd said he'd had to learn 'to leave the killers and those they killed' outside his home. 'If you don't, you go crazy,' he'd said with a wry smile. I hadn't fully under-stood what he'd meant at the time, but I did now.

I reminded myself that my immersion in these dark pools was entirely voluntary. I could get out if I truly wanted. Someone else could finish the documentary. Steve would do it if necessary. People like Larry McCann couldn't do that. Lives depended upon him and his colleagues staying in those awfully depressing mind zones, staying there until all the monstrous activity of a murder made sense to them and they caught people like Dennis Nilsen. And having caught them, they went back to the stack on the desk and started a new case, a new hunt for a new monster.

*

Stood in a clearing in a forest in Virginia, the scene of a past murder, McCann had chillingly explained to me a new category of offender appearing on investigatory radars. 'Some of us go to a ballgame, some of us sit down, have a beer and watch TV, and some people kill – just for the thrill of killing. It's what we call recreational homicide.'

I marked it out as the opening soundbite of *Murder in Mind*. Maybe that's what all the offender profiling analysis boiled down to.

Serial killers kill because they like it.

Like it as mundanely as liking beer. As watching sports. Certainly, Des Nilsen had talked about his crimes in that same disarming matter of fact way. Killing is what he did. Murder was his secret pastime.

And he was by no means unique.

After months of requests and correspondence, serial killer Robert Berdella had agreed to be interviewed for the programme. Briefed by Bob Ressler, I had flown to Missouri to do the interview myself. When I arrived, I had to lie and say that the woman journalist he'd been writing and had expected to see had been unable to come for personal reasons.

Like Nilsen, Berdella had grown up as a closeted homosexual in a deeply religious family feeling he was unloved, especially by his father. He had been bullied for being effeminate and was repeatedly called 'a sissy' and 'a faggot'.

Like Nilsen, he had done okay at school, but not exceptionally well. The only thing he seemed to have had a talent for was art. He progressed to art school but then dropped out.

Like Nilsen, he was of above average intelligence, exceptionally opinionated and narcissistic.

Like Nilsen, Berdella had preyed mainly on young down-and-outs, homosexuals and rent boys whom he picked up in gay bars while looking for casual sex partners. Once he lured them back to his home in Kansas City, with the promise of shelter and food and drink, he drugged and overpowered them.

Now the similarities fade. Berdella fantasised about live victims, not dead ones.

He gagged the young men and bound their hands and feet. He tied them to his bed and injected drain cleaner into their throats, destroying their vocal cords so that they could not scream or be heard if he took off their gags.

Then he used them as sex toys.

He beat them with boards, sticks and whips.

He anally raped them and had frictional sex all over their bodies.

He pushed his fingers through the eyeballs of some of his live victims and electrocuted their genitals. All the time, he photographed them and kept a diary detailing what type of torture he had administered and how the victim had reacted.

I interviewed Berdella in Jefferson City Correctional Centre, where he'd been sent after being sentenced to life imprisonment. He was tall and bespectacled like Nilsen, but chubby. He had big round glasses, swept-back thinning brown hair, and was clean-shaven, save a thick moustache.

'I never found bondage to be that exciting or stimulating,' he told me in a manner every bit as casual as Nilsen's. 'I'm much more turned on by very cooperative, consensual, mutually satisfying sex.'

'How do you reconcile that,' I asked, 'to what you did to your victims?'

'Don't have a clue.' He laughed. 'I don't have a clue. Don't-have-a-clue!' His grin widened. 'You know, to put it in rather simple language, tying up and beating somebody is not an aphrodisiac to me, it's not stimulating. It was done to perhaps control these individuals, to modify them, to make them controllable, so they would be consensual.'

Like Nilsen, power and control over a passive and compliant victim had been central to Berdella's crimes. He told me, 'I felt like I had little control on the rest of my life. I had to get a handle on something, have something that I could do what I wanted with, whenever I wanted.'

Berdella tortured his victims so violently that to all intents and purposes they were every bit as compliant as Nilsen's corpses.

'In one case, the only time my victim was tied down was when I left the house,' he said proudly. 'I slept with him in the bed, right next to me, the only restraint on him being a dog leash around his neck. His hands were free, his legs were free. If he wanted to do me harm, all he had to do was roll over and there I was.'

'Why do you think he didn't?' I asked.

'I don't know.' Berdella smiled. 'I guess at that point he was broken, he was afraid, he was under control.'

'And how did you feel about him?' I asked.

'That I had succeeded. That I had a willing sex toy. I had a sexual zombie under my control. No back chat, no complications, no objections, no resistance to my will.'

Berdella objectified his victims in the same way that Nilsen had. When it came to disposing of their victims, they were also remarkably similar. Berdella would dismember the body, wrap the parts in newspapers, put them into dog-food bags, then in thick, plastic garbage bags that he'd leave out for the weekly garbage truck.

'In my mind, I was putting trash out.' He waved a hand dismissively. 'This was just garbage to go to the city dump, that's all. I didn't enjoy it, I just got on with it.'

When Berdella was arrested, two heads that he'd kept as trophies were found in closets, while human remains were discovered in his back garden. Like Nilsen, he couldn't remember the names of many of his victims. He said he wasn't sure he'd ever known them. Names didn't matter to him.

Again, like Nilsen, there had been many other men that he'd lured back to his home, had tied up and abused, only to then let them return to their broken lives.

'They didn't fit the criteria,' Berdella explained to me. 'I had a certain criteria for victims, and these men, the ones I let go, didn't resist being tied up – in fact, some of them liked it – so I had no sense of exerting power, no satisfaction of conquering them, of gaining control, so there was no thrill to be had from retaining them after we'd had sex.'

I'd promised the serial killer I'd send him a tape of the transmitted documentary in the hope the authorities there would let him watch it.

I never did.

Robert Berdella died in jail of a heart attack less than a month after my interview with him and before I'd finished editing the documentary.

The Berdella section of *Murder in Mind* ran to just over five minutes and I decided it would come towards the end, just before the Nilsen interview, so comparisons could easily be made between the two men. The documentary would then end with on-screen conclusions from Britton, Ressler and Hazelwood about the value of psychological profiling in halting the run of serial offenders and saving lives.

In January 1993, the machinery of network documentary-making was running full tilt and I was in danger of burning out. Twelve-hour days had become eighteen-hour days that had somehow grown into sleeping for an hour or two on a back-breaking sofa in my office and then drinking enough vending-machine coffee to raise a corpse from a coffin.

I seemed to have an endless to-do list.

Title sequences had to be finalised, graphics double-checked for errors, voiceover scripts completed and then approved by internal and external lawyers. Music that I had commissioned for the documentary needed to be edited against particular sections. Sound effects had to be selected and dubbed into newsreel footage that was mute, or where recording levels were low or damaged. Library footage of Nilsen, Berdella and others needed clearing with the copyright owners. Video press kits containing clips from profilers, policemen, Berdella and Nilsen had to be prepared, cleared and sent to various media departments.

Then there were the final stages of editing the documentary and its various alternative versions. In my experience, there are usually at least ten different cuts from first cut to final cut – the one that goes into sound dubbing and is ultimately broadcast. Sometimes this can be nearer twenty. Uncertainty over the Nilsen interview meant we had to double this process, so that an alternative documentary would be ready if we were stopped in our tracks by a Home Office injunction.

Programme timing always had to be precise. If you were given a transmission slot of fifty-two minutes and six seconds, then that's exactly how long it had to be. Not a second more or less. Commercials had to be played before, during and after the show, and the durations of the ad breaks were sacrosanct. You couldn't cut an advertiser's slot. Not unless the whole of the earth had suddenly caught fire.

In the 1990s, advanced publicity for TV programming was obtained by sending a preview copy of the programme to national and local newspaper TV columnists, usually about six weeks before planned transmission. Something we couldn't risk doing because we didn't want to send up flares in front of the House of Commons and provoke legal action.

As it turned out, they'd already been provoked enough.

I was still editing when we were served with legal papers declaring that the Home Office had applied to the High Court for an injunction to stop the programme being broadcast. The case was listed for the day before intended airing.

I almost collapsed in a fit of ironic laughter.

After months of waiting, the government had deliberately got a court slot the day before broadcast. They knew that if the hearing lasted more than a day, we could miss transmission. And if we lost, then there would be no time to appeal against the injunction.

Their timing was masterfully brutal.

Once news of the application for the injunction became public, tensions rose among Central TV senior management, our owners Carlton TV, and the ITV Network Centre. Inevitably, national journalists were now all over the story and I was glad to escape our Nottingham studios, pack a suitcase and catch a train south to the capital.

On 25th January, the day before the intended broadcast, I watched the early morning TV news in a London hotel room. Bill Clinton had just begun his first term as the US President, with Al Gore as VP. The Monika Lewinsky scandal was still years away from breaking.

In the UK, there were reports that Princess Diana had declared she wanted a divorce from Prince Charles.* John

---

* Charles and Diana had separated in December '92. In November '92, the famous Camillagate tapes had leaked (intimate telephone conversations between Charles and Camilla).

Major, the prime minister of the UK government, was coming under growing criticism because of the country's economic crisis* and his lengthy affair with Health Minister Edwina Currie was about to become news.

In the taxi on the way to the High Court, the cabbie droned on about the weekend performance of Manchester United, one of the football teams I hated most in the world, and then hummed badly out of tune to Whitney Houston's 'I Will Always Love You' as it played on his tinny radio. I considered getting out and walking.

Britain's High Court is part of the architecturally magnificent Royal Courts of Justice, occupying twenty-four thousand square metres of prime real estate on the Strand in Westminster, just over a mile away from the Houses of Parliament.

Externally and internally, it has the appearance of a cathedral, all weathered stone and vaulted ceilings, hard, cold floors, soaring archways, gigantic Royal crests on walls as big as houses, labyrinthine corridors lined with sturdy stone pillars strong enough to support the universe, and multiple floors joined by cascading stone staircases.

After some searching, Steve Clark and I found a notification that told us the case of The Secretary of State for the Home Office Department v Central Broadcasting Ltd was being heard in the Chancery Division.

By the time we reached our designated court, I couldn't decide whether my heart was thundering from the exertion of the walk and the excitement of the scenery, or the fear that more than a year of hard work might within minutes be destroyed.

---

* 'Black Wednesday' had happened just a few months earlier – so-called because the British government had been forced to withdraw the rapidly falling pound from the European Exchange Rate Mechanism.

Our external lawyers were Mischon de Reya,* one of the most powerful law companies in the country, and just before the hearing began, we briefly discussed the case with our legal team, Peter Prescott QC and Alexander Drysdale Wilson.

Peter had been engaged because he was an expert in intellectual property and the main thrust of the government's claim was that they owned the copyright of the recording. It was built upon the shaky premise that they owned the jail in which the recording had taken place, and the interviewee, Dennis Nilsen, had only been able to appear because they allowed it. We, of course, argued otherwise, and additionally raised our concern that what the Home Office was really attempting to do amounted to state censorship and a denial of freedom of speech.

What unfolded beneath the elevated platform of Justice Aldous was courtroom drama of the highest order, complete with all the props, costumes, characters and legal scripting you'd expect of a primetime television show.

Appearing for the secretary of state was Michael Silverleaf, another IP heavyweight. He repeated the claims made in letters sent to us by the Treasury solicitor that the interview had never been intended for broadcast and had only ever been sanctioned for police use. Allowing the broadcast, he contended, would encourage sensational journalism, increase Dennis Nilsen's notoriety, flout Home Office policies and cause distress to the families of Nilsen's victims. Furthermore, he asserted that I had obtained it by deception, insisting that Home Office permission had not been granted and I therefore had no right to have been in the jail.

---

* Mischon de Reya also acted as divorce lawyers for Princess Diana in her settlement with Prince Charles.

Our QC, Peter Preston, pointed out that I had passed through prison security for two days running, had printed and signed my name in the visitor's book, and at all times had been accompanied by at least one prison officer, two senior policemen and a highly respected Home Office accredited clinician. It was left to the High Court judge to decide whether it was possible for me to have done that and carried out a lengthy interview with a Category A prisoner without permission.

To my surprise, and disappointment, permission didn't seem to be a big issue for Lord Aldous. Nor did our arguments about freedom of speech and matters of public interest. These, I had thought, were the three strongest tenants of our case. Instead, he seemed more interested in the issue of copyright, and this made both Steve and I nervous. It wasn't our area of expertise and we sat in anxious silence as arguments raged not over whether the contents of the interview were suitable for broadcast, but who actually *owned* the interview.

Did the Home Office own it because they had provided the venue and the prisoner?

Did Central TV own it because we had arranged the interview and had filmed it?

Did Dennis Nilsen own it because he was the subject of the interview and it was his image and voice that had been recorded?

Did Paul Britton own it because he had asked the questions?

My nerves jangled.

It seemed to me that one possible outcome was that *everyone* owned the interview.

Joint ownership would mean joint permissions would have to be granted and it was blatantly obvious the Home Office wouldn't now allow me permission to breathe, let alone run extracts of the Nilsen tapes on network television.

We countered claims that the interview glamourised Nilsen's crimes and injured the feelings of his victims' families and friends with sworn affidavits from two leading experts.

Bob Ressler's statement said:

As part of my professional work, I have had to interview numerous relatives of victims of violent crimes. It was part of my research for offender profiling. I have been specifically asked whether showing a programme like Murder in Mind containing the interview with the murderer Nilsen may cause pain and suffering for the relatives of his victims. I say not likely in the way this programme has been done, more likely the opposite. It might be different if the victims were identified but this is not so here. It is psychologically important to families who are victims of violent crimes that they feel something positive is being done about stopping similar criminals. Emotionally, relatives need to feel this. Given that their loved one has been killed, I believe most relatives would feel better if the loss of their loved one was in some way being used to prevent such evils, which is what is done in offender profiling.

Additional testimony came from one of the world's most respected forensic scientists, Professor Derrick Pounder, Head of Forensic Medicine at Dundee University.

I have been asked to comment on whether this programme, and specifically the Nilsen interview, would cause distress to the victims' families. I am of the opinion that Central TV has minimised any damage the Nilsen interview might cause to relatives in two ways:

   (a) Nilsen only talks about his victims after their deaths, as corpses; and

   (b) it is a very generalised interview with no names of victims mentioned.

Inevitably, some degree of pain and suffering is bound to be experienced due to the subjects that the programme seeks to cover. This will happen whether or not the Nilsen interview is included. Each relative will have a very individual reaction to the programme dependent on how he/ she has dealt with the grieving process caused by the loss of a loved one.

The hours bled away.

Attention swung to past cases. Legal precedents. Clauses from dusty old law books.

We got to late afternoon, and to my horror, Judge Aldous adjourned the case until the following morning – the day of transmission.

The worst of my fears were coming true.

There was now every chance that the case would continue beyond the next day and we would lose our slot in the TV schedules.

Steve called the Network Centre and updated them, advising that they needed to have a completely different programme ready to run tomorrow night in case we didn't have a court resolution.

We left the hallowed halls of the High Court in litigation limbo and, with the prospect of another day in court looming large, we resisted the urge to drown our sorrows in a pub.

Steve spent most of the evening updating everyone in the station's senior management positions who needed updating, which meant endlessly repeating all the legal arguments. I did the same with my production team, all of whom had invested months of their lives and astounding amounts of skill and patience in the documentary and were now wondering whether it would all amount to nothing.

Another sleepless night followed.

Staring at the ceiling of the hotel bedroom, I marvelled at the absurdity of it all. Four minutes of film had somehow managed to cause a heavyweight fight to the death between the country's biggest TV company and the government of the United Kingdom. Tens of thousands of pounds of taxpayers' money was being spent to stop us showing about two hundred and fifty seconds of footage.

Why?

All because it wasn't Home Office policy to allow prisoners like Nilsen to be interviewed for TV.

Maybe it was time to change that policy.

I thought of the man at the centre of it all. Dennis Andrew Nilsen. If he knew what was going on, I was certain he'd be roaring with laughter. I'd never seen him laugh. Nothing more than a thin smile. But this would have him beaming from ear to ear.

The Home Office's action in taking the case to court guaranteed that win or lose, Nilsen was back in the front-page headlines.

At 4 a.m. I abandoned all hope of rest and rang Bob Ressler to update him. He said if the worst came to the worst, he'd willingly go on camera and talk about what a bad decision it was not to show the footage. I thanked him and resumed the pointless task of trying to force myself to go to sleep.

My insomnia proved to be valuable. By the time the court reconvened, I was too tired to be nervous.

Bleary-eyed, I sat impatiently on the hard wooden bench reserved for defendants and braced myself for the inevitable. From the way the QCs were arguing, I could see proceedings dragging on all day. Maybe all week. The judge could so easily duck the issue of granting – or not granting – an injunction, simply by not coming to a decision quickly enough for it to matter. If we lost our slot, it might be months before we got a new one.

I looked at the clock and could see it would soon be lunchtime. That would mean another break. More delays. A mid-afternoon restart. Nothing was done at lightning pace in the High Court. Everything was measured. Considered. Painfully slow.

Or so I thought.

To our complete surprise, Judge Aldous announced that he'd come to a ruling.

'The injunction is denied,' he declared undramatically. He went on to say that he had decided that the extract contained in the documentary did not glamourise Nilsen, the facts about his murders had already been well-known and it was beneficial (as Bob Ressler had stated in his submission to the court) that the public could see how normal a serial killer might appear.

Great points, I thought. I couldn't have put it better myself. We were free to broadcast.

It wasn't even midday and we'd won. In a little over ten hours, the programme would go to air. We shook hands with our legal gladiators and focused on the most pressing matter.

Publicity.

Steve masterminded a plan to stage an afternoon pressshowing of the documentary at the London offices of our parent company Carlton Television. It would be followed by a questions-and-answers session with national news journalists and TV critics.

We phoned everyone that needed to be looped in and grabbed sandwiches for lunch. For the first time in weeks, I began to relax.

Oddly, Steve didn't.

'I don't think this is over yet,' he said, completely spoiling my mood.

'They *lost*,' I reminded him. 'No injunction. We heard the judge say it. No injunction.'

'It's the government. They won't let it rest there. They'll appeal.'

I thought he was nuts. 'They might want to, but there isn't time. You can't just get in the Court of Appeal at the drop of a hat. It takes months or years for appeal cases to be listed there.'

'Maybe it doesn't if you're the Home Secretary or prime minister.'

I wrote such a notion off as nonsense. Steve always saw another angle and planned for it. This was his pessimistic genes messing with his chemistry. I guessed he wouldn't unwind until the show had actually aired.

While the press screening of *Murder in Mind* began, I was checking that the right TX copy of the documentary was at the Network Centre and would be ready for playout.

Then came news from our legal team.

The government *had* appealed.

Steve was right.

The case was to be heard, virtually immediately, in the highest court in the land. Not only that, but we also had to halt the press screening of the documentary, otherwise we'd be in contempt of court.

In front of rolling TV cameras from the UK's top news stations, plus dozens of national news reporters, Steve had to literally pull the plug on the press-viewing and tell everyone that we were back in court and they couldn't report on anything they'd seen – or they too would be breaking the law.

14

JUDGMENT

The nervousness I'd experienced stepping into the High Court was nothing compared to the hand-trembling fear that gripped me at 2 p.m. on Tuesday, 26th January, as I settled into the echoey chamber of the Court of Appeal.

The three justices, mustered at little more than a moment's notice, were none other than the Master of the Rolls, Sir Thomas Bingham,* Anthony McCowan† and David Hirst.‡

These were the biggest of the big hitters.

The heaviest of the legal heavyweights.

I couldn't help but wonder whether they'd be truly impartial, or had they been called in because they would tow the government line in the case, now listed as The Secretary of State for the Home Department v Central Broadcasting and Another.§

The government had looped Britton into the action, presumably to ensure that he couldn't claim copyright either.

---

* Sir Thomas would go on to become Lord Chief Justice and be acclaimed as 'the greatest English judge since the Second World War'.

† Anthony McCowan had famously sat on the Official Secrets case (and acquittal) of Clive Ponting, the civil servant who leaked documents about the controversial sinking of the Argentine vessel the ARA *General Belgrano* during the Falklands War.

‡ David Hirst was the son of a former Master of the Rolls. As a QC, he had represented Paul McCartney, The Beatles and the Bee Gees and had only been appointed as a Court of Appeals judge in 1992, the year before our hearing.

§ 'Another' was Paul Britton.

Before the legal arguments began, we learned that the appeal had been granted because the Home Office claimed the High Court judge Justice Aldous 'had erred' by taking too little account of potential distress to relatives and friends of Nilsen's victims and of potential damage to Home Office research, and 'the fact that damage was irreparable in the sense that once the interview was broadcast it could never be withdrawn'.

Furthermore, Justice Aldous was said to have 'given undue weight to the evidence of two experts*on behalf of the first defendant'. And that 'the effect of refusing the injunction was to condone subterfuge by the first defendant'.

There was only really one exhibit for the Justices to scrutinise. The documentary itself.

A large TV on a rolling stand, complete with video playback machine, was wheeled in. Cue a moment's comedy. No one could make it work. The three wise men stared patiently at a blank screen as a court official turned the plug on and off, pressed a variety of buttons and became increasingly stressed.

'Your Honours, I can make it work,' I declared confidently.

An usher called me forward.

Fixing it was just a case of shifting a cable and selecting the correct input channel on the remote control. Only later would I learn that I'd broken strict protocol by speaking out directly and not through our barrister. Seems I was consistently breaking rules without even knowing they existed.

Tape watched. Battle commenced.

Both legal teams were the same as those that had appeared in the High Court and more than an hour was lost reiterating the old arguments to the new judges.

---

* The experts were Robert Ressler and Professor Derek Pounder from Dundee University.

Because no audio tape recording of proceedings was allowed in the court, I resorted to taking shorthand notes, which I later transcribed and kept on file. What follows is an abridged account of some *very* lengthy exchanges.

The judges were told that Paul Britton was a forensic psychologist engaged by the Home Office to provide consultancy services in relation to the technique of offender profiling. The contract the Home Office had with him provided for confidentiality and stated that all copyright in the work should become the property of the Crown.

'Mr Morley, a producer employed by the first defendant [Central TV]was working on a documentary on offender profiling,' Michael Silverleaf told the court. 'Morley discussed the programme with the second defendant [Paul Britton], and it was agreed that it would be desirable to include an interview with an offender. Morley obtained the consent of the serial killer Nilsen to an interview. Morley sought permission from the Home Office to interview Nilsen but this was denied. The second defendant also sought permission from the Home Office and stated that the first defendant had agreed that the film would be held in the second defendant's possession until the Home Office could consider it, and that if it was decided that the film was unsuitable for inclusion in the documentary, the first defendant would accept this. The second defendant was given permission to interview Nilsen and for the interview to be videotaped by Superintendent Laidler of Northumbria Police.'

As far as I was concerned, what I was listening to was *a version* of the truth. One I'd never heard as plainly put as this. I'd never been party to any discussion or agreement (verbal or written) about 'the ownership' or 'the copyright' of the interview. I'd repeatedly made it clear that without my involvement, Nilsen wouldn't cooperate and neither would I. There'd always been an understanding that I would record Paul interviewing Nilsen and would include a mutually agreed extract in the documentary. On the issue of exactly which sections were suitable, I would have gladly let the police and Paul guide me.

Michael Silverleaf continued to tell the court that the interview with Nilsen had been recorded on two cameras – 'A camera provided by the police and one provided by Mr Morley.'

This I had no argument with.

'Afterwards,' Silverleaf said, 'Superintendent Laidler took possession of both tapes. The tapes were given to the second defendant for evaluation in connection with his research. Later, the second defendant realised that he needed VHS copies of the tapes recorded by the first defendant. To make the VHS copies, the second defendant arranged to use the first defendant's video-editing room. Morley provided the blank tapes and showed the second defendant how to use the machines. Morley also arranged that a further duplicate was made without the second defendant's knowledge.'

Again, this seemed accurate.

Silverleaf then made the multilayered argument that I most feared.

He claimed that either the Home Office should legally be recognised as the owner of the film, since they had made the necessary arrangements, or Paul Britton should be recognised as the owner as he'd asked the questions – *and* – because Paul had at the time been employed by the Home Office; herein the copyright of the film lay with the Home Office regardless.

Trying to cover every possible eventuality, Silverleaf

alternatively argued, that the Home Office contended that Paul Britton or the prison governor were joint owners, so, come what may, that the Home Office was at least a joint owner of the copyright.

To my relief, our QC, Peter Preston, countered that Central owned the copyright outright, since I had been the one who had contacted Nilsen, persuaded him to participate, had liaised with Paul Britton and John Stevens and had made the most critical arrangements necessary for the filming, including actually recording the interview.

Michael Silverleaf insisted that 'such recording' had only been made possible, 'pursuant to an agreement with the first defendant that no part of it would be used without the plaintiff's consent' or 'without the plaintiff's consent which would not be unreasonably withheld'.

There then followed an argument that no 'formal *written* agreement' existed. And on this point, our QC stressed that even if there had been such an agreement, then it 'lacked consideration' and 'had been breached by the plaintiff, by them unreasonably refusing consent'.

Steve and I exchanged glances. This seemed like a minor victory.

Various letters and conversations were quoted by both sides, but one exchange surfaced that took me completely by surprise. It was a letter from Paul Britton to a senior Home Office official and while much of it was not read out in court, it concluded:

> *Mr John Stevens, chairman of both the Home Office/ ACPO Policy Committee on Offender Profiling and the ACPO Crime Sub-committee on Offender Profiling, is in full agreement that the proper recording of this interview*

is an important element of the United Kingdom offender-profiling initiative. He is clear that Central Television has behaved appropriately and with sensitivity throughout the preparation of the documentary record, and feels, as do I, that preserving this interview on film, aspects of which may be included in the documentary, can only enhance the reputation and actual work of offender profiling within the United Kingdom. Regardless of whether or not Central Television records the research interview, it will need to be recorded on video for our own purposes.

It may help you to be aware that, so far as this particular interview is concerned, the agreement with Central Television includes the provision that the film record will be held in my possession until due consideration of the content can be given by both myself and the Home Office/ ACPO parties concerned. Central has accepted that should it then be decided that no part of that particular film record is suitable for inclusion in the final documentary this will be accepted gracefully.

I am somewhat uncertain as how to best go forward, but am concerned that Dennis Nilsen's consent to be interviewed should be acted upon as soon as is practicable, lest it be withdrawn or modified in the light of his imminent transfer away from Albany. In this regard, it may help you to know that other people convicted of similar, or equally relevant offences have proved most reluctant to be the first to be included in this in-depth psychological research programme.

I would be most grateful if you could facilitate, in whatever fashion is appropriate, the completion of this aspect of the offender profiling initiative.

I had to swallow hard.

Again, this was another *version* of the truth.

What was missing from the letter was the fact that I had been the person to suggest interviewing Nilsen. Until my suggestion, to the best of my knowledge and the best of knowledge of senior policemen such as Don Dovaston from the Derbyshire force running CATCHEM, neither Paul Britton nor any other accredited profiler had been scheduled to interview any serial killers in the near future.

Additionally, there was no mention of the fact that I had been asked to be complicit in deceiving Nilsen as to the identity of the two police officers, who posed as camera crew.

And finally, there was the sentence, *'Central has accepted that should it then be decided that no part of that particular film record is suitable for inclusion in the final documentary this will be accepted gracefully.'* This was elegantly misleading to say the least. We all knew that there was no way you could interview Nilsen for four hours and *nothing* at all be suitable for broadcast, and there had just been the admission by Michael Silverleaf that such permission 'would not be unreasonably upheld'.

None of my thoughts mattered. I had no right to stand up in the court and shout, 'Whoa! Hold on a minute, let's just discuss this a bit further!' This was a rarefied chamber where only barristers had voices.

The court was told that almost a week before the planned filming, the governor of Albany Prison had been informed by the Home Office that in principle, approval had been given for 'Paul Britton's interview with Nilsen' (no mention of me or Central TV) to be recorded by Superintendent Laidler and Chief Inspector Cleugh of the Northumbria Police. 'The arrangement was that the police would videotape the interview and would certify in writing that they would accept responsibility for the videotape and ensure it was used only for the purposes of research.'

I recalled that at about the same time, I'd been *verbally* informed by a Home Office press officer that permission had so far been refused for the interview, but no confirmation in writing followed. I'd subsequently checked with ACPO and been told the interview was going ahead, so I presumed the Home Office had changed its mind.

The Court of Appeal was informed that on 4th September 1992 that the prison governor telephoned Superintendent Laidler (John Steven's staff officer) and told him permission for the interview had been given, stipulating that the recording should take place during the week beginning 7th September.

Part of my sworn affidavit was then read to the Justices:

> 'Paul Britton telephoned me again to say that the interview could go ahead but that the Home Office required that the equipment be operated by police officers. He suggested that I speak to one of the officers concerned, DCI Cleugh. DCI Cleugh explained to me that for police purposes he would be using a domestic camcorder (a small video camera) to record the interview. I pointed out to him that this was unlikely to produce usable material even for the purposes of a training film, and I told him that it would not be a problem as, for our purposes, I would be bringing a professional camera, lighting and sound equipment and they would have access to these tapes eventually.'

Sitting there as it was read aloud, I began to see things differently than I had at the time. Originally, I'd thought the Home

Office had withdrawn their permission *after* I'd done the interview. But now, I saw another possibility.

There was a chance that either *both* Paul Britton and John Stevens, or at least one of them, had realised that if I'd been told that I didn't have permission, in other words Central TV was being subtly squeezed out, then I might have informed Nilsen about the decision and that could have stopped him participating.

Given the fact that I'd spoken to both Dennis Cleugh (a DCI in Stevens' own constabulary) and Paul Britton just prior to turning up at Albany, they were either all aware that I shouldn't have been there, or there'd been a decision made between them, with ACPO's blessing, that I should be allowed to attend.

The remaining mystery was *how* – presuming the Home Office had secretly decided the interview should go ahead without me – was I allowed inside the prison for two consecutive days?

The prison was out of ACPO's control and out of Paul Britton's sphere of influence, so only the Home Office could have sanctioned my entry.

Michael Silverleaf told the court that I had signed the visitor's book at the gates on Monday, 7th September, along with Paul Britton, Dennis Cleugh and Wilf Laidler, but had written down that I was a psychologist, not a TV director. That just wasn't true. I had never written out the word psychologist. I had written my name in capital letters and added my signature immediately after Paul's, and I believe the police officers had followed suit. I could, at best, see the possibility that the guard at the gate might have thought we were all one big psychological party.

But surely, at a high-security prison housing murderers,

arsonists, rapists and child molesters, they'd have been informed of the exact *number* of people visiting for the interview (three not four), and the exact *names* of those people (Britton, Laidler, Cleugh – and not Morley)?

And surely, they couldn't make the same mistake two days running?

And – *surely, surely, surely* – given this interview was unique (no accredited profiler had ever interviewed a British serial killer before), then at the end of day one, there would have been at least one high-level discussion with Home Office officials about how the project was progressing?

On Tuesday, 26th January 1993, in the Civil Division of the Court of Appeal, none of those questions were raised. The next phase of the battle of the barristers had already begun, and it was all about existing legislation and previous legal cases.

Both sides claimed different rights and interpretations of the Copyright, Designs and Patents Act of 1988 and how it subsists in films and soundtracks.

Our QC then lobbed in the grenade of freedom of speech, the right to express opinions and disseminate information, quoting R. v Advertising Standards Authority Ltd, Ex Parte Vernons Organisation Ltd (1992) but it certainly did not seem to devastate the opposition.

The gist of our defence was that according to past cases, copyright lay with us because we had brought the material (the videotape) on which the interview had been recorded and we had owned and operated the equipment that recorded it. Furthermore, Paul Britton had completed his work for the Home Office in June/July of 1992 and his involvement with Nilsen, at our suggestion and ACPO's approval, hadn't taken place until September.

Put simply, *we* owned the copyright because we owned the tape on which the interview was recorded, and in the absence of any written contract between the parties saying otherwise, existing legislation seemed to support our case.

I looked at my watch. It was 5 p.m.

We'd been in court for three hours and were, as far as I could tell, a long way from the case being settled. The documentary was scheduled for transmission in five hours and forty minutes. Realistically, the Network Centre would have to know before *News at Ten* which version of *Murder in Mind* to transmit.

So, I guess we had five hours left.

Three hundred minutes.

Eighteen thousand seconds.

'You know, if we lose this, I'll get sacked,' Steve whispered as we listened to the legal debate. 'Someone's head will have to roll.'

'If they do that, I'll resign,' I replied bravely.

'No need for that,' he replied in an amused tone. 'They'll probably sack you as well.'

Summing up the Home Office's case, Michael Silverleaf said Justice Aldous had been wrong to deny the injunction, as broadcasting the interview would cause distress to the relatives and friends of Nilsen's victims, enhance Nilsen's notoriety and encourage sensationalist journalism.

The three Justices retired to consider their judgments.

Around half past six, we learned that the case was now dominating all the evening TV and radio news bulletins and the national newspaper press pack, complete with photographers who were now camped on the court steps awaiting the outcome.

Just after seven o'clock we were called back into court.

My heart was in my mouth.

I felt as though *I* was on trial for murder.

Sir Thomas Bingham, the Master of the Rolls, prepared to speak first.

I listened intently, hoping he'd kick straight off with a clear decision that the injunction had or had not been granted.

No such luck.

Sir Thomas gave his judgment in a steady, sombre tone in a pin-drop silent courtroom.

'This is an appeal by the plaintiff in this action against the refusal of Mr Justice Aldous to grant an interlocutory injunction restraining the broadcast of a film of an interview with Dennis Nilsen, the notorious convicted murderer. The plaintiff in the action is the Secretary of State for the Home Department and the effective defendants are Central Broadcasting Limited, who are franchise holders and programme makers with a base in the Midlands.'

I rested my head in my hands and massaged away a growing migraine as he summarised the day, noting, 'The plaintiff says that there was a contract between his department and the defendants which restricted the freedom of the defendants to broadcast any film, at any rate, without reference to him. He furthermore claims copyright in the finished film and alleges that the first defendants' possession of the completed film of the interview with Nilsen was obtained by means of a subterfuge, the suggestion being that a copy was taken at a time when it was unknown to the Home Office that a copy was being taken, and when the taking of a copy would never have been consented to.'

'D'you think we've won or lost?' I asked Steve, like a schoolboy whispering in class.

'No idea,' he whispered back.

I glanced across to Peter Preston and the look on his face told me he was as equally in the dark.

'All these factual and legal matters are the subject of challenge on behalf of the first defendants,' Sir Thomas continued. 'They deny the existence of a contract. They claim copyright in the film themselves, and they resist the suggestion that they were guilty of any subterfuge, at least to the extent that they claim that they were themselves used by the Home Office, in the sense of being induced to take part in this exercise of interviewing Nilsen on a basis that was not made clear and from which the Home Office subsequently departed. This court, like Mr Justice Aldous, is in no position to take any final view on these controversial matters. In the ordinary way one might very strongly suspect that the Home Office's account, at least of the circumstances in which the interview took place, would be right, and indeed, of course, that may turn out to be so. But it does seem at the outset somewhat surprising that a television crew, apparently with camera, should have been admitted at all into a prison in which a Category A prisoner of Nilsen's notoriety was confined. As I say, the facts relating to that cannot be reviewed in detail and certainly cannot be decided.'

I took this common-sense observation to be a positive point in our favour, but still had no real idea whether we'd won or not.

Sir Thomas turned his attention directly to the four minutes of interview with Nilsen and whether it could cause distress to the victims' families or the public. 'These are matters which the judge considered, and they are matters on which argument has focused. It seems to me that so far as distress to relatives is concerned, while that is of course a matter of importance, it is none the less a matter to which Mr Prescott, appearing for the first defendants, gives a convincing answer; namely, that it is quite unnecessary for any relative of any of Nilsen's victims to be distressed by this programme if broadcast in its existing form in any way at all, since all that anyone has to do is to switch off the programme. Mr Prescott has made clear that the broadcasters are willing to make quite plain at the outset of the programme that it will contain unpleasant scenes relating to Mr Nilsen which may be capable of causing distress, and that, he says, should encourage anyone liable to be distressed to spare themselves the unnecessary experience of watching the film at all.'

For the first time, I felt a genuine surge of optimism.

'So far as the damage to research is concerned,' Sir Thomas continued, 'the film does suggest that the profiling of serial killers and serial rapists is a scientific undertaking which can lead to the earlier detection and identification of those who commit, or are liable to commit offences of this very serious kind. It is on that basis that Mr Silverleaf suggests the damage will be done to such research if this interview is broadcast. For my part, I see little force in that criticism, save to the possibility of damage to research conducted by the Home Office and other official authorities in conjunction with broadcasting companies. I can, for my part, see no real reason why there should be any damage to research conducted by the Home Office or official bodies on their own, and it cannot, I suspect, be intended that research should, in the ordinary way, be conducted with the cooperation of broadcasting companies.'

Another brick in the Home Office's wall had been knocked out.

But it was almost 8 p.m.

We still didn't have the ruling we wanted.

The Master of the Rolls continued at a pace lacking the

urgency I craved. 'I was, initially, much impressed by Mr Silverleaf's submission as to the irreparable nature of the damage which would be done if this broadcast were transmitted. But on further reflection and further argument the point diminishes in force, in my estimation, for this reason. It is now quite plain that this film will be shown this evening at 10.40 p.m., whether or not this extract is included. While, therefore, such damage as the Home Office can demonstrate would be irreparable if it were included and broadcast, it seems to me that it would also be an irreparable loss to the broadcasters if this interview were excised and it were subsequently held that they were indeed entitled to broadcast it. There would be no possible practicable suggestion that this interview would be broadcastable on its own. I am not, therefore, for my part persuaded that this criticism of the learned judge's approach to the matter is made out.'

Now I fully sensed victory. A feeling that grew as he dismissed suggestions that Justice Aldous had given too much credit to the testimonies of Bob Ressler and Derek Pounder. 'The learned judge referred in summary to the evidence that those two witnesses had given on affidavit and concluded that his own view coincided with that of the two witnesses, namely: " . . . that the distress felt by the public, including the friends and relatives of Nilsen's victims, will come from the programme as a whole rather than the extract. I believe that friends and relatives of Nilsen's victims will understand that the interview was made as part of a research programme to try to help to prevent similar criminals carrying out serial killings. They will see Nilsen as a man without remorse. In the light of his crimes, they will realise that he does not appear mad but is and was a cold resourceful and dangerous man who should not be released from prison. They will see the extract as demonstrating that he should not be released. To that extent, I believe they will find the contribution valuable." It is not, I think, appropriate to say whether oneself is inclined, as the judge did, to express a view coincident with that of Professor Pounder and Mr Ressler. The question for us is whether the learned judge erred in his review of this matter by taking the view which he did and which I have just quoted. In my judgment it cannot be said that the learned judge fell into error in that respect.'

Another brick tumbled from the Home Office wall.

Sir Thomas added, 'The third major criticism which Mr Silverleaf advanced was to the effect that the learned judge's refusal of an injunction condoned the unlawful behaviour of the broadcasters in resorting to subterfuge in obtaining the tapes instead of going through legal processes in order to recover them. That submission has some appeal, since even if the broadcasters were not themselves guilty of any subterfuge, they certainly could have used legal means to establish the position. But it seems to me that the sting of that submission, in effect, depends on an allegation of impropriety in the broadcasters' behaviour, and that is something on which, at this stage, the court is really in no position to reach a concluded view.'

I guessed this was about as bad a public dressing-down as I was going to get for deceiving Paul Britton and copying the tapes. I consoled myself with the knowledge that if I hadn't done it, then the chance of ever getting the material from the Home Office was less than that of the proverbial snowball surviving in hell.

'The fourth criticism which Mr Silverleaf advanced, somewhat, I think, as an afterthought, was that to permit the broadcast to take place would be to enhance the status of the defendants as broadcasters, and he complains that the judge gave that consideration inadequate weight. It is, in my judgment, a point of very little weight, and I do not in any way criticise the judge for not attaching very great importance to it.'

And then came the magical announcement.

'I would, for my part, dismiss this appeal.'

My face lit up with relief.

'We need a majority,' said Steve, sensing my premature excitement. 'The other two judges could still back the Home Office.'

Our attention swung to Lord Justice McGowan.

'I agree,' he said.

I closed my eyes in relief. We had the majority.

The third and final judge also ruled in our favour.

We had a unanimous decision.

With just over two hours to go, the Home Office's attempt to ban the programme had failed. Their injunction had been denied.

We were free to broadcast the documentary, including the four minute Nilsen interview.

However, the three Lord Justices upheld a restriction which stands to this day, namely that *only* those four minutes of interview would be shown on TV and just for that one broadcast.

If Central TV wished to show more, then it would have to force a full trial over the matter, something which could cost them millions and bring prolonged conflict and bad feeling with the government.

Exhausted and exhilarated, Steve and I left court to face a barrage of cameras and journalists chasing deadlines. The victory was one of the lead stories on every radio and TV news bulletin from 9 p.m. onwards.

Within the hour, I was in a hotel bar in central London

drinking like a Viking. By 10.40 p.m., as the opening titles played out on ITV and Dennis Nilsen's voice was heard across the country, I was completely disinterested in what he had to say. I never wanted to hear the man's voice again.

I wrote to Dennis Nilsen several times after the interview and the broadcast of the documentary, even sending him a VHS copy of the programme. I never received a reply, and took the silence to mean the serial killer had wished to end all communication between us. It was only many years later, when I read Nilsen's account of the interview, given to author Russ Coffey* (and reproduced below with his kind permission), that I realised it was perhaps the Home Office that had decided the connection between us should be severed.

> '*The interview, recorded by two cameras, took one whole day. I asked for no payment nor did I wish to know the questions in advance. In the room were two men introduced to me as cameramen, Paul Britton (who asked the questions) and Mike Morley overseeing the whole production. I had also loaned Britton Parts I and II (of the autobiography) to help him with my background (I had a job getting these back. He returned these eight months later only when I wrote to Home Office HQ in complaint).*'
>
> Nilsen continued, '*So the interview was "in the can" and I awaited the finished product. In January '93, the shit hit the proverbial fan. The then Home Secretary, Kenneth Clark, had found out about the project and, politically embarrassed, sought a High Court injunction*

---

* *Dennis Nilsen – Conversations with Britain's Most Evil Serial Killer*, Russ Coffey (John Blake, 2013).

to stop Central TV using any of the footage. The Home Office's case (all news to me) held that the taped interview had been conceived and made by and for the purposes of police training by ACPO (Association of Chief Police Officers) and approved as such by the Home Office. It was never meant for public broadcast, as was wrongly claimed. So, it seems that Morley acted as a front man in a deal with the immediate organisers, and in return he was promised use of some of the footage. As all my letters are censored, it is clear that all in authority at Albany knew full well what was being organised. It also transpired that these two "cameramen" were, in fact, a chief super-intendent and a chief inspector. The deception had been thorough.'

Russ Coffey added:

Nilsen still seethes over the incident. His indignation, however, is less directed at Morley – to whom he was grateful for the gift of a typewriter – than towards Britton, who had held on to the manuscript for so long. In his writings, he points out that Britton – generally thought of as the inspiration behind ITV's Cracker *– was later widely criticised for his involvement in the arrest and then subsequent collapse of the case against Colin Stagg for the murder of Rachel Nickell on Wimbledon Common in 1992.*

Nilsen gave an even more expansive (and somewhat incorrect) view of the interview and the aftermath in his autobiography, *History of a Drowning Boy*, published in 2021:

Nineteen ninety-two folded and 1993 opened with a bang. Mike Morley from Central TV wrote and said they were having difficulties with the Home Office concerning the transmission of his documentary Murder in Mind, which included the interview they'd filmed with me at Albany Prison. These 'difficulties' would soon explode on to the front burners of national news and the decision to try to stop the documentary airing was taken by the Home Secretary, Kenneth Clark. I was handed a cutting from the Today newspaper headlined, 'Ban on Silence of the Lambs TV Talk with Killer Nilsen'. The piece told how 'television bosses were yesterday banned by a judge from showing journalist's . . . interview with serial killer . . . dismembering bodies . . . the Home Office changed its mind . . . was not policy to allow interviews with Category A killers to be shown . . . ' This came at me like a sudden sock in the teeth and was the first intimation I had that the Home Office were claiming authorship and copyright on my words. I had agreed to the interview in the express belief that they were recording for a publicly transmitted broadcast. Permission had obviously been given because the Home Office had allowed it to be made in the full knowledge of what I believed to be the case. All my correspondence with Central TV had been monitored by the usual censorship procedures in prison and I had no agreement or correspondence with the Home Office to give any interview. When one smells a rat, one has to poke around with a sharp stick to discover the source of the smell and, in the first instance, Mike Morley broke off all communication with me, but the press reports continued to flow. The Sun ran with a confused narrative, stating, 'Killer Nilsen Wants to be a Telly Star' in which 'Nilsen . . .

revelled in his chilling television performance' and claimed to have obtained all this from Lord Longford. The article finished on the note that the Home Office '. . . is expected to sue [Central TV] over copyright and breach of contract'. The more serious newspapers were at it too. The Independent told, accurately, how 'Nilsen TV Producer "Deceived" Prison' by their crime correspondent, Terry Kirby. The plot was, indeed, beginning to thicken with a fog of criminal deception. It went on, 'A television producer tricked his way into a top-security prison to film an interview with . . . Nilsen, the High Court was told yesterday.' The subject remained controversial news for some days and all sorts of irrelevant opinions were solicited on the matter – except for mine. By this time, it was clear to me that all the involved factions had been avidly deceiving each other, united only in the common goal of getting the interview, for their own diverse purposes, by deceiving me. In the end, the Home Office failed in its attempt to ban the broadcast and immediately lodged an appeal, which was also rejected, and the programme went out as scheduled. The brief, three-minute clip, selected from the four hours of tape, was not representative of the interview as a whole and was picked for its sensationalism, pure and simple. I solicited an explanation from the Home Office through the Request & Complaint procedure, but none was forthcoming, so I engaged the services of a local solicitor to make further enquiries. But all that they were able to uncover was an admission that the two cameramen were indeed senior detectives (who they named). When the Home Secretary, Ken Clark, was interviewed on BBC Radio 4 during the controversy, he avoided the main details of the issue and concentrated his attack on me and

*his public duty to prevent 'murderers like Nilsen from
happily describing their crimes in full view of victims',
etc. Anyone would have thought that the interview had
been my idea. Terry Kirby of the* Independent *was made
aware of the true facts through the agency of Mark Austin,
armed with a copy of my statement and all the correspondence I'd had with Central TV. Kirby, at first, seemed
keen to run with it as a legitimate news story but then
began to hum and haw, finally admitting his bosses had
placed an embargo on the revelations. So much for the
independence of the* Independent. *Following transmission
of the programme, the issue dried up and vanished into
the thin air of British hypocrisy. I gave my full statement
on the Central TV interview to the local Cambridgeshire
police for action but all they did was to send it to John
Stevens (the then deputy chief constable of the
Cambridgeshire Constabulary) who ruled that there was
no criminal offence. I then wrote to the Police Complaints
Authority who advised me to address my complaint to the
Cambridgeshire Constabulary, thereby neatly closing the
establishment circle. Only one good thing came out of
the Central TV interview fiasco and it was that Mike
Morley sent me a manual typewriter that he'd found lying
around in a cupboard at the office. They no longer used
them – being into word processing PCs by then – and I
was thankful for this kind gift.*

The above extract is insightful for a number of reasons, not
the least that it is evidence that Dennis Nilsen's memory was
not as good as he thought, and he had the habit of presenting
false assumptions as truths.

Aside from the incorrect view that I hadn't written to him

post-transmission, John Stevens hadn't been the deputy chief constable of Cambridgeshire at the time Nilsen said he wrote to him (he was chief in Northumbria and had been so for a long period of time) so he couldn't have ruled 'that there was no criminal offence' as Nilsen reported, and of course the Home Office had never achieved a ban on the programme, their attempts to obtain injunctions had failed.

These were only small details.

But as the FBI's Terry Green had taught me, every small detail mattered. Every detail had meaning.

15

THE SHOW THAT
NEVER GOT MADE

*M*urder in Mind had been transmitted as part of ITV's *Viewpoint* series, a prestigious curation of factual-event programming, that had included works by *Death of a Princess* producer Anthony Thomas, and John Pilger the producer of *Year Zero, The Silent Death of Cambodia.*

It had been watched by a record number of viewers, caused inevitable controversy in the popular press, was the subject of most current affairs chat shows on radio and TV, and was nominated for a BAFTA.

The only disappointment was that, internally, there was no top-management appetite to go to full trial and contest the court ruling that we couldn't ever screen more than the four minutes of interview we'd shown.

To me, this added insult to injury. I'd been emotionally and physically exhausted by making *Murder in Mind* and almost two years of increasing closeness to Nilsen and his crimes. The darkness that came parcelled with his murders and post-mortem acts had worsened my insomnia, triggered bouts of depression and left me restless. I needed closure. And closure would only come with the knowledge that all that effort and hard-earned understanding amounted to something substantial, something more than two hundred and forty seconds of airtime.

I'd already received feedback from Bob Ressler and Roy Hazelwood on the interview in its entirety and I tried to argue a case for a follow-up programme that would use the transmitted material, plus have an actor voice sections that we hadn't been allowed to screen. I was told in no uncertain terms that this was a non-starter. No one, it seemed, wanted the cost and stress of going back to court again, let alone the political heat that would come from it. Nevertheless, I obsessively planned the programme out on paper, piecing together Nilsen quotes with analysis from the profilers and hoped at a later date to have Paul Britton, or another UK profiler, provide one coherent final analytical view of view of the serial killer.

In 1992, during the months when I was shooting *Murder in Mind*, Central TV had been taken over by Carlton Communications, a powerful UK media group led by Michael Green, a businessman widely reported to be an influential Conservative Party supporter. In 1994, Green appointed David Cameron – a future Tory government prime minister – as his director of communications and all hope of me making another Nilsen-related programme, let alone fighting the Home Office for full exploitation rights of the interview tapes, disappeared forever. Frustration cut deep. Left a scar that just grew ugly, rather than faded away.

Had I produced that show, I would have sought to have used experts to come to conclusions about what had made Nilsen a serial killer. I'd have focused particularly on ten key factors that either Nilsen or expert profilers had cited as contributory to his deviancy, and I probably would have dealt with them in this order:

1. MATERNAL NEGLECT
2. THE DEAD GRANDFATHER
3. NON-INTERVENING PARENTS

4. CLOSETED HOMOSEXUALITY
5. FANTASIES
6. NECROPHILIA
7. KILLING FOR COMPANY
8. BODY DISPOSAL
9. CANNIBALISM
10. MAD OR BAD

Ideally, I would have liked Paul Britton to have at least been party to examining this top ten and would have valued his assistance in formulating an overall conclusion – a definitive answer to the question he'd asked in Albany Prison on Tuesday, 8th September 1992 – 'Who is Dennis Nilsen?'

But it was not to be.

Paul and I last met in 1994. I had been given exclusive access by Nottinghamshire Constabulary to film a fly-on-the-wall network documentary about the police hunt for a newborn baby called Abbie Humphries. She'd been kidnapped from the maternity wing of the Queen's Medical Centre, one of Europe's largest hospitals.

Paul had been called in as a consultant profiler and I was told by officers he did the best he could to have me excluded from as many critical meetings as possible, which given his recent experiences was highly understandable. I was, however, there with the direct blessing of the chief constable and I made sure we filmed 24/7 so nothing was missed.

When the police swooped on the home of a twenty-two-year-old local woman, we were camera-to-shoulder with the arresting officer as baby Abbie was recovered, unharmed. The documentary went on to win several major awards including one from the Royal Television Society.

I'm saddened that Paul and I never met after this, never talked and never exchanged so much as an email about the contents of the Nilsen interview. I would very much have liked to have known what conclusions he'd drawn after that lengthy interrogation. I contacted his agent several times while writing this book, and was told, 'Paul has no enthusiasm for the idea of drawing more attention to DN than has already been generated.' That's a laudable position to take, but it's perhaps not the only reason for his silence.

In his excellent casebook publications, *The Jigsaw Man* and *Picking up the Pieces*, Paul draws a lot of attention to other offenders but doesn't make a single reference to our interview with Dennis Nilsen in Albany Prison. I can only imagine that he still sees it as a potato too hot to publicly handle, perhaps one too uncomfortable to touch, if you still wish to deal with the Home Office.

I have nothing but respect for him. Nothing but gratitude for the fact that he helped me create a piece of television history. And I am sorry that I had to betray his trust when I copied the Nilsen tapes without his knowledge. I suspect he finds that act unforgiveable. But then again, we had both betrayed Dennis Nilsen's trust in presenting two 'crew members' who were actually undercover policemen. And I strongly suspect that a number of people conspired to betray my trust when they decided that, after having secured Nilsen's cooperation, I could be squeezed out of the picture and the interview kept solely within the control of the Home Office.

In the absence of Paul Britton's analysis, I fall back on comments made to me by Bob Ressler and Roy Hazelwood. Additionally, I've considered (but not always believing) Nilsen's autobiography, *History of a Drowning Boy*, published in January 2021, plus his personal letters to me and those published by others such as Russ Coffey and Brian Masters, and also invaluable advice and insight from Professor Guy

Rutty, one of Britain's most eminent chief forensic pathologists. To illustrate the conclusions drawn, I'm also going to recall direct quotes from Nilsen made in either interviews or letters he sent to me.

1. MATERNAL NEGLECT

From all the interviews and reports that I've read, Betty Whyte/ Nilsen/Scott certainly didn't see herself as a neglectful parent, and it seems harshly unfair to accuse a young woman, who'd been burdened with raising three children without the help of a remotely supportive first husband, of anything approaching neglect. By Nilsen's own admissions, she did the best she could 'to put food on the table' and 'keep a roof over our heads'.

But neglect, like abuse, takes many forms.

And what about love?

What about emotional care?

Did party-loving, job-juggling, struggling-to-make-ends-meet Betty, living in one room at her parents' home, have the opportunity, ability and capacity to uniquely provide for the different loves and needs of all her children?

Probably not.

Outgoing, manly Olav obviously required completely different parenting to her youngest child and only daughter, Sylvia.

But what about stuck-in-the-middle Des?

Here was a sensitive, introverted, uncertain boy, who looked so unlike his older brother and father that he was not alone in thinking he was someone else's son. He was undoubtedly in need of extra affection, special attention and specific TLC if he was to develop a strong and healthy personality.

NILSEN: 'My upbringing was loveless. It was emotionally frigid. There was no warmth in the house, just religion and restrictions, do this, do that, don't you dare do something I told you not to . . .

'If someone walked in here and said to me, "Des, your mother's dead in Scotland," I wouldn't cry. I wouldn't shed a tear . . .

'I don't know what it's like to have been hugged and loved by a parent, the notion is alien to me.'

RESSLER: 'The original profiling study the FBI did was of serial offenders born immediately after the Second World War and in the 1950s, so people of about the same age as Nilsen. They had commonalities in their childhood that are mirrored in Nilsen's. In almost half the cases, the father had left before the age of twelve – and it was the same with Nilsen. More than half said they had a domineering mother who showed little or no affection – again the same with Nilsen. Around three quarters felt their childhood had been psychologically abusive – again this applies to Nilsen. Just under half reported having a negative relationship, not a positive one, with their mother – that's another box ticked. So, yeah, you have to say that, if a number of other negatives were also in play, then a lack of maternal love and attention, in addition to an absent father, those factors are damaging.'

HAZELWOOD: 'I'd say the fact that Nilsen *felt* unloved by his parents, is maybe more important than whether he actually *was* unloved or not. Psychologically, moms have always been seen as the ones who teach sons how to love, how it's okay to be vulnerable. They play big in our lives. As a kid you run to mom and get hugged and kissed and made to feel better when you've banged your knee or hurt yourself somehow. Dad, on the other hand, he's more likely to just dust you down, tell you you're okay and send you back out there. But single dads, they can fill that nurturing role just as well. Big brothers can do it. Sisters can do it. Even friends can do it. Usually, if we can't get that kind of support and nurture from one source then we find it in another. In Nilsen's case, I'm not sure that he found it. I should also say, I don't think emotional neglect on its own is as singularly corrosive in formative character development as, say, sexual abuse can be. But it has an effect.'

2. THE DEAD GRANDFATHER

When Brian Masters interviewed Nilsen in the eighties, the Scot clearly identified the death of his grandfather as injurious to his development, and in particular, he cited the way the news of the death and the viewing of Andrew Whyte's body in a coffin affected him. A decade later, Brian told me, 'Well, there's no doubt that it did have an impact. He told me that he believed his troubles really started there, that his grandfather's death blighted his personality forever. Andrew Whyte had been a father substitute, someone he spent a lot of time with, and his death at sea opened a void in Des's young life. I think he failed to comprehend what death was, and to some degree interpreted the absence as an example of another person, like his father, just deserting him and his mother.'

By the time Paul Britton and I interviewed Nilsen in Albany Prison, he had downgraded the loss of his grandfather in his life, but still maintained he'd been confused and traumatised by being suddenly shown Andrew Whyte's corpse, without any real understanding of what death was.

NILSEN: 'Did I weep for him? No. No. Never . . .

'No one took the time to explain to me what had happened. I was completely unprepared. My mother asked me if I wanted to see Grandad and I still didn't know what death was so I said I did. I was taken into this room in the house and there he was in his coffin. I didn't understand what I was seeing. It looked as though he was sleeping, but I could tell that it was a different sleep, a strange sleep. And then I was taken out again and that it was it. No one explained to me what it meant or what had happened and all that had a profound effect on me. I remember, soon after that, asking, "Where's Grandad? Why doesn't he come for me anymore?" and I was told "You won't be seeing him again. Your Grandad's gone." I asked, "Where?" and my mother said, "He's gone to a better place." And I wondered where that was and why hadn't he taken me? We went lots of places together. What had I done to make him not want to take me to the *better place*?'

Perhaps more significantly (though I didn't realise it at the time), Nilsen had already begun to intimate that all of his recollections of his grandfather *hadn't* been confined to happy walks. He said he remembered him '. . . regularly taking me for a wee when we were out. He would take down my pants and hold my penis while I did it, and I used to say, "I can do that Grandad," but he'd say he'd do it, because he didn't want me to get any on myself.'

If you were on a jury, would you decide that was evidence of sexual abuse?

Or would you think it was just an attentive grandad trying to make sure his four- or five-year-old grandson didn't pee all over himself and then become distressed afterwards?

It wasn't until decades after the Albany interview that Nilsen would drastically revise his memories and dogmatically assert in public that he'd regularly been given drugged drinks and seriously sexually abused by his grandfather. By the time he finished writing his autobiography,* this suggested abuse had (to Nilsen) become unquestionable fact and was presented in a way that clearly portrayed grandad as the villain, not hero, of his childhood, and himself as an innocent child deeply damaged by the old man's actions. 'Seeing him laid out in his coffin brought to me a great earthquake of excitement. I had lost the good aspect of him as well as the painful trauma of his abuse. I had wished him gone and he had gone and the guilt came from this and my excitement and sense of loss at viewing the mighty fallen, slumbering in that coffin in the room where I had been born. I was not that clear on the full meaning of death and felt that he could have still "got me" if I revealed our secret.'[†]

RESSLER: 'The death of a grandparent is something pretty much all grandchildren face at some point. Properly handled, at any age, it is just a sad event. It's the viewing of the body by a very young child that is

---

* Before editing, Nilsen's autobiographical writings are said to have run to more than 60,000 pages and in excess of three million words.

† *History of a Drowning Boy*, Dennis Nilsen (RedDoor Press, 2021)

dangerous. If that's going to happen, then it has to be handled with due care and sensitivity. From what I've been told, Nilsen, at six, was way too young, too unprepared and too vulnerable a child for this to have occurred without a risk of serious psychological damage. If the grandfather abused Nilsen, then that would have a very big effect. Sexual abuse in childhood was a common element found in the early years of about half the serial murderers we studied.'

HAZELWOOD: 'Traditionally, grandparents are big on love, care and attention, and not as hot on discipline as mom or dad, so kids feel very free and happy when they go round to see them. They develop special bonds, and losing a grandparent means losing that special bond. That's not so bad if there are lots of other emotional ties in the kid's life. If it's the only one, then what might well be their first big trauma is somewhat amplified. As to the alleged sexual interference by the grandfather, I'd need to ask more questions and be given a whole lot more information about what actually happened to verify it. The urinating story sounds innocuous enough – with kids that age, they pee everywhere if they're not helped. Maybe more than that happened. Maybe Nilsen told his mom something more than that had happened and she shrugged it off. If he *was* abused, then it would potentially be quite damaging to his development. We see that in serial sexual offenders around half of them were abused as children.'

3. NON-INTERVENING PARENTS

Sat with FBI profiler Larry McCann in a diner in Quantico, Virginia, we got round to talking about the childhood of serial killers. Larry made a point that stuck in my mind. 'There's not a kid alive that hasn't done something he or she shouldn't, that hasn't come off the rails, gotten into some kind of trouble, maybe more by accident than design. Usually, there's a red flag waved when that happens, a warning sign that they're struggling, that they're depressed, they're frightened, they're angry, and natural parenting or good schooling picks up on it and has every chance to correct it. What we've found, time after time, is that in the case of serial killers, there's been an absence of watchful eyes and those red flags either haven't been waved or have been missed.'

Larry's comments reinforced Bob Ressler's remarks about there having to be 'at least one pair of safe hands in a family, someone to catch a kid when they come off the emotional or disciplinary rails'.

Where were the watchful eyes and safe hands in the life of young Dennis Nilsen?

What were the occasions when red flags should have been raised? And who should have done that?

With the benefits of hindsight, we can easily point at people who perhaps should have been more vigilant, and we can pin down key moments that needed different actions, but back in those instances, young Des's persistent melancholy, his slow-growing depression following his grandfather's death, his repeated wanderings-off on his own, his gradual underper-formance at school and his tensions with his older brother might have been harder to spot, or just didn't seem important enough to do anything about.

NILSEN: 'How I felt, or what I thought, was of no consequence to anyone but me. There were a lot of voices in my childhood but mine wasn't one of them. I was the only person listening to me, the only person I could have a conversation with . . .

'Never a day passed when I wasn't reminded of how insignificant I was when I was a child . . .

'I was happiest when I was left to my own devices. As soon as I could walk, I'd get out of the house and get as far away as my legs would take me. I wanted to be on my own, not to be under someone's thumb, and I think it suited the women* that I was out of the way. They were firm believers in the old sayings, "Out of sight out of mind", and if you were around, then "Children should be seen and not heard".'

RESSLER: 'Bad parenting contributes to delinquency. Abusive parenting – beating, sexually or emotionally abusing a child – that's the worst that can happen. But not doing the basics, that's bad as well. Not watching and asking what a child's doing, listening to, why they're doing it, where they're going, who they're seeing, when they're coming in, what they've been up to, how they're feeling, what they're planning, what they're hoping for – that kind of negligence is bad as well. Moms, dads, grandparents, have to be alert. They have to see the signs, and they have to react when they see them. They won't always be right, but they do always have to be watchful. In Nilsen's case, that doesn't seem to have happened.'

---

* A reference to his mother and his grandmother.

HAZELWOOD: 'Parenting is primarily about nurturing, but it's also about teaching what's right and wrong, setting boundaries and checking moral compasses. You can't do that if you don't know where your child is and what they're thinking. Dennis Nilsen seems to have been a complex and unhappy child and people would have needed to watch out for him. By that, I mean teachers too. Teachers have these children under their scrutiny all day and they're well placed to see behavioural changes. That's not to say that there are not serial offenders who came from homes with diligent parents and great schooling – there are – but in Nilsen's case it appears no one spotted any of the signs that we can now see were there.'

4. CLOSETED HOMOSEXUALITY

Dennis Nilsen's generation was the last to grow up in the years when homosexuality was illegal in Britain. Not just illegal, but horribly punishable by imprisonment and a type of public shaming via some newspapers of the era that was uniquely English in its prejudice and prurience.

Any child growing up feels some uncertainty and pressure as they hit puberty and they seek to establish their first sexual relationships. Fantasies change from childhood imaginings to adult cravings. It's a time of awkwardness for almost everyone. Personal embarrassment and fears are usually overcome through discussions with peers who are going through the same experiences, along with family members offering guidance and reassurance.

Nilsen told me, 'I came of age in the wrong era in the

THE DENNIS NILSEN TAPES

wrong part of the country. There were third-world tribes with more enlightened sexual views than those in the east coast of Scotland when I was a kid getting horny. If you so much as said the word homosexual in Fraserburgh you burst into flames, at least that's what we were led to believe.'

In *History of a Drowning Boy*, he pens an even more telling experience of how sexually frightened and confused he'd felt during his teenage years and how that confusion pushed him towards criminality:

The year before I left school, my sexual notions took a new turn concerning another beautiful boy when I was in the grip of puberty. His name was John Beech* – a year younger than me – and I almost collapsed into a fainting spin when I saw him in white shorts, socks and PT vest. His beauty sent my pulse racing and I ached for physical intimacy with him. However, being shy and withdrawn, I couldn't even summon up the courage to talk to him, let alone go some way to express my feelings, which had, thus far, been confined to playful wrestling bouts with other boys and exploring my half-brother's body when he was asleep. I longed for contact and the very thought of John Beech made me sickly dizzy. At one point, I teetered on the brink of criminality but drew back, shocked and afraid by my own ambition. I imagined that if I hit him on the head from behind and knocked him unconscious, I could have him to caress. I raged at myself for such a thought, not because of any injury it might cause him but because of the risk of being found out and exposed as being gay. I had a vision of him lying there, oblivious

---

* Not his real name.

to my actions, as I pulled down his white shorts and fondled his unconscious body. His would have been just the physical body of an imaginary friend created in my mind. The aim would never have been to harm him but to express tactile tenderness towards his physical body.

RESSLER: 'Being told his sexuality was illegal and that the feelings he had were criminal, will have damaged Nilsen's sexual and emotional development throughout his adolescence and adulthood, de-socialising and alienating him. Can you imagine if you were in his position and you were mocked, bullied and prosecuted for being attracted to someone? Being forced to keep your feelings secret would have made you both depressed and angry. At some point, that anger's gonna come out. When it does, it's often in the form of self-harm or violence towards others.'

HAZELWOOD: 'The laws of the time would have caused intense internal conflict for him. The absence of real relationships would also have increased his fantasies about obtaining intimacy with someone. We have a saying, 'Dead men tell no tales' and I think this [reasoning] was also partly responsible for shaping Nilsen's fantasy about having a partner who was dead and therefore unable to tell anyone of their gay relationship.'

RESSLER: 'Serial offenders I interviewed were, as adolescents, most likely *not* to have joined peer-related activities such as going out in groups and seeking partners. Instead, they started their own little fantasy worlds and immersed themselves in them. As young kids, they'd gotten used to playing on their own and inventing friends and fun scenarios in their heads, maybe using toys or dolls. Then, in puberty, they stimulated themselves by imagining sexual scenarios, fantasies in which they had control, maybe over things that frightened them, like girls or boys or death. These fantasies were escapes from the pressures they were feeling in the real world.'

HAZELWOOD: 'The images people use for masturbatory purposes, be they commercially produced pornography or just thoughts they have, these are things that mentally excite them, and the more they masturbate the more they reinforce their attraction to those images. Being frightened is so close to being excited it can sometimes be hard to tell the difference. We scream on rollercoasters because we're scared, but we call it fun. Nilsen's fantasy life, his use of mirrors and cosmetics to make himself appear dead while he stimulated himself, was him overcoming a fear of death, of him mastering and conquering it, taking on the power and control that in real life he hadn't felt he'd had. In that process, he'd locked in his sexual attraction to corpses, to their passivity and his power. This is the most likely source of his necrophilia. When he took photographs of the corpses of his victims, he was creating his own pornography and further embedding his necrofetishistic fantasies. There are some cultures in the world where people still believe photographs capture the spirit of the subject, and serial sex offenders often get off on the idea of *the complete* capture of their victim, including their image.'

5. FANTASIES

Thankfully, we live in an era when it's okay to say that fantasies are common. They are healthy. Everyone has them. They come in all forms, frequently and fleetingly, from all ages.

I'm not sure that in the 1950s there was the same level of liberal understanding.

Our dreams and wildest imaginings fuel social aspirations, solve problems, push scientific boundaries, invent wondrous objects, create cures to awful diseases and achieve a myriad of other marvels.

Our sexual fantasies help us develop our individuality, build romance, nurture desire, build intimacy and sustain long-term relationships.

But when sexual fantasies become obsessive, they can lead to illegal, dangerous and deadly acts.

In the more vulnerable individual – the type of person for whom reality is unbearably lonely, isolating and humiliating – paraphilic, deviant fantasies can much more easily leap from fiction to fact.

When profiling serial offenders at a murder scene, the FBI has traditionally looked at five aspects –

1. Situational – where did the offences take place? In Nilsen's case, always inside the privacy of his own home.
2. Paraphilia – what was the deviant sexual component? Nilsen's was necrophilia.
3. Relational – what relationship did the offender fantasise about having with the victim? Nilsen always cast himself as dominant, caring, even heroic.
4. Self-perception – What role and actions does the offender imagine he is going to perform in the fantasy? For Nilsen

this was the undressing, bathing, carrying and redressing ritual.

5. Victim Demographics – what is the age, sex and appearance of the person in the offender's fantasies? Nilsen always imagined a younger male victim and an older male abuser.

Dennis Nilsen spoke and wrote copiously about his fantasies. They were so obsessive, compulsive and extreme, that at least one psychiatrist who examined him in prison doubted that he could always discern reality from fantasy. This was borne out when Nilsen admitted that the story he often told about an older boy in Fraserburgh saving him from drowning and then abusing him, had in fact not happened at all but had been imagined.

Commonly, Nilsen fantasised about young men or boys being 'passive' (for passive we can also read 'dead') participants in homosexual acts. Variously, *he* was either the passive boy, or the powerful instigator. Occasionally, he was both at the same time. His grandfather would sometimes be cast as the older male and he as the younger. There were also fantasies in which he and his grandfather 'shared' the younger male. Fantasies in which bodies were buried, unearthed and abused. Fantasies in rooms, on sand dunes, in deserts, in seas and all over the world. As diverse and depraved as they were, death was a constant plot point.

NILSEN: 'Death is not frightening. I've never found it frightening. Fascinating and mysterious. Powerful. It's like the sea, it can thrill you or drown you without a moment's notice . . .

'The world inside my head has always been far friendlier to me than the one outside. The capacity to use my imagination to escape an oppressive and threatening reality has been integral to my survival and my development as a functional individual . . .

'My fantasy life has always been rich and daring, with the sea often present, flowing through my imaginings, whether I wished it to or not. There are often older men and younger boys, sometimes myself, sometimes my grandfather. And death. Death is omnipresent.'

In his letters to me, and in the interview in Albany Prison, Nilsen made countless references to how *beautiful* he found the corpses of his victims, and how he would dream romantically about dead young men in a variety of locations and scenarios. In these dreams, he would often be both the onlooker and the victim – like an actor playing multiple roles in a film. His theatrical fantasies were extended by elaborate props, costumes, make-up and rituals that he would stage when he decided to masturbate. The practice was most vividly illustrated by a written account he made to Brian Masters, published in his book *Killing for Company* and reproduced below with Brian's kind permission.

I put talc on my face to erase the living colour. I smear charcoal under my eyes to accentuate a hollow dark look. I put pale blue on my lips. I rub my eyes to make them bloodshot. I have put three holes in my old tee-shirt. I make a mixture of cochineal and saffron to synthesise blood. I soak the blood into the holes and the liquid stains my shirt and runs down my body. I lie, staring-eyed, on the bed in front of the mirror and let my saliva foam and drip from my mouth. I stare in fascination at the *shot body of me in the mirror. I step outside myself in detached imagination. There is another imaginary person in the room who finds my body out in the woods. I have been executed and left there by the SS. I am a French dissident student. The other person, an old hermit who lives in the woods, drags my dead body back to his old shack. He is wearing rags and he decides that I have no further use for clothes and begins to strip my limp body. He is speaking to me as though I were still alive. He pulls my now naked body off the bed on to the floor. He washes me. He ties my penis and puts some wadding in my anus. He sits me on a chair then he puts me over his shoulder and carries me back into the woods and buries me. Later he returns and digs me up* and takes me back to the shack. He masturbates me and my penis comes to life and I ejaculate. It is over. I tidy up the room, replace the mirror and have a bath. I turn on the TV and call the dog over to me.*

RESSLER: 'Studies of serial offenders like Nilsen have revealed common patterns when it comes to their fantasy lives. These offenders often have excessive fantasies, vivid nightmares, recurring daydreams. The themes that keep coming up in their fantasies are ones of dominance, power, control and molestation and they are themes that we then find in their crimes. These individuals require higher than normal levels of arousal to become sexually stimulated and these tend to be more extreme, such as bondage, torture, visual suffering and acts of death and mutilation.'

---

* Necrophilic arousal from being buried alive is known as taphephilia.

HAZELWOOD: 'Props, costumes and pornography are often conduits that carry fantasy into fact. A man who's never raped may regularly masturbate to videos or pictures of men having sex with women who have been tied up. He may then get himself some rope and tie himself up while he looks at his pornography. It could be that he keeps the pictures and the rope in his car, so his wife or girlfriend doesn't find them in the house and ask about them. Then one day, he's out driving around and he's thinking of sex. He's somewhere remote and he sees a woman walking by the side of the road and she fits his fantasies. He imagines her tied up and thinks how great the sex would be for both of them, just like in the pornography he'd seen. Then he gets to thinking how easy it would be to take his rope out of the trunk, tie her up and actually live the fantasy. Now maybe, that particular day, nothing happens, he thinks better of it all. But the thought is now there in his head. Next time he's home alone and gets out his pornography and rope, he now imagines the woman on the road, and that gets him even more excited, because that's an image from his own existence. He's pulled her into his fantasy. A few days, or weeks, or months, or even years later, he's no longer getting the excitement he needs from porn, and while he's out driving, he comes across another woman on a remote road. And this time, that fantasy becomes reality. Only, he's not thought it through. The woman puts up a noisy fight, and in trying to control her, trying to keep her quiet he strangles her. This guy, when he first got out his bondage magazine for a little private relief, he'd never even imagined he'd become a rapist, let alone a killer, but now he is. He's crossed over. There's no going back to how he was and who he was.'

6. NECROPHILIA

Generally, people are either quietly respectful when viewing the dead body of someone they know, are somewhat shocked, or even frightened or repulsed. Seldom are corpses the centre of their sexual fantasies. But this is a paraphilia that has long been recognised. It's certainly nothing new.

As far back as 450 BC, there were accounts of embalmers being known to have intercourse with the bodies of the newly deceased, considering it to be almost 'a perk of the job'.

Ancient Polynesian tribes and some indigenous people of British Columbia approved of men copulating with their dead wives as a way of coming to terms with their loss, a physical act of 'saying goodbye' to their loved one.

In the nineteenth century, Native Kanakas* reportedly indulged in necrophilia with the decapitated corpses of white women.

During the Russo-Turkish war in 1877, there were reports of dead soldiers being sodomised on the battlefield by their victors, as they performed what became known as 'warm necrophilia'.

In India, the Hindu sect of *Aghoris*, devotees of Shiva, became famous for living in cemeteries, meditating while sat on corpses and performing a variety of necrophilic acts on cadavers.

---

* Kanakas were workers from various Pacific Islands employed in colonies such as British Columbia, Queensland, Papua New Guinea, Fiji and the Solomon Islands.

In Berlin's red light district, alongside the more severe S&M dungeons, there were also 'mortuary chambers' that catered for pseudonecrophiliacs and allowed them to act out zombie and vampire fantasies. These dimly lit brothels were decked out in black cloths, silver candlesticks, caskets and other funeral paraphernalia. Prostitutes would dress in white shrouds and play dead for their clients. They would use white, blue and grey make-up to create deathly flesh tones and use cold compresses to render their skin cold to the touch.

Infamous cases of necrophilia include reports that the body of Eva Peron, the much sung about First Lady of Argentina who died when she was only thirty-three, was abused by several different men after being embalmed and her body hidden from the public by the military.

More recently, there was, according to the deputy coroner, evidence of necrophilic acts having been performed on the corpse of Hollywood icon Marilyn Monroe after her death in Los Angeles in 1962.

In China in 1994, a thirty-nine-year-old driver from Canton was arrested for serial rape, murder and necrophilia relating to more than a dozen women. In his home, police found video recordings of the crimes, dismembered body parts preserved in antiseptic that he kept for sexual rituals, and mannequins containing skin and sexual organs from some of his victims.

Cultural history is also rich in necrophilic referencing. On doing a lazy internet search with the keywords 'necrophilia in music', I was surprised to find close to two million hits and numerous Top Tens of necrophilic songs.*

---

* https://www.ocweekly.com/i-want-to-hold-your-dead-hand-10-best-songs-about-necrophilia-6597705/

Books, plays and movies are also abound with necrophilic plots, themes and undertones. From Hamlet in Ophelia's grave, through the works of the Marquis de Sade, to Bram Stoker's creation of Dracula in 1897.

The non-speaking walking dead, immortalised in the twenty-first-century binge-worthy TV box set of the same name, first came into vogue after Victor Halperin's 1932 film *White Zombie*, complete with its catchy poster hook lines: 'With these zombie eyes he rendered her powerless. With this zombie grip he made her perform his every desire.' It's worth noting the coupling here of *powerlessness* and exploitation of *desires* – both are central pillars of necrophilia.

In 1958, when Dennis Nilsen was twelve going on thirteen, two major Dracula films were released, *The Return of Dracula* with Francis Lederer and Norma Eberhardt, and more influentially, the iconic Hammer Horror production *Dracula*,* with Christopher Lee and Peter Cushing. This was followed two years later by the sequel *The Brides of Dracula*. Nilsen's early teenage years coincided with the beginning of the golden age of Dracula films, with the UK studios Hammer Horror producing one almost every two years until the mid-seventies, with Cushing and Lee scaring kids, teenagers and adults alike right off the cinema scare scale. This was an age when cinema was the most powerful media force in the world. A time when television sets in the UK were as small as an average oven – and twice as heavy. During the late fifties there were only two TV channels in the UK – BBC and ITV. The BBC didn't launch its second channel until the mid-sixties. It wasn't until the seventies

---

* The poster strapline for *Dracula* was 'The Terrifying Lover Who Died – Yet Lived'.

that colour television sets and colour broadcasting became affordable and commonplace.

Cinema – the picture house – the movie theatre – was the focus of event viewing. A big day out. And during this time, other UK and US studios were pumping out their own Dracula and vampire offerings.

I'm not for one moment going to suggest that this film genre was *the* cause of Nilsen's necrophilia, far from it, but I am going to assert that the giant-screen impression made by the Count who couldn't be seen in a mirror, and who 'slept' in a casket (like the one Nilsen had seen his grand-father in), also influenced the developing fantasies of the film-loving young Des, raised in the cultural backwater of Fraserburgh.

The 'undead' of the Dracula world are always seen as unblemished corpses save for a fanged bite mark on the neck. Similarly, Nilsen recounted the beauty of the dead young men he repeatedly abused after strangling or drowning them. But that's not the truth. The corpses that he stored beneath floor-boards in the ground-floor flat at Melrose Avenue, or in the attic at Cranley Gardens were all unrefrigerated and therefore would have quickly putrefied.

The dead companions Nilsen interacted with will have had marbled, green or blackened flesh, blistered eyelids and puffed-up lips. Their bodies will have bloated because of the production of abdominal gasses, and they would have been infested by wave after wave of carrion-seeking flies, spiders and beetles.

To better understand the forensic taphonomy of Nilsen's decaying corpses – and put in perspective that throughout this period the serial killer remained sexually aroused by the sight of them – I sought the advice of Professor Guy Rutty MBE, one of Britain's most experienced and respected chief forensic pathologists.

'The putrification would start after about twenty-four hours and the corpse would rapidly be infested by flies and insects, they will have migrated to the body from all over the dwelling. Within twenty-four to forty-eight hours, the skin would have started to turn green, then it will have marbled and blackened. Very quickly there would have been the distinctive reek of death. It's unlike any other smell, and is so strong that it creates a nasal sensory overload. If Nilsen bathed the corpses in warm water, then the top layers of skin would be expected to quickly come away, so he may have used cold water to try to preserve the flesh.'

I pointed out that Nilsen had sprinkled talcum powder over the dead bodies, which I thought had been to make them fit the white corpse mirror fantasies that he'd had before he even started killing. But it seems there may have been an extra reason.

'In mortuaries we also use talc or similar compounds. We use it to absorb fluids seeping from the corpse, and it would to a small degree have helped reduce the smell as well. To understand what the flesh of a corpse looks and smells like, you'd have to buy an uncooked chicken and leave it in your lounge for days, weeks and months at room temperature. That cringingly *off* smell, that extreme rancid stench, that's what it's like.'

Professor Rutty noted differences in the way the bodies in Melrose Avenue and Cranley Gardens would have decayed.

'Beneath the floorboards of the ground-floor flat, there could have been an airflow, and this may have had a mummifying effect on the corpses. The skin would have become very stiff, like unprocessed leather before it's been worked into being flexible. Bathing would for a short time have rehydrated it, but then the skin would have quickly come away to reveal a slimy subcutaneous layer. In the attic, there would likely have been no mummification, unless there was a draft or airflow over the body, and the decomposition there would be expected to be much faster.'

This comment is valuable because it may, at least partly, explain why Nilsen's killing was more frequent and his mental state more unbalanced in his short time at Cranley Gardens – the corpses just didn't last as long.

Throughout the ongoing process of decomposition, and Nilsen's continual sexual interaction with the corpses, the dead bodies of his victims would have not only been infested, but as the blackened skin and subcutaneous layers fell away, large parts of the skeletal bone would have been exposed. I mention this not to shock, but to give insight into both the dubious state of his mind, and also the enduring and overriding power of his fantasy.

Professor Rutty has for decades worked key murder cases, providing expert insight to police homicide teams and testimony in murder trials. He made several observations about Dennis Nilsen that I, and others, had missed.

'After death, muscles relax and blood and bodily fluids flow out of orifices. A corpse often looks like it's just been very badly assaulted. As well as practicality, there is a profoundly religious overtone to the washing of a dead body, cleaning and purifying it, usually carried out by members of the same sex. One of the reasons Nilsen will have had difficulty with anal sex and would have resorted to frictional sex between the victim's limbs, is that the anus would have had no tone or reaction to penetration and would have just been an opening in the body.'

Revealingly, he added, 'I would have expected Nilsen to have constantly smelled of death, it would have permeated his clothes, his hair and his skin. He could bathe in an attempt to prevent the odours being noticeable but even when he thought they'd gone, they probably hadn't. He would most probably have become 'nose-blind' to it, just as a dog owner doesn't notice the smell of their own wet dog after a while, but others coming into the house instantly spot it; colleagues must have noticed that there was a strange smell to him.'

Professor Rutty, who is an acknowledged expert on body dismemberment* saw a clear reason for Nilsen's eventual dismemberment of the corpses. 'It was ritualistic. It enabled him to keep the parts as trophies. After retaining the bodies for so long, the bones would have disarticulated and he could have simply pulled them out of their sockets. It's what chefs do when they have hung meat for twenty-eight days.'

Necrophilia seems to have been repeatedly (and sometimes confusingly) reclassified since the landmark Krafft-Ebing categorisations in 1886, the Wulfen revision in 1910, Jones classification in 1931, Hirschfeld's definitions in 1956 and Rosman and Resnick's classifications in 1989.

In trying to determine an accurate classification for Nilsen, on Professor Rutty's advice I studied a scale (with multiple subcategories) in Dr Anil Aggrawal's book *Necrophilia: Forensic and Medico-legal Aspects*, a scale that even he thought needed further and ongoing revision.

The categorisations run as follows:

Class I: Role Players (those who need sexual partners to play dead and sometimes act out zombie, vampire fantasies).

---

* *Criminal Dismemberment: Forensic and Investigative Analysis*, Rutty, Black, Hainsworth, Thomson (CRC Press, 2017).

Class II: Romantic Necrophiles (usually, but not exclusively, bereaved people who can't bear to be separated from deceased loved ones, but also necrophiles who wash, dress and embellish corpses and have a reluctance to dispose of the remains).

Class III: Fantasisers (these are offenders who don't have intercourse with the dead but fantasise about it and sometimes visit graveyards for sexual arousal, or even masturbate at the back of funeral services).

Class IV: Tactile Necrophiles (offenders who need to touch, kiss or lick cadavers in order to achieve orgasm).

Class V: Fetishistic Necrophiles (might not kill, but they may remove objects or clothing from dead bodies for sexual gratification and/or dismember and preserve body parts for sexual arousal. The primary motive is not to mutilate the body, but to keep at least a part of it).

Class VI: Necromutilomaniacs (offenders driven not by urges to have sex with the corpse, but to achieve orgasm through the excitement of destroying it – they often masturbate during the mutilation/dismemberment).

Class VII: Opportunistic Necrophiles (offenders who are usually sexually functional with living partners and only discover necrophilic arousal by accident – i.e. through a partner dying during intercourse).

Class VIII: Regular Necrophiles (these people do not enjoy sex with living partners).

Class IX: Homicidal Necrophiles (offenders sometimes called lagnonectors, who are prepared to kill for the thrill of having necrophilic sex. They are particularly attracted to 'warm necrophilia' sex with the just dead, and this urge often drives them into serial killing).

Class X: Exclusive Necrophiles (necrophiles who are – or become – unable to have sex with the living).

Nilsen seems to have graduated from a Class III fantasist to perhaps (and it's a big perhaps) an opportunistic Class VIII, someone who didn't plan to kill but having done so found the post-mortem sex addictively arousing.

Having broken these taboos, he developed the serial offending urges of a Class IX Homicidal Necrophile, the collective traits of a Class V necrofetishist, and the reliance of Class IVs who can only orgasm providing they can somehow touch a corpse.

This combination of categories – five of the ten – would also go some way to explaining Nilsen's comment that he was unable to have sex with the living while the dead were in his flat. Basically, his sexual predilections were in the process of shifting him to Category X – the type of offender who only wanted sex with the dead.

NILSEN: 'I would get an erection immediately after I was certain he was dead – it was excitement because I knew I could now perform the rituals I had fantasised about. Rituals he would participate in, both as himself and as me. It was consensuality of a unique kind.'

HAZELWOOD: 'Nilsen wasn't originally only a homo-sexual necrophiliac – that is to say, he wasn't only capable of sexual interaction with the dead. There's evidence that he had living sexual male partners as well, it's just that his preference was increasingly for dead ones. His masturbatory fantasy life and each victim increased the level of this preference. The rituals he developed lead me to classify him as necrofetishistic and exceptionally dangerous. This kind of individual is so motivated to achieve his sexual ends he will walk through the fires of hell to do so. It's a level of paraphilia that's incurable. Necrofetishistic killers never stop.'

7. KILLING FOR COMPANY

Over several decades, Nilsen gave the impression that his motivation for killing was that he'd reached such levels of acute loneliness that the mere thought of being rejected again, of someone once more leaving him alone in the flat, was just so unbearable that he killed them rather than let them go. This notion became engrained in public consciousness when Brian Masters named his bestselling Nilsen biography *Killing for Company*, and ever since has been an easy explanation of his offending.

> NILSEN: 'The loneliness I felt was at times as extreme as physical pain. It was like being winded but in the mind not in the stomach. It was so intense it would physically and mentally immobilise me, leaving me deeply depressed for days on end. If I was in the flat, then I would try to fill the emptiness by drinking and listening to music or to the radio. I'd put it on and imagine the voices were people in my room sitting and eating with me. I'd sometimes take myself away from there and go into town to try to get as pissed as possible, to drink myself out of the despondency. Initially, this would work, but more often than not made things worse in the long run.'

> HAZELWOOD: 'Dennis Nilsen didn't kill because he wanted someone around to talk to – [he wanted]

someone who couldn't talk back. He didn't kill because he couldn't bear the thought of being lonely. That wasn't the case. Nilsen was a serial sexual offender. He was a necrophile. Corpses aroused him. He killed because he wanted a dead body he could use for sexual relations, without them hanging around and talking to him afterwards.'

RESSLER: 'The road to necrophilia is a long one. It's not one event at one period of time that short-cuts an offender to this kind of activity. Sure, there are some factors that may impact one individual more than another, but it's always factors, plural. Generally, necrophiliacs come from an ineffective social environment – by that we mean the kind where bad behaviour was tolerated, parents weren't around or didn't care much, the child didn't have good models to get guidance from. There's usually some evidence of abuse or neglect, a lack of close parental contact, failures to develop emotionally, express love and kindness, to form family bonds. In adolescence they become isolated, rebellious, they lie a lot, grow more secretive and begin to believe they can only trust themselves. In puberty, they indulge in autoerotic fantasies and develop fetishes. Increasingly they need more extreme fantasies, pornography or props to become sexually aroused. When they start offending, they mitigate and justify their acts, they try to make it seem as though the offences somehow victimised them. They lack empathy or genuine regret. Offending provides them with higher levels of arousal and satisfaction than their fantasies did and this increases their feelings of power, control and dominance – things often lacking in their lives. And they learn. From offence to offence, they sort out their problems and refine rituals to best serve their needs for sexual satisfaction.'

8. BODY DISPOSAL

Dennis Nilsen was caught because of one single factor – the manner in which he disposed of the bodies.

There had been no substantial manhunt for any single one of his poor victims. Efforts to investigate their disappearance paled into insignificance when compared for example with the hunt for the killer of Caroline Hogg, Susan Maxwell and Sarah Jayne Harper, when detectives appeared almost nightly on national and local TV news bulletins and claimed front-page newspaper coverage with their multimillion pound searches for the killer.

So why did a man intelligent enough to hold down good jobs in the army, police and civil service just simply flush flesh down the toilets and hope to get away with it?

At first, you can explain his seemingly poor judgment by saying that when he moved to the attic in Cranley Gardens, he had no access to a back garden, and so couldn't burn body parts as he'd done at Melrose Avenue. And you can factor in that he didn't have a driving licence or access to a vehicle.

But I don't believe those were the reasons.

At his previous flat, Nilsen also buried organs and body parts in the garden soil, as well as staging bonfires there and on neighbouring wasteland for larger disposal. On occasions, he carried bags of decomposing human organs and entrails to local parks and put them in places he hoped hungry animals, not inquisitive humans, would find.* But he could have been much cleverer than that.

Nilsen explained during our interview how, after keeping a body, the severed parts were like butchered meat and there was little or no blood.

Wouldn't it have been easy for him to wrap those 'cuts' in black plastic, stick them in a backpack and catch trains to all corners of the capital – or indeed the country – and randomly dispose of the pieces on recycling tips, deep in holes in forests, or in the capital's plethora of waterways? Nilsen was clinically of above average intelligence, forensically aware and smart enough to know that.

The only conclusion that can be reached is that he *chose* to keep the body parts for as long as possible – meaning, until their state of decay had created such a stench and hazard to health that he had no option but to get rid of them. This theory is supported by his post-dismemberment ritual of masturbating over the corpses, as a means of saying goodbye.

> RESSLER: 'Even without a vehicle, Nilsen could, if he had wanted, disposed of the body parts of his victims far from where he lived, and in doing so minimised the risk of being apprehended. In every other aspect of his offending, he appears to have been organised – he'd known where to go to select his victims, he'd chosen people he was sure wouldn't be missed, he'd disabled them through drink so he couldn't be overpowered, and he'd strangled them with ligatures that he always had to

---

* Nilsen says that in the summer of 1981, prior to moving to Cranley Gardens, after a drinking binge he took a plastic carrier bag of human entrails to dispose of in Gladstone Park while walking his dog, but absentmindedly left it in full view on an adjacent public road.

hand. Afterwards, he'd kept the bodies for sexual exploitation as fulfilment of his fantasies. Everything is planned
up to and including this point. Intelligent serial offenders
learn as they go along, they refine their practices and
make fewer mistakes. If they didn't have a good plan for
body disposal after the first kill, they sure did by the time
they carried out the second. Nilsen's plan was to hold
on to every part of his victim for as long as he possibly
could, and then dispose of them only when he absolutely
had to. He'd been emboldened by doing this during his
first kills and had developed an arrogance that he could
get away with it. I've known plenty of serial killers keep
body parts as souvenirs. They kept heads, hands, feet or
other parts of the individual that they had found arousing
when they'd been alive, parts that were sometimes distinctive to the individual they killed. Killers like Ed Kemper
kept body parts, like the head of his mother, because he
wanted to continue to vent his anger at her. Arthur
Shawcross kept sexual body parts such as vulvas and
nipples because he found them stimulating. There's a
reason why these guys keep such things for so long.'

HAZELWOOD: 'Dismemberment is practical or paraphilic. Some offenders hate the process but do it so they
can more easily dispose of body parts. Others experience
power and satisfaction during dismemberment. This final
destruction of the human body completes their mastery
of the victim. If body parts are kept as trophies, then it's
often ritualistic, something that wasn't in their original
fantasies but became so. Necrophiliacs generally don't
fantasise about the dismemberment and disposal, but
once they've done it, it becomes part of the ritual, and

having accomplished it, they maybe keep trophies to celebrate their achievement.'

9. CANNIBALISM

It's difficult not to imagine that Nilsen the chef, the man who cut and cooked his victims on his stove, who pared skin from bone, didn't consume any of their flesh or feed any to his dog Bleep. His statement, 'The bodies are all gone but I feel a spiritual communion with these people. They are a part of me', implies that he did.

In *History of a Drowning Boy*, Dennis Nilsen went to interesting lengths to try to end suggestions that he'd been cannibalistic.

There was certainly no suggestion of cannibalism, nor did my dog eat any human remains. When dissecting the corpses of the first two victims at Cranley Gardens (on the wooden board across the bath), I was able to reflect, rationally, on the culinary possibilities of fairly fresh, human meat but the thought only engaged me for a few moments. When I sliced through human buttocks, the meat looked just like beef rump steaks, with the colour being slightly lighter than in beef. Similarly, the pieces boiled in the pot (on the stove at my flat in Cranley Gardens, in 1981) looked just like boiled beef. The thought of giving a small chunk to Bleep crossed my mind but I didn't want her to acquire a taste for human flesh, though she looked interested enough at the prospect of getting a piece. In any case, food was never an important feature of my life and I was content to have everything I ate served

with chips; fried egg, bacon or chop or hamburger or
sausage, with baked beans or tinned tomatoes.

One of the tips I picked up from profilers at the FBI was that when interviewees greatly embellished denials – when they added colourful details, as Nilsen did in this account – then it was often a sign of lying. The liar intends the details to be so familiar and interesting to the listener that as a consequence they believe the whole statement.

I don't.

And not for one moment am I deceived by the protestation that food was never an important feature in his life. He'd chosen catering as a career. He'd become a very accomplished chef, being left in charge of some prestigious army functions.

I'm highly suspicious of the beef and steak language used above, when he described the destruction of the body parts. And let's remember, this wasn't about food – it was about power, total domination, or as Nilsen himself put it 'spiritual communion'.

I'm totally convinced Nilsen lied about his cannibalism. Not only because it was something he might have been ashamed of, but because of two other main reasons. Firstly, he felt such an admission damaged the image he was trying build of himself (both inside and outside prison) as an 'intellectual' rather than a 'crazy' or a 'paedo' – the kind of categorisations that in prison put a target on your back. Secondly, secrets were power. Retaining this secret, and a possible one or two others, was the last power he had.

Conversely, I don't think Nilsen was frequently cannibalistic. Certainly, he could not have consumed flesh that had badly decayed, so this limited the practice to only those few bodies that he dismembered soon after death.

RESSLER: 'There are so many similarities between Dennis Nilsen and Jeffrey Dahmer that it's hard to believe Nilsen wasn't at least an occasional cannibal. Dahmer was smart, he was gay and a necrophile. Both men lured their victims back to their homes with promises of favours, both had sex with them after they were dead, both concealed evidence of their crimes, both kept body parts as sexual souvenirs and trophies. Given all those similarities, plus commonalities with other cannibalistic offenders – such as the slicing and cooking of body parts – it's hard to believe Nilsen wasn't also cannibalistic.'

HAZELWOOD: 'He at least tried it. That's the bottom line here.'

10. MAD OR BAD?

Despite sitting with detectives and voluntarily confessing to numerous murders and attempted murders, when Nilsen came to trial in 1983, surprisingly he pleaded not guilty to all charges.

His QC, Ivan Lawrence, argued he'd suffered from personality disorders that diminished his responsibility to the extent that he'd been rendered incapable of forming the intention to commit murder, and therefore should be convicted of the lesser charge of manslaughter. Legally, it was a crucial move. Murder carried an automatic tariff of life imprisonment, whereas the length of a manslaughter sentence was at the discretion of the presiding judge.

In tabloid terms, the question to be answered by the jury was whether he was mad, or bad? Predictably, both the prosecution and defence teams called eminent psychiatrists to give evidence.

Dr James 'Jim' MacKeith, universally regarded as pioneer in the world of forensic psychiatry,* told the court Nilsen had trouble expressing any emotions other than anger. He depersonalised people and treated them as components of his fantasies. He said Nilsen displayed signs of maladaptive behaviour, narcissistic traits, an impaired sense of identity and suffered from an unspecified personality disorder.

Under vociferous cross-examination from the prosecuting QC, Allan Green, Dr MacKeith refused to say unequivocally that Nilsen had suffered from diminished responsibility on *all* the occasions that he had offended.

The defence's second psychiatric witness was Dr Patrick Gallwey.† He said Nilsen had false self syndrome, a condition in which people create an artificial self to protect their true self from reliving traumas experienced during their childhood years of emotional development. He thought he suffered from schizoid disturbances and an arrested development of his personality.

Interestingly, Gallwey made a point that more than a decade later Bob Ressler would make to me. He said that that the good behaviour of sufferers of false self syndrome was likely to break down if they became socially isolated. They were, he claimed, in need of healthy relationships, attention and affection (what Ressler called 'safe hands').

---

* Jim MacKeith's psychiatric evidence helped expose a number of false confessions and wrongful convictions, most notably Engin Raghip, wrongly convicted of the murder of PC Keith Blakelock at Broadwater Farm, London, and Judith Ward, wrongly convicted of IRA bombings.
† Dr Patrick Gallwey was an internationally respected prison doctor (Wormwood Scrubs), psychoanalyst and forensic psychiatrist who specialised in treating violent sexual offenders.

Like MacKeith, Gallwey found himself subjected to bludgeoning cross-examination and forced to admit that he did not dispute Nilsen had been 'intellectually aware of what was going on' when he killed or attempted to kill.

The prosecution's expert, Dr Paul Bowden, was said to have examined Nilsen on numerous occasions over about eighteen months while the Scot had been on remand in Brixton Prison. He implied that Nilsen was manipulative when recounting events from his childhood and, unlike MacKeith, he found no evidence of maladaptive behaviour, no evidence of undue amounts of loneliness, no paranoid tendencies, no impaired sense of identity – in short, no mental disorder that would have diminished his sense of responsibility.

On 4 November 1983, the jury agreed with Bowden, not MacKeith or Gallwey. They returned guilty verdicts on all charges. I can't help but wonder if they would have come to different conclusions if they'd fully understood the physical state of the blackened and almost skinless, decayed corpses that Nilsen had continued to interact with sexually and socially.

NILSEN: 'Sometimes when people mention the crimes that I have been convicted of, I feel I must have sleepwalked through them. At those precise moments, I was at my most imprecise. I know I did those things, yet I do not feel it was the conscious me, the absolute me, that participated. It was a different me, a me that surfaced amid the momentum of the ritual that engulfed me . . .

'I have been seen by many psychiatrists on many occasions and the only thing they seem to agree on, much to my relief, is that I was not and I am not insane, though I fear there is a real danger that if I am forced into their company again, I may be driven mad.'

RESSLER: 'UK law is different to US law. In certain states, we have a plea of guilty but insane and I feel that Nilsen, like Jeffrey Dahmer, might, and I stress *might*, fit this categorization. It recognises that some people at some times under some circumstances are unable to resist impulses to offend, to rape and to kill, and instead of prison they need to be admitted to a secure place where they can receive psychiatric care.'

HAZELWOOD: 'One thing for sure, wanting to kill people and have sex with their dead bodies is not the act of a sane person. Different courts in different countries will all come up with different views on whether someone is legally or clinically insane – and those are usually two different things. What matters most with serial sexual murderers is that they are kept off the streets, because, while maybe treatable, they will always be incurable. Given freedom, Dennis Nilsen would reoffend, I have no doubt about that.'

16

ANY LAST WORDS?

You must make your own mind up on what turned Nilsen the innocent child into Nilsen the guilty-as-hell serial killer and necrophile. After reading a book like this, you deserve closure. And for that, you need conclusions.

As do I.

Your journey has lasted around three hundred pages. Mine, three decades. It's spanned a painful divorce, a second marriage, the birth of my third son, and the joy of being a grandparent. Despite all those years, my meeting with Dennis Nilsen is as vivid and deeply felt as a near-fatal car crash. The trauma is numbed. But nothing is vague. Nothing forgotten.

Over these final few pages, you'll find bold statements about what made Nilsen the offender he was. They're drawn with the benefits of hindsight and new research, and bring what I hope is a valuable perspective on one of the century's most baffling serial killers. Inevitably, some psychologists, psychiatrists, sociologists and criminologists will disagree with these findings. It would disappoint me greatly if they didn't. After all, they spend most of their careers disagreeing with each other.

Dennis Nilsen died in 2018,* and ironically, for a necrophile, almost as many words have been written about him

---

* Nilsen died in hospital in York, aged seventy-two, after being admitted for surgery with a ruptured abdominal aortic aneurism. A post-mortem examination cited cause of death as pulmonary embolism and retroperitoneal haemorrhage. His body was cremated.

post-mortem as since his conviction. He's been subject to front-page headlines and lead news items the world over. A major three-part dramatisation of his crimes aired on ITV, the UK's largest independent television channel. A new network documentary followed on the same station. Books about him were updated and reissued. Nilsen's own autobiography was published. The global documentary for the streaming giant that I participated in was also produced.

In 1993, the world saw Dennis Nilsen interviewed about his life and crimes for the first and only time, and because of that interview we've been talking about him ever since. TV exposed his full monstrosity and mundanity. It showed a middle-aged man talking intelligently and calmly about killing a dozen young men so he could enjoy 'the beauty' of their corpses and satisfy himself sexually.

It was unspeakably gripping television, watched by a record number of viewers and probably even more closely by the lawyers and members of the government who'd failed to stop it being broadcast.

Britain has a vast and terrible pantheon of serial killers that stretches back centuries. Doctors and nurses like Shipman, Allett and Cotton. Lovers like Brady and Hindley. Married couples like Fred and Rose West. Gangsters such as the Krays and Richardsons. Psychopaths like the London and Yorkshire Rippers. But, unlike Nilsen, few of these people wrote anything of worth about their lives and crimes. None were interviewed on camera by a psychological profiler, knowing policemen throughout the country, and the British public at home, would sit in front of their televisions, scrutinise their every word and pass damning judgment on them.

Whether we like it or not, Dennis Nilsen is the UK's Ted Bundy. A vile, serial murderer who has become a mass-media personality because of the extremities of his crimes, his distinctive personality and disarmingly articulate explanations of what drove him to commit them.

Nilsen, like Bundy, was more than happy to open the door to his house of horrors, welcome us in, chat away about his murders and study our shock and repulsion. It was always up to us whether we accepted his invitation or not.

FBI profiler Roy Hazelwood told me, 'Nilsen was a narcissist and craved attention, probably because he didn't get it when he was growing up. He was a ritualistic serial sexual criminal, rare in that he was a homosexual necrophiliac. Most necrophilia is male-on-female. There isn't a huge database on homosexual necrophilic behaviour, but post-mortem predilections apart, Nilsen behaved a lot like a common paedophile. Paedophiles are narcissistic and are highly motivated to carry out their crimes. They will invest considerable amounts of planning, patience and money in achieving their ends (grooming, buying drinks, etc.). Their regular paraphilic fantasies are increased by masturbatory rituals and they develop distinct mental scripts that when acted out give them high levels of satisfaction. They are usually of more than average intelligence, and they mix so well at work and in society that they are never suspected of criminality. They will often hold trusted positions such as charity workers, treasurers, union officials or neighbourhood watch organisers but they are not good at maintaining meaningful relationships with partners. They lack empathy for their victims and seldom experience any remorse or guilt, often blaming circumstances beyond their control for their crimes, rather than their own planned actions.'

Even more tellingly, Roy added, 'These types of criminal often photograph or film their sexual offences so they can masturbate to them, and they then extend and worsen their fantasies and offending. Most serial sexual criminals slow down as they become older, but that's not the case with paedophiles, and it didn't appear to be so with Nilsen. Once men like this kill for the first time, and as a result achieve their desired fantasy, they will carry on into their sixties, seventies or beyond, possibly until they are physically no longer able to take a life, or until God takes their own.'

Bob Ressler echoed his former colleague's thoughts and added: 'Nilsen was what we termed an "organised" offender. That is to say he planned his crimes and he carried them out precisely in a way calculated to fulfil his fantasies. He only used two methods to kill his victims, and his post-mortem rituals were consistent throughout his offending. The disposal of his victims initially appears "disorganised", in that he kept bodies and body parts in his home for long periods when, logically, to avoid detection, he should have disposed of them much earlier. But this behaviour turns out to also be "organised", in that it went as he'd planned, it's what he'd wanted, because he'd wished to retain his victims as long as possible. Given that he removed organs, boiled skin off of skulls and cut and cooked flesh from his victims, I think that like Jeffrey Dahmer, as a way of finalising his power and completing his abuse and exploitation, he also participated in cannibalism.'

Nilsen would have been horrified to have been talked about as a paedophile and cannibal. In prison, such labels mark you out for regular beatings if not worse. During his time at Full Sutton Prison in York, he mixed with child-killer Colin Hatch, who was seventeen years into a life sentence for child abuse and the murder of a seven-year-old boy when he was taken captive by a fellow inmate and strangled to death.

I suspect Nilsen was pleased to have kept his secrets from

other prisoners and to have taken them to his grave after dying at 9.19 a.m. on the 12 May 2018, in the same prison Hatch had met his fate.

After questioning at length, and listening intently to the answers of all the psychologists, psychiatrists, policemen, profilers, pathologists and authors listed in this book and elsewhere, there's enough direct and circumstantial evidence to come to some detailed conclusions.

There wasn't one singular event that turned baby Desmond Andrew Nilsen, born in Fraserburgh in November 1945, into that thankfully rare human specimen we refer to as a serial killer.

There was a perfect storm of events.

A storm that began in his childhood, grew in adolescence, and erupted in full hurricane horror in his adult years.

One or more of the following characteristics are commonly found in the backgrounds of serial murderers – an absentee father, a neglectful mother, sexual abuse (or even believed sexual abuse), feelings of loneliness and social isolation throughout childhood, adolescence and adulthood, depression, introversion, death of someone close to them, inadequate emotional care during a grieving process, a period of cruelty to animals, a lack of strong emotional ties to any family members, academic underperformance, repressed sexuality, strong visual fantasies involving fetishes and paraphilias, use of prostitutes as a substitution for relationships, uncorrected behaviour in formative years, overuse of alcohol and, most of all, a lack of a stable, long-lasting relationship that both partners find intellectually, emotionally and sexually satisfying.

In Dennis Nilsen's case, *all* of the above contributing factors were applicable.

All of them.

This combination constituted that perfect storm.

Nilsen's own accounts of his childhood, adolescence and adulthood are largely truthful but, almost inevitably, through the truth seeps streams of self-serving, self-aggrandising, self-mitigating lies, fantasies, embellishments, and fallacious memories. That said, Nilsen consistently quoted a specific trifecta of 'circumstances beyond my control' that he felt particularly contributed to his offending:

- A lack of affection and love in his childhood.
- The trauma of losing his grandfather, the unexpected viewing of his dead body and the lack of a proper explanation of what death meant.
- Extreme loneliness and depression from childhood to adulthood, to the extent that he feared the young men he invited back to his home would reject him and leave.

The coldness of his childhood – whether perceived or actual – is as equally damning in development terms. The death of his grandfather undoubtedly was another emotional landmark. And the loneliness and depression was unquestionably present. Left to his own devices Nilsen drank heavily, his personality deteriorated, and his fantasies increased. I think Bob Ressler was right in saying you can't blame drink for his crimes – they were premeditated, fantasy-driven and too well organised.

No discussion on Nilsen can conclude without noting that over the final years of his life, he dramatically changed his recollections of his grandfather from the benign and caring picture he'd painted of him when talking to Brian Masters during his time on remand in Brixton in the early 1980s. A decade later, when I filmed him in Albany, he declared a vague memory that when he was only five years old, Andrew Whyte had held his penis while he'd urinated and he'd wondered whether this had been a mild form of child abuse.

Several decades later, by the time Nilsen finished his autobiography, he more graphically recalled Andrew Whyte repeatedly plying him with 'drugged tea', taking him into an old WWII bunker, pulling down his trousers, handling his penis and fondling his buttocks. Additionally, when they were back home, Grandad would often bathe him, take him to bed, embrace him and then penetrate his anus with a finger.

Evidentially, I have major problems believing these stories. Not just because memories tend to fade over time rather than become more accurate, or, as Paul Britton spotted within hours of first meeting Nilsen, he was forever 'working on an image', but because there is absolutely no corroborating evidence of abuse, no corroborating testimony from any family members or friends, and because, *had it been true*, I'm certain Nilsen would have mentioned it much earlier in his life, as he was always ready to portray himself as a victim.

I'm also sure that the stories of abuse, if they'd been genuine, would have surfaced in a consistent form, in the early letters or essays he wrote, or conversations he had with myself, Paul Britton, Brian Masters, Russ Coffey or others.

And finally on this issue, it's difficult to believe that had his grandad been a lifelong paedophile, no one else would have raised suspicions about his behaviour, and the only offence he'd ever be accused of would be the abuse of his own five-year-old grandson. As Roy Hazelwood pointed out, paedophiles are lifelong offenders, they never only offend once – and they never stop.

After consulting many psychologists and profilers, I do, however, think Nilsen was adversely affected by the death of his grandparent. I suspect he really missed the older man and genuinely struggled to understand both his death and the deep feelings (grief/sorrow/depression) that he felt as a result.

My youngest son, Billy, a bright and happy child, lost *his* beloved grandfather when he was ten years old. The impact on him was so severely upsetting and depressing that at times he was unable to face the journey to school, because the school bus passed the cemetery where Grandad was buried. His teachers were as diligent as we were in recognising his grief. They suggested the creation of a memory box, and into it Billy put his grandfather's old tie, some football memorabilia from their favourite soccer teams and other personal items representing moments they'd shared. By working with the school, Billy's daily custodians, and talking sensibly and consistently with him, we were able to gradually ease his pain.*

I don't believe Nilsen received anything approaching this normal level of support. Not only had there not been any 'safe hands' to catch him when he'd emotionally fallen, no one had even noticed him tumble, and certainly no one picked him up.

The final part of Nilsen's trifecta of traumas was downplayed by every psychological profiler I consulted. None of them believed he killed for company – because he was lonely and desperate for companionship. They all insisted he had murdered people for his own sexual pleasures and needs.

That's not to say that Nilsen hadn't desired company, craved attention and been desperate for affection. He very obviously had. But those weren't the reasons he turned to murder.

Bob Ressler put this into perspective. 'Had Dennis Nilsen

---

* Nilsen said he had no recollection of ever being taken to see the grave where his grandfather had been laid to rest.

kept his victims alive, had he restrained them solely as companions that he then interacted with, then you could argue that what he had wanted was company. He hadn't. He'd killed them at the first opportunity, and he'd done that because he wanted corpses not company. For him, these people needed to be dead so that he could sexually satisfy himself by acting out the fantasies he'd mentally scripted.'

Aside from a necrophile, what else was Nilsen?

In letters to me, in the interview in Albany Prison and in his autobiography, Dennis Nilsen insisted no fewer than six times that he had only killed twelve people, not fifteen. Nine at Melrose Avenue (five of whom were identified) and three at Cranley Gardens (all of whom were identified). Over more than thirty years, he maintained that he'd originally mentioned fifteen or sixteen to the police as a general number but had later tried to correct the total. 'It suited the police to go with the higher figure,' he claimed, something detectives have always refuted. But there really was no incentive for the police to lie about this. A few more or less unidentified murders over a decade or longer makes no difference to their crime clear-up rates, it closes no files, relieves no stress on staffing and makes no positive headlines.

So why was Dennis Nilsen so insistent he 'only' killed twelve people?

This question bothered me from the moment he made the assertion during our meeting in prison. It was, to my knowledge, the first time a notorious serial killer had sought to *lessen* his total of victims. Generally, publicity-seeking narcissists seek to *increase* the number to heighten their notoriety.

I think the answer is simpler than it seems.

When a killer says there are *more* bodies, then the police have to begin formal and rigorous investigations. They are obliged to search. Compelled to go back in time and examine records of unsolved murder cases and missing persons.

Nilsen didn't want that.

He didn't want it, because he was afraid that such operations would unearth crimes that he was hoping would remain secret. Crimes that he was either ashamed of, or crimes that held precious memories that he never intended degrading by disclosure (and the condemnation that would come with it). Serial killers like secrets. Secrets play to their needs to have power and control.

In December 2020, news broke about a pregnant neighbour of Nilsen's going missing during his killing spree at Melrose Avenue. This was in the eighties when he owned the ground-floor flat and could burn human remains in the garden. Although surrounded by a six-foot fence, the space was over-looked by several multiple-occupancy homes in his building and surrounding houses. It is entirely possible that neighbours confronted him about the bonfires and the terrible stench that they would have emitted.

Some criminologists have dismissed the possibility of Nilsen's involvement in her disappearance, saying a single, pregnant woman didn't fit the profile of his other victims, but if his liberty had been threatened by exposure, then I'm sure he would have taken her life – and later, perhaps, been so ashamed of what he'd done that he would not want to admit it – not even to himself.

'There are times,' he wrote, 'when I reflect on what I have done and I cannot reconcile those acts with the person I know I am. Those actions were not ones I recognised of the person I was or believed I was. With all honesty, I contest that I was not myself at those times. They were actions alien to me and all my values.'

Back in '93, Bob Ressler told me, 'There's a high probability that there were other victims, ones earlier than the first recorded murder in 1978. It's unusual for men to begin killing in their mid-thirties without there being prior murders or attempted murders that are later discovered. If I was working this case, I'd look very closely at his activity during the decade when he was overseas in the military, concentrating when he was just about to move from one country to another and believed his chances of not being apprehended were at their highest.'

This overseas period will include his time in Aden, Yemen, when he admitted sexually abusing a boy 'prostitute' whom he acknowledged might have been as young as twelve. Tellingly, nearly all of Nilsen's age estimations when it came to those he killed or attempted to kill were inaccurately high. The victim often turned out to be considerably younger than he described.

Dennis Nilsen undoubtedly took secrets to his grave – his last grasp of power. There will have been more victims – possible ones he forgot about – potentially victims of sexual assault or attempted murder, people who do not want to be identified and have not come forward.

He will have indulged in more depraved practices than he admitted. Conversely, he will have done many kind things that will go uncredited, because as a society we have profound difficulties reconciling such contradictions.

Nilsen said something to me that stuck. He claimed he'd only really been in love three times in his life. Maybe that's more than most. Maybe it isn't. Usually, once is enough – providing the love is reciprocal, circumstances don't screw things up and the couple grows together with shared goals and values. Clearly, that didn't happen for Nilsen. And it's something that's also absent in the lives of most serial offenders. Sure, some of them might have been married, but not so happily that they stopped offending, and in some instances the deteriorating relationship contributed to the offending. What all this amounts to is a way of saying that had Nilsen found true love in his adulthood, it might have filled the childhood void and prevented his offending. Love can do that.

In the winter of 2020, almost two years after Nilsen's death, I took part in the latest documentary on his life and crimes. The director asked me about the interview in Albany Prison and as I answered, I found my views had changed over the decades.

In 1992, I didn't believe Nilsen had been criminally insane at the times he'd committed his crimes.

Now I do.

It's hard to list all the factors that contributed to his offending without believing that professors Gallwey and MacKeith might have had valid points in claiming his sense of responsibility had been diminished by some form of 'maladaptive behaviour . . . impaired sense of identity . . . unspecified personality disorder . . . and false self syndrome.'

I still believe Dennis Nilsen should have been jailed for life. Locked away until his dying day. But inside a secure psychiatric ward, where clinicians could have studied him in greater depth, and maybe helped society find the real answers to what made him commit his terrible offences and destroy so many lives, including his own. Answers that might have stopped others stumbling murderously through life in his psychological footsteps.

Given there are said to be at least two serial killers operating at one time in the UK (though by the very nature of their crimes they are not discovered simultaneously, or until many years later), I deeply regret that the world never got to see all four hours of the interview I recorded with Dennis Andrew Nilsen. The footage was far more educational than shocking. Much more important than gratuitous. The faint-hearted could always have chosen to give it a miss.

Greater still, I regret that the interview did not, as planned, lead to a large-scale FBI-style study of serial criminals in the UK, from which an invaluable database of homicidal behaviour, perhaps even culturally peculiar to Britain, would have been compiled. Such a project might have saved lives. Perhaps have caught first time murderers before they became serial offenders.

It may even have prevented the creation of another Dennis Nilsen.

As it is, out there amongst us are other recognised pillars of society, possibly army chefs, police officers, civil servants, doctors, nurses or other professionals, who are secretly fighting their demons, secretly about to start killing, for reasons we don't understand, and may never fully understand unless we more closely study those who commit such crimes.

*

'Right at the end, the pressure was getting worse and worse. I could see it all accelerating. If I hadn't been caught, then it could have been one a week. There could have been hundreds of bodies.' – Dennis Andrew Nilsen

ACKNOWLEDGEMENTS

This book wouldn't have been possible without the professionalism and encouragement of Joelle Owusu-Sekyere and her team at Hodder, my excellent agent Luigi Bonomi and his superb LBA colleagues. I'm grateful for the patience and cooperation of authors Brian Masters and Russ Coffey, their publishers and agents, and also Mark Austin, holder of Nilsen's copyright and Clare Christian at Red Door who published Nilsen's autobiography. Forensic pathologist Professor Guy Rutty gave me invaluable perspective on post-mortem offending that greatly shaped many of my conclusions. Additionally, I'm thankful to Sol Kaufman who provided specific legal research and Billy Morley for editorial research and support.